A portion of the proceeds c
"Operation Giveback," w
of Phillip Hatfield anu ʌic ʌigiai ʌcaiii.

OPERATION GIVEBACK

Operation Giveback is the official charity of Ziglar, Inc., established by Chief Sergeant Major Jose L. Garcia-Aponte by the inspiration of Zig Ziglar and his proud son, Tom Ziglar, President and CEO of Ziglar, Inc.

The MISSION of Operation Giveback (OGB) is to raise awareness, finances and resources for our wounded warriors, who, in turn, raise money to support "The GOLD Star Widows, Families and Children of our FALLEN HEROES"—Those who gave their lives for OUR freedom.

Operation Giveback for Wounded Warriors, Inc., is a Non-Profit 501(c)(3) organization created by veterans of Operations Enduring and Iraqi Freedom. It is composed of military veterans, Department of Defense (DoD) civilians, and defense industry contractors, and is based in Orlando, Florida. Operation Giveback (OGB) is committed to helping the men and women of the U.S. military who have been wounded in action, recognizing they have served our country with pride, distinction, honor and, in some cases, paid the ultimate price.

Ziglar, Inc., also provides training, mentoring and business coaching to these soldiers through various Ziglar programs.

Our heart at Ziglar is to GIVE back to these men and women who gave so much for us; to impact their lives in a POSITIVE way and help them to IMPACT their families and community and their world; to help these dis-abled men and women who are GIVING all they have to help take care of the Gold Star families.

The MISSION of Operation Giveback (OGB) is to raise awareness, finances and resources for our wounded warriors, who, in turn, raise money to support "The GOLD Star Widows, Families and Children of our FALLEN HEROES"—Those who gave their lives for OUR freedom.

CSM. Jose L. Garcia-Aponte
Founder of OGB

After 28 years of honorable service to his nation as a US ARMY soldier he retired in 2009 as a Command Sergeant Major at Program Executive Office of Simulation Training and Instrumentation (PEO STRI) in Orlando, Florida. In June 2005 Jose was awarded the Soldiers Medal for saving the life of another soldier.

L-R: Andrea Castillo, Chuck Armstead, Veronica Ortiz Rivera (Gold Star Mom), Tom Ziglar, me, and an unidentified man. Veronica received help from OGB, then Veronica joined us to help other Gold Star families Christmas 2012. Then she joined us and raised money for other wives who lost their husbands in the war and ran the 197 mile race with us.

FINISH LINE! 197 mile Ragnar relay Miami to Key west in 36 Hours with Tom Ziglar and OGB Wounded Warriors January 12, 6:30 pm 2013

L-R: Phillip Hatfield, Command Sergeant Major Jose Garcia Aponte (in cap), Sergeant Lito Santos ~ on one leg, E-6 Clifford Bruto ~ carrying Flag of The United States of America, Staff Sergeant Will Castillo ~ on one leg, Sergeant First Class (Chuck) Charles Armstead ~ on one leg

CARRIED by *Angels*

Dr. Blake

You have

Blessed me

As LA-!

PhilliP

Eph: 6: 18-20 KJV

I Am A Life
That Was
CHANGED!

Soon to be released books:

Leadership Explosion
"Leaders that will 'Rock your World!'"

"Charassō" Chiseled Character
Changes in Your Life and Business Open the Door of Opportunity for HUGE Success.

Go Ahead! Open That Door!
Get FIRED –UP and make an IMPACT for Christ!

I've often said, "You never know what you miss...until you miss." With that in mind, don't miss reading this book by Phillip Hatfield...or you'll miss a blessing.

Brad Strand
Author Strand Study Bible
Sr. Pastor Harvest Bible Church

What an amazing story. Carried by Angels *is a story of faith, persistence, mentors and friendship that have shaped the destiny of a man who has found what his purpose in life is all about. And what greater purpose in life is there than that? Phillip sets a high bar for us all in finding the best in every situation and making a difference in so many peoples lives."*

Kyle Wilson,
Founder Jim Rohn International
Author of *52 Lessons I Learned From Jim Rohn and Other Great Legends I Promoted*

CARRIED by *Angels*

Phillip Hatfield

HATFIELD
HOUSE
PUBLISHING

Cover Photo by Tom Watson Photography

For Speaking Engagements
Travels worldwide
From Dallas, Texas
www.PhillipHatfield.com
Phillip@PhillipHatfield.com
214-912-5795

Library of Congress Control Number: 2013903931

10 9 8 7 6 5 4 3 2 1

978-0-9846732-0-9 Softcover
978-0-9846732-1-6 Hardcover
978-0-9846732-2-3 E Book

Table of Contents

Dedication

This book is dedicated to all of the hundreds and hundreds of people who literally came rushing to my side during my tragic accident. To those of you who took care of my family and me, those of you who stayed with me and my family all the way through from the first night of the accident and the months that I was in Parkland Hospital and my recovery afterwards. There are hundreds of you and I cannot possibly list everyone's name. Prestonwood Church, Dallas Christian Singles, American Homestar Corp., John Browning my attorney, and on and on the list goes.

This book is also dedicated to Parkland Hospital and all of its employees and staff, from the doctors, nurses and nurse aides, to the physical, occupational and speech therapists who worked with me to regain my life and day-to-day activities. The trauma team also deserves recognition as well as the orthopedic surgeons and their team from Dr. Adam Starr's department. This includes the janitors and the dishwashers, too, as well as all the office and administration personnel. It took the whole team of you at Parkland Hospital doing your job for me to receive the lifesaving care and nurturing that I received from you. God used all of you to help save my life. Thank you so much Parkland Hospital.

This book is also dedicated to all my doctors from UT Southwestern School of Medicine and Doctor Frank Gottschalk.

Acknowledgments

There are so many people to thank I cannot possibly get them all in! Many of you will see your name in this book. Thank you so much to everyone for being a part of my story.

I am so thankful to Laurie Magers, at the Ziglar Corporation and personal assistant to Zig for over 35 years now. Thank you for all your hard work on this project with me, all the hours in editing. Thank you so very much for your encouragement all along the way. You have done a wonderful job.

John Caton, thank you for the phone call and re-igniting me, and inviting me back to Ziglar offices for that Monday morning meeting last May.

Thank you Larry Chapman of Rood Scholar Press for helping me complete the process and all that you do for me. Even taking me on those long walks, or I should say my one-legged hops in the park on my walker, after my release from the hospital and the amputation of my leg.

Thank you Amanda Boyd and Janet Long for this beautiful book cover design, and Janet for the book layout.

Thank you to all the people who serve in the *media departments* of your local church, as well as the people who put the Gospel on the airwaves from TV and radio to the Internet. Thank you all for giving your selfless gift of service. I always call you media guys "the faces with no names," because I always passed you in the hallways and you were always smiling as we passed by each other. You are always so busy working while we are enjoying the services. We see your faces yet we never seem to know your names! Thank you for your service. Yes, your contribution in media does pay off, because I am a life that was changed. Thank you to the media team at First Bossier, Eddie Anders, Daniel Dooly, and all the rest of you guys.

Thank you, especially, to First Word in Bossier City, Louisiana and Dr. Fred Lowery. "The First Word" got my attention and brought me home! Thank you for your television ministry.

Thank you, my wonderful, beautiful, sweet and awesome bride, Erika, for your support and words of wisdom. Thank you for your encouragement to keep working on this book and the other books that are in the works. Thank you for pushing me to get the story out. I love you dearly.

Thank you, my kids Jeremy (Mr. Magoo) and his wife Stine; Emma and Christian and my precious grandkids Cameron, Matthew and Lily. I love my blended family; God blessed me to have all of you in my extended life by God's amazing grace!

Thank you to the greatest parents who ever lived, Dan and Rosa Hatfield. I never could ever put all the words on paper to express my love and gratitude to you both. I was so blessed with a dad who has shown me the love of Christ in action because you "chose" to be my dad when my own dad didn't want me. You "chose" to love me, just as Christ did. Thank you, Mom, for staying all those agonizing days and long nights by my side at the hospital and the many months afterward when you were taking care of me at home.

To my wonderful sister, Sharon Gibson. Thank you, Sis, so very much for taking care of me when I could not help myself through all the long days in the hospital, and for making those life or death decisions that had to be made and saved my life. Thank you, Sharon, for all you have done. I love you so much and words can never tell.

Thank you to my pastors, mentors and friends, Dr. Fred Lowery, Dr. Jack Graham, Steve Stroope, Wes Hartley, Brad Strand, Todd Bell, Ray Raney, Don Dixon, and the Gideons. Thank you Zig Ziglar and Tom Ziglar. A special thanks also to Eddie Faith, Pat Worley, Robert Finley, Willie Buffington, Ron Lewis, Lee Phipps and Carlos Meza for being men who walked the new walk with me and mentored me along the way! Yes, I am still a work in progress. I have not arrived yet.

Thank you & God bless all of you,

Phillip

<(((><

Foreword

Have you ever prayed *for a passing ambulance? When I was 30 years old I was playing in a golf tournament and I remember looking up and seeing a Careflight helicopter fly over us. For some reason it struck me and I couldn't get it out of my mind. Later that day when the tournament was complete I learned that it was my sister in the helicopter being transported to a hospital in downtown Dallas. Something in my spirit knew that the helicopter was carrying a loved one. Now when I see an ambulance on the road I often think that someone's loved one is in there and perhaps someday it will be my turn.*

The reality in life is we don't know the future. Our turn for something is coming! So, I have a question for you; when your turn comes, will you be ready to be "Carried By Angels"? As Dad says, your past is important because it is what has gotten you to here, but it isn't nearly as important as the decisions you make today about the future you will have tomorrow. The message of this book is simple. Regardless of your past you can start today, right now, and create an incredible future. And the circumstances, even if your body is crushed in a motorcycle accident, do not determine your joy and happiness in life. Read the first few pages and I know you will want to read more. And, like me, you will come to love the phrase "trouble grace." Grace is amazing as the song goes, but "trouble grace" sustains you when you have nothing left. Read this book, buy into what it says, and when your turn comes, you will be ready to be "Carried By Angels."

Tom Ziglar,
The Proud Son of Zig Ziglar

Introduction

Do you believe in *Angels?*

If you ask me, the answer to that question is a resounding, *YES!* Absolutely! I believe in angels as much as I believe in the air that I breathe and the unseen oxygen that is in the air that sustains the very life that you and I are so blessed to live today.

Angels are sometimes just like the oxygen that is in the air; they can be all around, and you do not even see them or know they are there. Then there are times when angels just suddenly appear! Possibly angels arriving on the scene to render aid like when we are in traumatic situations, or sometimes angels come to give us encouragement or even to lead us or guide us in certain situations or circumstances. Then there are the times angels are there just to comfort us. Knowing that angels are only sent by God to carry out His divine orders and purpose and that He cares so much to send them is overwhelming. Just to feel the powerful presence of God and know He is near, tending to our needs is an indescribable feeling.

No matter what we may think, angels are beings that follow the directions God gives them. He gives them a mission and they carry it out to completion! Yes, *they are as much alive as you and I are. Angels are spiritual beings that sometimes cannot be seen at all, yet they sometimes will just appear and take on human form, just like they did in the Old Testament, and again taking on human form in the New testament of the Bible, too.* We will get more into this a little later.

I want to tell you that after all of the things that I have been through and all of the things that I have seen, I have to answer *yes. I have seen angels and I have heard their voices, too.* No, I am not losing my mind! Stay with me here and take a look for yourself! If you open up your Bible, it is full of angels from Genesis all the way to the end of Revelation, and what better place to get the information on them than the Creator Himself. After all, God created angels before He laid the foundation of the world, and that would make Him, God, the ultimate authority on the subject of angels. Wouldn't you agree that God is the Authority on the subject?

So, Absolutely, Undeniably, Emphatically! *YES*. **I believe!**

However it does not really matter if I believe in angels or not! There are angels and they are all around us! My belief has nothing to do with "The Truth." As the saying goes, "*It is—what it is.*" God said it so many times and in so many ways all through His Word, and that alone makes it so.

One of the main things that I have learned through my walk with God is that **"if I will do the possible…God will do the impossible!"** God will use His messengers (angels), people, situations, and circumstances; God will use everything in His power and all that He has to do impossible things for YOU and for me.

God is always working *on our behalf and He will bless us in the toughest and the worst of the deepest and darkest times of our lives. He will also bless us in the easy times too.* No, it is not about us! But then again *YES, it is. It is, **all about us!*** He blesses us and uses us to bless other people. God blessed me to be a blessing to YOU, and he blessed you to be a blessing to me or someone else.

God never, ever leaves us alone or asks us to carry out any mission alone. No matter what is happening or going on in our lives, God is there! Sometimes when we think we are all alone—BAM, God shows up. He may be ever so quiet when He arrives on the scene and you never even know that He has arrived, or He may show up with a BIG BANG. Then again, God just may send one of His Heavenly angels on mission to carry out a task for you or just to walk along beside you. So absolutely, life is all about YOU and me. As my friend Zig Ziglar told his son Tom Ziglar, "God don't make no junk." WE are not an accident! We are purposefully created to be an instrument to help other people and to be a blessing to others and to be blessed as we live lives that bring honor to God. So God may send those angels to us at any time.

Angels are such a wonderful, fantastic and magnificent creation; they operate only at God's command! They will only follow His divine direction. We cannot pray to angels and have them come to our rescue, so there is no need to pray to the angels. They will not answer or respond to your command. NOPE. We are to pray to God. He is the only one who sends the angels! After all, He did promise to supply *all* of our needs, didn't He? So we do not even have to pray for help sometimes, God just sees the need and responds. However, God does like to hear from us and He loves us to ask Him for help. God loves being a father, and a dad; He loves to have us ask Him for our needs and wants, just as He loves for us to tell Him about our day. He loves for us to just commune with Him and have conversation.

God always chooses the best way to help us, and how to grow and strengthen our faith in the process of the trial that we may have. So whether His help is by the Holy Spirit or an angel, or however God chooses to respond to our needs, it is all His decision. But He will always come through for us; for you and for me, and sometimes God chooses to use His angels to respond.

Once God has given the directive and the angel has his mission then *bam*, they come rushing in faster than anything you could possibly imagine. As a matter of fact, *it is unimaginable how fast, strong and powerful angels are*; yet how softly and gently they can carry out their mission as well.

Yes, as believers we are surrounded by angels on every side. As we will see later, *angels are one of the most powerful instruments* in "God's Holy Tool Box." Have you ever stopped and thought about that? Think of all of the tools and instruments God has available to Him. You never really thought about all of the tools God has in His toolbox, have you? Well you are one of those tools, too.

Yes, I believe in angels as much as I believe in Jesus' resurrection from the grave and the angel that was sent from God above that sat there on that tombstone the third day and announced to Mary, *"He is not here!"*

"He has RISEN."

Yes, angels start to appear in the very beginning of time, in Genesis and all through the Bible to Revelation and even still to this very day. There are also many accounts of angel appearances and sightings by hundreds of very credible people. Here is a recent true story from a friend of mine, Zig Ziglar.

Zig's Angel

Zig tells the story of when he was in the hospital on February 22, 2002, and had lost six pints of blood from the complications. The doctors called out a "Code Blue, Code Blue" alert. Zig was completely out; however, he had been silently praying while he was unconscious, "Lord let me live! I still have some things I need to do for you." Then an angel appeared!

The angel was a man about 65 years old, tall and slender, wearing a tan hat and a tan suit. The angel looked at Zig dead in the eye and shot him the ok sign with his thumb and index finger with a smile on his face letting Zig know everything was going to be ok. But as Zig says, "God was not satisfied with that." He wanted to give him a second indication of an angel.

On the tenth day he was in the hospital, Zig received a phone call from a good, close friend of over 40 years. He is a Jewish man named Bernie Lofchick from Winnipeg, Manitoba, Canada. Bernie said "My brother Zig, I had a dream last night and it was the first time I ever had a dream so clear! I dreamed Suzan (Zig's deceased daughter) came to me and she was dressed like an angel. She looked right at me and said, "Brother Bern, don't worry about Dad, he is going to be with us a long time."

I agree with Zig 100%! God sends angels to look after His own. The question I have for you is, *are YOU one of His own?* If you cannot answer the question with a definite yes, then please pick up that phone and give me a call. Today! My number is right here in this book, or send me an e-mail. As Joan Rivers says, "Let's talk."

Today is December 1, 2012, and I just met Bernie at Zig Ziglar's visitation at the funeral home on Friday night, November 30, and I heard the story from Bernie, FIRST HAND.

Bernie said he was on his way to visit Zig in the hospital and his flight out of Winnipeg, Manitoba, Canada was delayed. There were problems getting the flight out and he had to wait until the next morning to fly out. Bernie said, " *I finally got to sleep and I was in the deepest sleep I have ever had. While I was asleep I saw an angel; however, it was Zig's daughter Suzan from Heaven. I know Suzan so well, with her being Zig and Jean's firstborn and being friends with Zig for so long. Suzan was like a daughter to me. I knew every detail about Suzan.*" Bernie went on and described her to a "T," right down to her beautiful eyes. He said she told him, "Uncle Bern, don't worry about Dad, he is going to be with us a long time." Bernie said when he woke up, immediately he knew it was not a dream but God had sent an angel to him. Bernie got on the phone right away to call Zig in the hospital here in Dallas. He said when the phone rang a miracle happened, Zig answered the phone! He said Zig was sitting up in the bed as he listened to the story from Bernie, and Zig started laughing and shared with

Bernie his angel story.

YES that was not a coincidence. As Zig says, "Coincidence is God's way of remaining anonymous." However, this time God was showing Himself to two men hundreds of miles apart.

But let's not just go with that one credible experience from Zig. Let's continue to explore as we read about what God and the Bible itself says about angels. You will be amazed. Let's start right here and take a look. In the book of Hebrews, the Bible tells us to *"be careful because we entertain angels unaware."*

Hebrews 13:2 says *(ESV)*:

> *"Do not neglect to show hospitality to strangers, for thereby some have entertained angels unaware."*

So what does that tell you?

Sometimes we encounter angels when we do not even know it!

That is what this story is all about! Encounters, sometimes when I was not even aware of them! Then there were the times when I knew full well that God had sent an angel to me at that very second! You see, God is always at work in our lives. He is always here for us as a loving Father, supplying all of our needs! Not necessarily all of our wants! But He promises to always be right there with us, just like the Scripture in Psalms 34:1-22 *(ESV)*. I love the whole chapter but especially verse seven when it says,

> *"The angel of the Lord encamps all around those who fear Him, and He delivers them."*

This is my story and about those angels that are all around us, and the story of entertaining angels when I was not even aware they were there. You are about to read an amazing, fun and exciting true story, and in this story you will see *triumph over tragedy* and real *success over failures; victory over a selfish and conceited pride.* You are going to see many things in this story like *bikers, gambling and murder,* all ending in a genuine salvation experience of a life that was truly changed. Then there was the fulfillment of His promise that He would never leave me. God took special care of me when I needed it, and I was *"Carried by Angels"* at a time when I could not help myself. You will also get to see how "My Greatest Tragedy truly is My Greatest Blessing." Oh yes, and there is a real love story in this book, too. So get ready—we are going to have some fun!

Walk with me on this awesome journey. We are going to be side by side and you will see it all through my eyes. You will get to see my experience of "**Trouble Grace.**" Yes, a grace I am sure you have never heard about before. We will also explore the times of my life before I became a Christian. Uh-oh, that is going to be a very rough ride so you'd better buckle up. Then several years later my salvation, and the story of being "*Carried by Angels*" in the midst of that very terrible, traumatic and tragic storm. This whole unbelievable story is about to unfold before your very eyes.

Are you ready?

Let's go!

<<<(><

The Story

This story is about God, angels and people, all of them coming together in the process and redemption of a 39-year-old man, me. Then, **bam**, they all come alive together in a time of extreme need and when you least expect it.

Then you rise up, and bursting through the unexpected battles and the ups and downs of life you stop to realize that the supernatural power that you have just encountered is not your own power. It is an *empowerment* from God above that is delivered by His Holy Spirit or by His angel messengers. Who knows, *I bet you too may even be able to see yourself at times having been picked up out of a storm*, and see times when you were "Carried by Angels" too. Then you can see how "**Your Greatest Tragedy really can be your Greatest Blessing**," too.

Oh, yes, I believe angels will carry you through that valley that you may be in right now, too, no matter how deep or dark it may seem to you at the moment. Maybe it is the Holy Spirit at work right now, helping you through that tough time you are in and not angels. No matter what, God is still at work! So the question you will have to decide for yourself is whether you believe it is angels or the Holy Spirit. But that is not that important of an issue, because *the real issue is that God fulfills His promise to never leave us or forsake us*. **The message here is not all about angels, it is about God's provision!** However, God provided for me through His angels.

As you read this story you may say, "No, you are wrong! That is not an angel; it is the Holy Spirit at work!" You may well be right! However, personally, I believe God sent angels to raise me up and to give me a message that He is faithful and true and I can trust Him in all walks of life, from the start of my salvation journey and even in the deep, dark pit of despair of my own personal tragedy.

So Father, Son, Holy Spirit or angels makes absolutely no difference to me at all. It is simply the promise of Scripture fulfilled of my deliverance and protection. Then being cared for, encouraged and comforted, never being left alone. God supplied all my needs. So however God chooses to take care of me is all right by me! I am just happy that He is always there in one form or another and that all of His promises are true; especially, the promise that He will never leave me or forsake me. Guess what? He did it! He provided for me in unbelievable ways! It is TRUE! His promises are TRUE! I am living proof! He never once left me alone. He sent angels to carry me in the toughest of times when I could not help myself at all!

God is there by your side, too! So no matter what YOUR situation or the circumstances are, trust His heart. As Dr. Fred Lowery used to say, "*When you cannot see Gods hand, trust His heart!*" Sometimes God works through regular, common and ordinary people just like you and me! Then there are times God also works through the Holy Spirit and there are the times when He chooses to work through His angels, too.

God has so many tools at His disposal to use. I am just asking you to use an open mind and survey the Scriptures for yourself. *Just like in Elisha's situation when he could see the angels all around to protect him*, but his servant could not see them and Elisha prayed, "God, open his eyes that he might see." Read it here and see for yourself.

2 Kings 6:17 says *(ESV)*:

Then Elisha prayed and said, "O LORD, please open eyes that he may see."
So the LORD opened the eyes of the young man, and he saw, and behold,
the mountain was full of horses and chariots of fire all around Elisha.

Yes, these were angels God sent for Elisha's protection. Elisha had the faith and could see them, but his servant needed some help. The servant needed his eyes to be opened to spiritual things! Sometimes we need our eyes to be opened, too.

Angels are ministering spirits that will bring us to a presence of knowing God's dynamic love, even when "bad things happen to good people." Many times I am asked that very question.

"*Why does God allow bad things to happen to good people?*"

To quote Brad Strand from *The Strand Study Bible*:

Contrary to popular belief, bad things don't happen to good people.

According to the Scriptures, there are no "good" people (Job 5:7 & 14:1, Psalms 14:3 & 51:5, Eccl. 7:20, Jeremiah 17:9 and Rom. 3:10,23).

So **"*Why does God allow bad things to happen to good people?*"**

I also believe the answer to this question lies in the eyes and in the heart of the beholder of the tragedy.

Sometimes we may not know the answer. Sometimes it may be years before we can answer that question, however, I would like to answer that question for you right now.

I would like to think for me it is because...*God knows He can trust me!*

OUCH! I know! You are saying, *"Hold on right there, buddy."*

I know that sounds so bad and so self-righteous, too! That is a terrible sounding answer and I know exactly what you are thinking. But please hold on just a second and let me explain.

I really think God knows you or I will turn all honor and glory to Him. God knows you or I will share that triumph with everyone all around you (or me) to bring encouragement to other people or to bring people to see God for the God that He is. I believe He knows we will share the story of Christ with everyone.

The Scriptures say for a man not to think too highly of himself and not to think he is too righteous or he may stumble and fall. I know the previous paragraph sounds so bad and self-righteous, but I pray and I ask you to pray that I always know and that I always give all credit to God and never try to ever claim any credit for myself.

I am the most unworthy and undeserving person ever to receive the magnitude of grace that I have been given. After all, as you read the story and see God everywhere, if any of that power was mine I would not be alive today to tell this story! I would be dead! To God be all glory! The only power I have is to praise and worship God Almighty.

To be available and usable.

To give thanks and submit to Him.

To be a vessel that is open and available to be used by God. That is my prayer...to be faithful.

My life's verse that I chose to live by many years ago is found in Ephesians 6: 18-20

"18 praying always with all prayer and supplication in the Spirit, being watchful to this end with all perseverance and supplication for all the

saints—19 and for me, that utterance may be given to me, that I may open my mouth boldly to make known the mystery of the gospel, 20 for which I am an ambassador in chains; that in it I may speak boldly, as I ought to speak."

As my new friend Les Brown, the famous speaker says, "**Tell the message, sell the messenger!**"

Jesus is for real and FREE!

So, yes, I am so very well aware that it's not about me. It is about Him! God.

When bad things do happen in life, we have to realize that God allows all of us to have and use our own free will. God has given us that free will so we can choose to show Him and other people just how much we really do love Him, and how grateful we are for our salvation experience and that no matter what, we really do trust Him. It does not matter if we are in good times or bad times, we make a conscious choice to worship and praise Him no matter what. So I choose personally to give all honor and glory of **our** victory to Him.

Whatever that bad thing is that has happed to you, that is the open door and the opportunity for others to see that God is real and moving in your life!

It is time for other people to see *God is alive and miracles still do happen today.* **So, get yourself out of the way and let God use you**. Get out of that pity party of your bad situation and let God do a miracle that will draw people to Him. He will flat out *blow your mind*; God will amaze you and strengthen your faith as well as the faith of all of those people that are all around you. Let God amaze all of those watching and praying for you. **Let God *blow* their minds and amaze your family and friends, your co-workers and neighbors**. *Get out of the way so God can do a miracle through you!* Who knows, God may be using *you* and that bad situation you are in to bring someone else to Himself right now. *So what if you become disabled in the process? OUCH!* That is even more power for God to show Himself. *Trust me on that.* God will bring you so much joy to see Him using you to bless so many other people in ways you never thought possible. You get to see God use YOU.

The truth is, *I should not even be alive today!* I am alive by His mercy and grace.

Grace is *NOT getting what I deserve but getting something I do NOT deserve.* So, I am living on " EXTENDED grace time." This breath I take right now at this very moment is NOT mine. It is a gift I do NOT deserve. My life is "Extended Grace"! God's amazing and wonderful gift of mercy, giving me living a longer life here on this earth. But why? If I had died that day, then GREAT, I would be in Heaven today celebrating right now. So what is the significance of my life? Why would God save my life?

So why am I still here?

Why *did God leave me here?*

What *exactly am I here for?*

Who *am I here for?*

*What is my **new** purpose or mission?*

Well, one thing is for sure! I know my purpose and my place more today than at any point ever in my life!

What about you?

God left me here a little longer to proclaim that He is everything. **I know God left me here to serve.** I am here to encourage you and others, too. I am here to be a Barnabas. I am here to help people see all of the blessings that we all really have! I am here to witness to anyone who I can and to plant the seed of the knowledge of a risen Savior, Jesus Christ. Who knows, I may be here just to water the seed that you planted in someone else's life years ago. No matter what, *I am called to be a Barnabas, and encourager!*

Let me tell you something. My being disabled and this prosthetic leg that I wear and this limp that I have, opens more doors for me than I can ever even begin to explain to you!

No, not doors of prosperity, but doors to encourage people just like you.

I LOVE this leg I have! And...I HATE this leg I have.

Sometimes life can be so tough and the pain is just unbearable sometimes. But that love/hate relationship is what keeps me at the foot of the cross on my knees. Jut like the apostle Paul and that thorn in his side.

The truth be told, I LOVE this leg and this journey I am on.

This new way of life is NOT my cross to bear!

Absolutely NOT! This leg and life I have is "MY Blessing"!

This is MY privilege!

This leg and my disabled life are MY tools and my special gift from God. This is my testimony! As you have heard before "If there is no TEST, there can be no Testimony." I LOVE my Testimony. NO you cannot have it. This one is MINE.

Go get your own testimony.

This one is mine!

Just take a look and see how God uses this prosthetic leg of mine and this good-looking, short, fat, one-legged guy! Me.

Little children will be walking by me and say *"Look Mommy, what is that? What happened to that man?"*

Then bam, *the door of opportunity is now open.*

I can get down on their level, look them in the eye and explain, "The car did not stop at the red light. That is why Mommy and Daddy tell you to stay away from streets. Mommy and Daddy love you too much to see you get hurt! So listen to your parents and stay away from the street, because sometimes those cars just do not stop at the stop sign and red lights." I can tell them Jesus loves me! And I can tell them that Jesus loves them, too. *They listen intently and the smallest child and I are communicating on a level that I have never seen before in my life. They understand, listen and talk back. I never knew children were so intelligent and understanding, and feel such love and compassion. It is like they are feeling the conversation we are having. I cannot explain it. I am not a child psychologist.* But I have a new understanding of children too. **Oh, yes, I can definitely see why God left me here. I am a child ambassador for Christ sometimes.**

This leg opens the door for all kinds of ministry and encouragement opportunities!

This prosthetic leg of mine opens the door for adults as they are looking at my leg or me. I get reactions that will crack you up laughing, and sometimes I get that weird look of disgust, like I am a freak, too. No matter what the look I get, they will almost always ask, "What happened to you?"

Bam, *the door of opportunity is now open.*

All I have to do is walk right through it and tell them what happened to me and that I am so blessed just to be alive! God has blessed me beyond anything I could ever have imagined. At this point I can be an encourager to them. *So many times it opens the door in conversations where I can seize the opportunity* and ask them, "Where do you go to church?" and I get the response, "We do not go any more!" or "I do NOT believe in God. I do not believe in Jesus."

*Bam, the door is now **wide** open.*

*I want you to see God has given me a tremendous **gift** and a tool as well as a tremendous blessing! However…with this gift comes a tremendous **responsibility**, too!*

God has given me a "Visual Tool"! Yes, a special tool to witness for Him!

I have been given a powerful and wonderful gift! I get to tell the stories of Jesus and His love and grace and His mercy given to me. Y*es, I have a life and I have a tool to share with the whole world more about the abundant life that I have.* No, my life is not easy now; there are tough days still. There are still those days of being back in the wheelchair, or days back on a walker again. YES, yes, there are still days I cannot walk because of infections in my leg and many other issues I could sit here and cry about. *But I **choose** to be a blessing and a conduit that God can use.* I choose to tell the story and live the story of GRACE.

That is why I have to share this story!

The story is about Faith, Family and Friends, and all of us together being the "Hands and Feet" of Christ!

I want to share my story so you can see it is about picking yourself up, too, and dusting yourself off when you do not have the strength or power on your own to *get up*. Yet, for some reason, you have that power and strength to get up. Even after that devastating storm that leaves you knocked down in the dirt and feeling like you were just run over by a freight train, then hit hard by an 18-wheeler and it backed up and ran over you all over again. Then you GET UP and get FIRED up. You rise up! You can see God has blessed and empowered YOU and now you are *exploding* through the barriers that are before you, too, with a power and strength that is not humanly possible. It is the strength and *power* of God, and of His Son Jesus Christ!

You are not only surviving but now you are thriving! You are now enjoying a new and fantastic life living in this new journey right here where you are at this very moment. Please, ***let God raise you up*** for His glory and you will be blessed. **All we have to do is the Possible and God will do the Impossible!**

So whether you are able-bodied or disabled like I am now, you can *thrive.*

Yes, *now* after that life-altering tragic storm of life that you have just encountered or the storm that you may be going through right now, you are empowered right now, too, JUST like me!

So have FUN, have Faith and "BE Blessed."

Get up! Get back in the game of living and have a great life. John 16:33 says:

Have peace, because in this life you will have trouble.

He did not say pray for peace. He said:

"Have peace"!

Do not let Satan rob you of your life and the *"gift"* of that tragedy or that storm. We all have trials and tribulations; we all get knocked down, so *get up* and get with it. Come on! I am right here with you. Pick up that phone and call me, email me. You have my address right here in this book! I want to hear from you and I want to encourage YOU or whoever you know that I can be a blessing, too. So contact me today or tonight!

This story is about *YOU* finding a "new dream" and a "new vision," and getting a "renewed passion."

This is about you seeing where I have been *"Carried by Angels."* You probably have been, too, just like my friend Zig.

This is about YOU using your tragedy or trial as a tool to encourage other people and taking your focus off of yourself. When you do that you will find you are receiving so much more than you are giving. I *promise.* When you give, it is like Christmas all year long. You start receiving blessings every day. No, it may not be money; no, it may not be physical gifts, but you receive inner peace and more blessings. The more you give, the more you want to give, and then the more you receive.

By getting involved in your new passion you will find FREEDOM and happiness that you did not even know existed. That is what you hear about, right? So why not reach out there and grab a big ol' fistful of happiness for yourself? Go ahead, be selfish! *Get you some!* Grab you some of that peace, happiness, joy and FREEDOM. I dare you!

Once you engage and **embrace your tragedy** or trial, and when you are executing your action plan, you will find that you are now living your life to the fullest and way beyond your imagination and you are having a blast doing it, too! That is when you have a life of fulfillment and lots of fun, too, plus living in real heartfelt peace and genuine happiness!

That is when you are living a life of HEART and with HEART!

Notice: I did not say a problem-free life! Nope. Even though we are Christians LIFE still happens, but we get to choose to be a Blessing or a Burden

Yes, this story is about living life through a life-changing tragic event that took place ten years after my salvation experience. *That is when God sent angles in to carry me through the most tragic storm of my life!* Becoming a Christian does *not* give you a perfect, problem-free life! It gives you salvation and a promise of eternal life without all these problems, pains, and issues we have to deal with now here on this earth. Becoming a Christian gives you a whole new way of living life and a new way of handling your own situations in life. Becoming a Christian and imitator of Christ gives us all a life of eternity to be with Jesus and hear those awesome Bible stories come alive, and to hear it all firsthand from the Bible characters. We get to hear their stories. We get to see Jesus and talk and walk with Him. We get to live through all of eternity with our friends, family and people who we may have had some impact on in their life, and they will all be there to welcome us into Heaven to see Jesus and live an abundant eternal life.. Yes, we get a whole new life.

Yes, bad things do happen to good people!

So no, I am not talking about a perfect, or problem- or trouble-free Christian life, but a life that shows how *"My Greatest Tragedy truly is My Greatest Blessing."* You can have the exact same thing, too. Those terrible changes of life that happen to you really can bring you amazing and awesome blessings, and *you will find talents that you never even knew you had!*

I have heard it said, **"God does not call the equipped, but he equips the called."** Sometimes that requires some adjusting on our part. God is equipping you for a special mission just like mine. **Sometimes that may mean going from being a perfectly healthy and able-bodied person to becoming *disabled or physically challenged just like me.*** Who knows?

God sometimes has to do some chiseling on us and on our character, too. I needed some chiseling. I did not say I wanted it. **I needed something that I never thought I needed or even wanted! No, I do not want to be where I am today. But I would rather be here like I am and be used by God than to just**

be going through life not knowing my true direction or purpose. God had to do some chiseling on me. Just like those presidents' heads in Mt. Rushmore that were there in the mountainside all the time; they just had to be carved and chiseled out so that all of the beauty could be seen and admired by everyone all over the world.

That is what God does with us; He has to chisel on us sometimes and even a little pruning of us, too. He does this to make us happy! Yes, it makes us happy to be more like Christ. Or it is to make us more usable, and when God uses us, let me tell you, it brings a joy to you that I cannot even begin to explain to you.

Yes, God holds the chisel and God holds the hammer, too, and sometimes we need to be chiseled a little bit so everyone all over the world can see and admire all of our real, natural beauty! We are so beautiful and fearfully and wonderfully made in His image. We are a masterpiece underneath that hard old crusty exterior that life has caked up on top of us! God chisels away the junk in our lives and polishes us up so He can show us off for His glory! He is proud of us. He admires His Creation, YOU! Yes, you are that diamond in the rough.

This story really is not about me but about God! After all, He is everything and all that I am is because of Him. This is about God and His angels, along with the Holy Spirit and ordinary people just like you doing truly extraordinary things.

The Scripture in Hebrews in chapter 1:14 says:

> *"Are not all angels ministering spirits sent to serve those who will inherit salvation?"*

You will see where God and His angels, as well as the Holy Spirit, brought me to the place in my life where *I would finally accept Christ as the Messiah.* I would finally really accept Jesus at 39 years old and my life would radically change.

Those angels that seemed to appear in my salvation story and seemed to be all around <u>vanished</u> just as fast as they appeared, only to reappear again 10 years later when I was *"Carried by Angels"* through the most difficult fires and the most tragic storms of life.

So let me ask you again. Do you believe in Angels?

"Oh, Yes," as you know by now I certainly do!

After all, angels are listed in 34 books of the Bible from Genesis to Revelation, from the oldest written book of the Bible, Job, to the newest book written by Apostle John, the book of Revelation.

I have learned that there are angels on every side of us, and on every front surrounding all of us.

All that we have to do is open up our spiritual eyes. No, we are not walking this walk alone. So whether you are going through a terrible storm in your life right now or just living out your daily life, then "*be encouraged.*" Stop! Look! Listen! **You may even see, hear or feel the brush of angel wings all around you, too**.

Yes, there are those beautiful Heavenly celestial beings, some with six wings, that transcend the Heavens and come to dwell among us here on earth. I also believe that there are "*angels with skin on*" who walk side by side with us on two legs like you and me through this journey that we have here on this earth. Hmm, I just had a crazy thought, but since I am now an amputee with one leg, maybe God has some one-legged angels walking down here, too. *So now you see that you have a leg up on me already.* I love to think and wonder how I will get to dance when I get to Heaven. I don't know, but what a thought. But, I'm gonna be dancing somehow. Hey, ya wanna loan me a leg? Oh, yes. Just as King David danced before God in the streets, I will be dancing, too, but I will have my clothes on. Poor King David lost his clothes.

In this story you will see and hear from my own experiences.

I also will share stories of other people, friends and family members that are as true as I know them to be.

I have tried to be as accurate as possible.

HOWEVER, If I have made a mistake in any way, please forgive me and let me know and I will make corrections in the next printing.

All I know is what **I have seen with my own eyes** and what I have experienced in my own life. I have not only seen angels, but I have been "**Carried by Angels.**" That is the story I want to share with you. I want you to see that "**My Greatest Tragedy is My Greatest Blessing.**"

<((><

Prolog

It all started when a good friend of mine, John Caton from Kansas City, called me and said, "I am coming to Dallas to see Zig. Do you want to meet at the Ziglar offices on Monday morning, May 23, 2011?"

John is a close and personal friend of mine and so is Zig. It had been over a year since I had been able to see Zig myself. My life was pretty hectic and busy then, with all of the therapy and recovery from my accident, and I was still getting used to being a new amputee, too. Plus, I had gotten married *(Woo Hoo)* and moved to Rockwall on the other side of Dallas. So I said, "Yes, John, I would *love* to meet you at Zig's office." It was a date, Monday, May 23, 2011, at 8:00 a.m. Another date, another marker that now marks a significant change in my life!

I went to the meeting and had a great time. We were wrapping up everything and standing in the hall when Zig asked me, *"Now, just when are you going to write that book?"* I said, "Zig, you have me confused with someone else. You know I cannot even spell!" Zig said, ***"I didn't ask if you could spell! I said when are you going to write that book?"***

Zig tells lots of people to write a book and that is what he has been telling me since 2004. Every time I saw him he would ask, *"When are you going to get started on that book?"*

"What are you waiting on?"

But this time it hit me like a ton of bricks right smack in the middle of my chest. I knew immediately that I needed to share this story about what God has done for me. I was still recovering from my accident that almost killed me and left me disabled. But yet I am still so much more alive today than ever before, and I am blessed way beyond my wildest dreams! I am so happy even after all of the major changes in my life. No, I am not defeated; I am living a life of victory! My body has literally been destroyed, but my life now has a whole new meaning and purpose to it, and I have a new mission to accomplish. I have a whole new story to tell of God's grace that no one else has. **I have been able to experience**

God like very few people on this earth ever have! I got to brush by the gates of Heaven. So today Zig's question resonated in me all day long. This time he struck a chord. I got home later on that Monday afternoon and told my wife Erika (who I call my Bride) what Zig had said. Then she replied, *"So, when are you going to get started?"* Hmm…ok, so, here it is! I finally got the courage to give it a try and started writing the very next week, Monday, May 30, 2011.

In this story you are going to see everything from an *ego-driven, conceited, confident yet egotistical man, driven to succeed in business and in life by a selfish, arrogant and obstinate pride.* Then when Christ enters the equation the Bible and the Scriptures literally jump off the page and burst into life. Everything comes alive. You will see that God has given me undeserved mercy and grace. That is what this story is all about—grace.

After I became a Christian in 1998, that famous quote I had heard since 1993 began to make sense. *"You can have everything in life you want if you will just help enough other people get what they want."* Zig Ziglar. We will explore more about that later. But it is amazing: the more you help others, the more you get back in return.

As you start this journey with me, don't be thrown off as you are reading the story. There are going to be segments that at first may seem totally meaningless at the time, or they may seem completely out of place. You might think it is just a random rambling, or possibly even a wandering of thoughts. But, if you think about it for a second, just as in our own lives there is a continual progression of life's daily situations and circumstances, all of the details make our lives come alive.

Life is one continual story made up of several short stories all intertwined together to make up the one big story we call life. So do not skip through those short segments or you will miss some key elements. There is a progression in this story as life unfolds. So in order to understand it all you will have to see each piece of the puzzle and how it fits. Plus, all the short stories make it fun and exciting, too.

Come on this journey and you will be blessed. You are going to see some pretty funny things, too. You will get to witness everyday ordinary people come alive, do some *"extraordinary"* and *"amazing"* things. You will see angels come to life and just show up.

As you dig in, remember this story is about a basic guy, a regular good-ol'-Joe. A good person just like you or the guy next door, but I am being very transparent and letting you in to see the deep, dark secret places of my thoughts and actions. I am exposing my true self! You will get a glimpse of who I really was in real life. You will see angels all through this book, so keep your eyes wide open and be blessed.

After seeing and experiencing God and angels in my life, I want to share God's greatness with you, but most of all, His redemption story. I have a "*burning passion*" to share Christ and His story with everyone now more than ever before. I have a need to share His encouragement that He will never leave us or forsake us. Even in the darkest times of our lives. The passion here is to share and encourage everyone, both non-believers and believers, too. I hope to encourage you to get up and keep living the dream that you received when you first came to Christ, and rekindle the passion of that first love. I hope this story will inspire you to use your own *disabilities or abilities* to see all of the possibilities that you have standing right in front of you right now. But, if you are not a believer or do not know Christ, I hope this will inspire you to seek Him out! After all, He said if you would look for Him you would find Him.

So are you ready for the ride of your life?

Here we go…"*Sharing Christ*" and "*His story*" through my story.

Open your eyes and you will see why *Carried By Angels* is the title. I hope that you will see God at work and possibly even be able to see God and His angels all around you, too.

Come on, let's get started.

Here we go!

Carried by Angels

<(((><

BAM, Crash! Hissss...

November 9, 2008 7:24 p.m.

"HOLD ON, STEPH! Hold on as tight as you possibly can! Stay with me and stay with the bike! Do not lean at all just hold onto me as TIGHT as you can!"

I grabbed hold of both brakes, I squeezed my front right-hand brake HARD and I stomped my right-foot brake for the back tire as hard as I could. I was using both of my brakes and gearing down too for maximum stopping power. I grabbed the clutch with my left hand again and pulled it in, clicked down on the floor gear shift lever with my left foot again, gearing down to slow us even more. The car beside me was in the left express lane heading north with us and had braked already and slowed way down. Now the car was just slightly beside and behind us. We were still in the center lane but were fully opened and exposed to full impact on the left side if that car did not stop.

As I slammed down hard on the foot brake again and squeezed the hand brake harder, I felt the front bumper of that big Ford F-350 pickup truck as it tapped us and hit us on the back tire and on the rear fender of the motorcycle. The bike began to wiggle back and forth, side to side, in a fishtail maneuver.

The truck could not stop that fast. The back tire of the bike was just wiggling back and forth as the truck was pushing us forward. We were both trying to stop. The truck was doing all he could to stop but he was about to run completely over the top of us. *So I twisted the throttle all the way down again, wide open, and fired the Harley engine all the way back up to full throttle.* I now had no choice! I had opened her up all the way; there was nothing more I could do. She was SCREAMING with POWER as that Harley engine was WIDE open.

All we could do was hope the girl in the red car *talking on the cell phone* would take her foot off the gas just a little bit and just touch the brake. *If she would just get off the stinking phone and get off the gas, we would all be ok*! If she would just pay attention we would not have an accident!

She was STARING, looking right dead at us but not responding at all to what she was doing.

It was like she could not even see us! She was just looking through us like we did not even exist. *If she would just open her doggone eyes and pay attention, I knew she would see us and STOP!*

As soon as the light bulb went off in the girl's head, she saw what was going on and all the rest of the traffic that was all around her. She could see exactly where she was! *NOW she saw us on the motorcycle*; she could see where we were in the flow of the oncoming traffic in the northbound lane. Now she was aware of the entire calamity, and the destruction on the horizon if she did not STOP!

Then she panicked! **She floored it**, *giving the car all the gas she could. It was pedal to the metal for her. She now was fully alert and wide awake, but now she was committed and trying even harder to outrun us and go all the way across right there in front of us!*

She was trying to go all the way across all three of the northbound lanes of the oncoming traffic, **while she was still talking on the stinking cell phone**, and her traffic light was RED!

STOP! ...STOP, Lady! ...PLEASE STOP!

But she never even noticed or looked up at the red traffic light that she was running.

I had already committed to my plan, too; **I had no other choice**! I was blocked in. With that big truck eating up my back tire, and the back end wiggling as I tried to recover from the truck hitting us, I had just accelerated with all the power the motorcycle had to give. *There were no other options at all.*

The big truck had already tapped me on my back tire with his front bumper once; so I knew what was next. If I did not get the bike going faster right away, we would be run over and be underneath that big truck. And I mean get going faster *"right now!"*

The bike was still wiggling even more on the back end after the truck had pushed even farther up on us. We were now 100% committed to avoiding an accident any way that we possibly could. Somehow, we had to try to get past her because there was just nowhere else for us to go.

That big Ford truck could not stop!

He was right there on my tail still with his tires squealing. They were screaming, burning as they slid on the pavement and *smoking* from him standing on his brakes trying to STOP!

You could hear it and smell all of the burning rubber of his tires. I quickly dropped again into another lower gear, first gear this time, as we were at 20 miles an hour now, **so I busted out and opened up the throttle again** as wide and as hard and fast as it would go. Now I was in the most powerful gear I had.

The bike lifted up, it rose up off the front end with the front tire just barely touching the surface of the street. The back tire of my motorcycle was *biting down hard* and grabbing all of the road it could possibly grab. WE WERE ALMOST IN A WHEELIE POSITION. The engine was now ROARING and SCREAMING.

There were loud bellowing sounds coming from the full throttle of the 103 horsepower Harley engine and with the wide open tailpipes, it was SCREAMING and sounded like a LOCOMOTIVE barreling down fast and hard, full steam ahead, with its horn BLASTING and blowing. It was so LOUD.

I was now leaning over the top of the handlebars, leaning into the wind and over the front of the bike. I was leaning far over the front of the handlebars, trying to push the motorcycle ahead. I lowered my head into the wind to reduce the wind resistance. Steph was leaning forward and pushing hard with me. I leaned even more and pushed and jerked it forward even harder. I was now *trying to push the bike forward with all my might*, weight and strength, pushing as hard as I possibly could.

We were now at maximum power and full throttle. The screaming engine sounds, **horns honking, squealing tires** and *burning smells* of the rubber tires and exhaust fumes were in the air. We were now at 100% maximum power, all we had, 103 horses strong, when all of a sudden it happened!

BAM! Slam! CRASH! SCReeeCH!

Hissss...Hissss...Hissss... sssss. Sssssssssssss.

We were hit HARD!

We were hit, and hit so HARD.

It was the loud sound of impact, the crashing sounds of steel, the sound of the metal from the car hitting the steel frame of my motorcycle, and then the sounds of all the metal hitting metal. We were still in FULL motion FORCED by the IM-PACT.

I was hit hard, too. There I was with my body right there in between all of the crashing steel of the car and motorcycle. I was right there in between the car and the motorcycle frame and HOT engine and exhaust pipe. I was now caught in the front bumper of the car and the hard steel motorcycle frame and that scorching *hot* motorcycle engine.

The squealing of all the tires and the smoke and the smells of all the burning rubber tires were thick in the smoky air. **The hard crash from the car and the sounds of the crashing and crunching continued while the metal was still crushing in and we were falling down to the pavement below.**

That hot motorcycle engine was now BURNING all the way through my jeans and *sizzling into the skin* on the inside of my left knee and leg.

OH, the crushing pain of my knee and my thigh in between the bumper of that red car and the motorcycle crushing on in on the outside and digging deep into the flesh of my leg and body, too! **We were still moving and the car was still *crushing* in**. The burning and damage to my body was getting worse and going deeper and deeper. The hot burning engine was now all the way through my jeans and burning deeply into the flesh of my leg.

Oh, the smell of burning flesh and the smell of that hot burning rubber from our tires skidding down the road, the sounds of all the squealing tires from everyone trying to stop their cars and trucks were awful.

We were hit so *hard*! **Stephanie went flying in the air on impact!** The young girl driving the car was still on her cell phone talking, and had now panicked even more after impact. She was continuing to talk on her stinking phone! She kept her foot on the gas even more after impact, with the car still floored moving full force hard ahead with me and the motorcycle still in her bumper! She was not backing off or slowing down at all!

The car's bumper had now broken all the way through and was all the way down deep into the flesh on the outside of my left thigh. *OH my thigh, it snapped in half like a twig.* My femur bone was broken and the bottom half that was attached to my knee was now pushed all the way up and into my groin! **OH the pain!**

The left side of my body was now completely crushed, my knee snapped and broken from the side, my left leg now deep into the *hot* motorcycle engine even more on the inside of that same left thigh.

The car and the metal of the bike had dug deep in from my thigh all the way down to the calf of my left leg. The bottom of my left leg was crushed and broken in several pieces, all the way to the bottom of my foot.

OH, the pain. My ankle was now crushed and *pushed into the hot motor even more*, and the car's bumper was on the outside of my leg and ankle.

My left foot had now been forced down and had slipped off the gearshift and through the bottom of the floorboard of the motorcycle. *My left foot went straight down to the ground and was caught in between the motorcycle and the car as it was caught between the motorcycle and the pavement below, too.* **The force was now literally ripping my left foot off at my ankle and tearing it all the way through my boot as it filleted and ripped the bottom of my left foot from above the heel of my foot all the way through the Achilles tendon and all the way down to the ball of my foot.**

As the bike and I were still going downward from the side impact of the T-bone crash, I was now headed down toward the concrete pavement.

My *ribs*, at car height and impact level with the front bumper, were crushed. The car was pushing ahead still full force even as we were going down under the front edge of the bumper. **All my left ribs broke on impact**. The bike then slid on down and tumbled as it slid down the road sideways, flipping side over side.

Then the bike hit the concrete and was sliding on down the road. I hit the road skidding, sliding and tumbling too. The **bottom of my back had now broken** above the tailbone and the tailbone itself had broken, too, as I continued tumbling and sliding on down the road.

Stephanie was thrown way off the motorcycle on impact. **She flew through the air way off in the opposite direction of the force of impact.** She hit the pavement hard and broke her pelvis on impact. She flew in a totally different direction from where I was being thrown and where the force of the car was pushing me. We both continued sliding and rolling on the concrete as we were tumbling down the road. *Steph's body was twisting and tumbling like a rag doll!* She was rolling and flipping and flopping as she slid and tumbled towards a clear spot in the roadway, where she finally stopped. Her body was all mangled. I was still tumbling, flipping, sliding, and rolling with the motorcycle, finally skidding and slowing down. The metal of the bike was still crashing and scraping on the pavement, as it was slowing down, too.

I finally came to a skidding/sliding stop just as the motorcycle landed right there by my side. I landed approximately *250–300 feet from the initial point of impact.*

Shhhhhhh! It is quiet.

It was all quiet now...shhhhh

So quiet just for a second!

Everything was now all a blur.

There was almost a complete silence.

It was a really eerie and awkward silence!

* * * * *

All I could hear now was a ringing in my ears and in my head.

I could hear the hissing of the motorcycle, *the rumble of the idling Harley motor*, and the hissssssss.

The fuel was dripping down from the gas tank and the ripped fuel lines and the fuel sizzled as it was hitting and splattering on the hot parts of the engine and hot exhaust pipes.

SPIZZZ, spizzz, as it sizzled even louder and faster.

The smell now all mixed in with the other smells in the air of the burning rubber from tires. The spizzz, spizzz, spizzz splattering right there by my head, as the engine was still running and idling. It rumbled that deep Harley rumbling sound. Then the smell of the gas was so sharp and crisp in the air as it was pooling there by my head on the pavement.

The eerie quiet...

The faint noises and the voices in the background.

I could not hear very well at all, I was dazed. My head was RINGING. Things sounded muffled, and there were loud whistles and noises in my head and a ringing noise in my ears getting louder and louder as I could hear less and less what was going on around me.

It is completely and totally impossible and inconceivable to explain the sounds and the atmosphere at the time. This is one of those times you just have to be there to experience it.

I could hear Stephanie way off in the distance somewhere way behind me. *She was screaming and crying and wailing.*

She was begging for someone to come and help her. She was closer to the traffic as cars were all stopping now by the intersection and the point of impact. The people were running to get to her as fast as they possibly could.

She was lying on that hard, cold concrete street screaming to the top of her lungs at times from the MASSIVE pain and the shock of what was going on.

My heart sank to my toes as I heard her scream and I could not help her!

"Oh, My God, what have I done to Stephanie?"

She was screaming and crying out as loudly as she could,

"DOCTOR, someone call the DOCTOR, get me a doctor, PLEASE!
Someone, help me please! PLEASE HELP ME!" she cried.

The experience was surreal. It was like I was living a terrible nightmare.

I was in pain, yet I felt so guilty at that instant; *I knew I was responsible for Stephanie and that I let her get hurt on my watch, on my motorcycle!* Oh, My GOD, what have I done to HER!

How badly did I let her get hurt? The thought whizzed by very quickly in my head while I was coming to grips with what was going on. It was like a NIGHTMARE!

The experience was way more than possibly could ever be described. *The massive, excruciating, gut-wrenching, agonizing pain was more than I thought was humanly possible to bear!*

*My mind was now rushing; my heart was JUMPING, pounding and thumping, beating hard and **slamming inside up against my chest.***

My body was quivering and jerking and shaking uncontrollably! I knew what had just happened; yet, at the same time, I did not really comprehend what had just happened at all! Everything was all such a blur after the impact!

Then came the realization, even more of that massive, excruciating pain, the throbbing HEART BEAT. PAIN was now blasting hard down on my chest. I felt my HEART BEAT all over my body from head to toe as I was shaking uncontrollably.

I felt my heart beat banging, and the pounding of the pain. My heart was racing and there was extreme pain to the entire left side of my body. I felt my pulse as it was throbbing, too, and beating hard in my neck.

Then the excruciating and agonizing pain as it was building. I felt my heart beating HARD in my chest, my back, my thigh, my leg and foot. *I felt my heart beat all over my body as it felt like it was bursting to get out of this body.*

* * * * *

The PAIN

Oh, my back hurt so badly and I could not breathe in at all; it hurt so terribly that I could not take in a full breath. *The pain was so acute, the sharp pain of trying to suck in air;* it was almost impossible to even take a breath. All of my ribs were broken and I could not breathe; I felt like I was suffocating. I was sucking in for air over and over again, *but there was very little air coming in.* My asthma now kicked in, along with my broken ribs that were pushing deep into my chest.

The pain was so severe and was so sharp! Each breath I took was just a tiny, slim, slight sucking of air. It was just so unbelievable and unbearable. It is just completely unexplainable. I rose up just a little and was trying to look around and see what happened, and all I could see clearly was deep, dark crimson thick red blood, and it was everywhere that I looked!

There was blood all over the place, everywhere; it was in the road and all over me, too. Everywhere I could see there was blood. I saw pools and streams of blood running and channeling away from me through the lines of the concrete street. Then I realized!

It was mine! I was bleeding out, right there in the street!

As I lay there, I was not sure anyone saw me. I was all alone and I didn't know if anyone was even close to me at all. I heard Stephanie still screaming, and I was not able to get a strong enough breath to holler out and cry for help. I tried to scream out but nothing came out.

When I had finally stopped, I had landed with my body all mangled up in all different directions. My hips were facing one direction; my legs were lying in two totally different directions. I landed on my left shoulder blade. The left side of my body was lying on the ice-cold concrete pavement; my chest was facing forward, up toward the sky a little bit. My right side was facing up, yet lying back toward the pavement. I was all twisted up. I stretched out my right arm. I lifted it up to the sky as high as I could with all the strength I had, hoping someone would see me out here in the distance away from the accident.

I remember crying out as loudly as I possibly could, **"AMBULANCE!"** I cried again in as loud a voice as possible, but since I could not breathe it wasn't very loud. *It was not much louder than a whisper.* So I knew I had to holler louder if I wanted anyone to hear me, so I cried out again

"AMMBBUULAANNCCE!

"AMMBBUULAANNCCE!!!!!" I cried out again as I raised my right arm up to the sky as high as I could reach. I was looking for help and I was praying.

Oh, God, help me, please. *Am I going to die right here? Please, Lord; forgive me for all my sins. Take care of my son Jeremy and my mom and dad.* FORGIVE me please.

Then once again I cried out as loudly as I possibly could. I **screamed** once again **"AMBULANCE!!!!!!!!"**

As I lay there on that ice-cold street I knew I was going to die there all alone.

I knew it was over, and I KNEW that I was dying!

* * * * *

I heard all of the voices way back behind me in the background that sounded like they were way far off somewhere. I could hear the people but I could not move to look back and check it out. *I was just lying there all broken up!* My glasses had been knocked off and my head was pounding with pain. I felt my heartbeat in my head and beating in my eyeballs, too. My view was so distorted from the impact; I was just lying there trying to figure it all out as best I could. What happened, what is going on? Is this REAL? As I heard voices way in the background nothing was making any sense to me at all.

Everything was just spinning all around and everything was so fuzzy and continued spinning, and spinning and spinning around, faster and faster, and moving up and down and in all weird directions; all of the colors and everything I could see were all blending in together. All I could see were images that looked like the psychedelic color patterns of the old tie-dyed shirts of the '60s. Everything was so scrambled up in my head; I could not think at all or even collect my thoughts. All I remember at that moment was, *"I just hurt Stephanie. How is she? Is she going to live?"*

My vision was way out of my control. I could see only a very tiny little bit, I still did not know if anyone was there with me; *I still did not know what my surroundings were.* **I literally had just been knocked into oblivion!** I was lying there trying to collect myself, thinking, "What has really just happened to me?"

What is really going on?

Is this all really for real?

The relentless pain was so bad and I was so tired. As I was lying there, the pain was getting worse. I knew my blood was still pouring out all around me as I got weaker and weaker and more tired each second. **I knew I was bleeding out and I knew that I was dying, too.** I now was welcoming the time for the pain to end and everything to make sense. I was ready to go.

The pain was just unbearable; it was a severe and agonizing pain. But, **the pain could no longer keep me awake!** I felt completely exhausted and tired. I began fading in and out and was losing consciousness! Things were happening and everything was still spinning all around me, faster and faster. I still did not know what was going on. I did not understand or comprehend anything at all of what was happening. But, **all of a sudden, it really didn't matter to me anymore! It was time to lie back and give in to it!** *I knew it was getting close to time to lay my head back and surrender my life.* **It was time to let go.**

I was just so tired now; no one was coming to help me!

I was flat exhausted. I knew I was going to die and I knew I was going to Heaven!

It was almost time to go. It was time to get ready to see Jesus soon.

I was so exhausted, and I could not stand it any longer.

I was just going to lay my head back down, close my eyes, and go on to sleep. Then the pain would all be gone.

I was just worn out…I just needed to rest…rest…rest.

My Angel has Arrived!

I knew it was over, and my time had come, and I was ready to go!

As I lay back there on that ice-cold concrete road, dazed out of my mind, I had been begging for someone to please come and help me. But I knew it was over, and my time had come, and I was ready to go! I was passed out cold when I heard the steps of someone who came running up by my head. Someone came rushing to my right side. **I opened my eyes and, standing tall above me, looking straight down at me with his head all aglow, was a man! He was so radiant and bright!**

It was a tall man. He very quickly dropped and fell to his knees and knelt down by my side. All I could see at that moment was his brilliant, bright shining bald head. Then I looked more closely at him, looking for a response, but I could not see well at all. I listened, but he did not say a word. He then paused, as he looked deep into my eyes. I looked and I gazed into those beautiful, brilliant, deep ocean-blue eyes. It was such a sweet, gentle look. When he spoke he had an urgent, yet calming, voice. He said *"Phillip, Phillip…it's me, Buddy…I am here for you!"*

I knew, *he was my angel*; I thought he had come to take me to Heaven! My escort had arrived!

He very quickly leaned in closer to my face and I could see the concern all over his face. There was a quiver in his lips and tears in his eyes, but I saw a wonderful radiant and brilliant glow all about him, too. It shone so bright all around his head and his face was just all aglow. There was a countenance on his face and an aura, a sweetness and gentleness all about him!

Then he slowly and gently reached down his strong arms and he stretched them out, reaching down for me!

He slowly and gently wrapped his big, strong and powerful arms all around me. *I knew right then that God was for sure there on the scene!* No doubt he was an angel.

His wonderful strong arms were now wrapped all around my shoulders with one hand placed in the center of my back. Then he gently placed his other hand on the back of my head. I could feel the strength in his right hand as he gently cupped it to hold underneath the back of my head!

His touch was so gentle and soft, yet I could feel the magnificent power and strength in his touch, too. Then he began lifting my body and my head up so slowly. *He was gently and easily scraping me up off that ice-cold slab of concrete.*

He raised me up and pulled my upper body close to his and cradled me deep into his chest. Then he ever so gently and tightly just held me. *He just held me there in his comforting arms.* Then he pulled me closer and even deeper into the bosom of his chest. He clutched me in a comforting and assuring hug for several seconds. Then he ever so slightly and gently rocked me back and forth, back and forth, as he stroked my hair on the back of my head.

I felt warmth and comfort like I was being held in the arms of God and in the hands of Jesus!

He was holding me a little more tightly and securely in his arms now. It was like he was holding me and communicating with me, saying, *"I am so sorry it had to be this way, but this is the way it had to be! I will NEVER, EVER let you go. Everything will be ok, just trust me!"* No he never said a word that I heard at that point, but that was the message I was receiving from his loving embrace.

He gently laid me back a little so he could purposefully look and see my face. He just stared deep into my eyes. I could tell he was surveying my deepest innermost thoughts as a tear flowed down from his cheek.

I could see his face again, as we were face to face. I began to focus a little and I saw his bright, shiny and glowing head and his beautiful, tear-filled, deep, blue eyes. He just kept gazing and looking deep into my eyes. It was like Jesus was looking at me through those beautiful eyes. It seemed he was still trying to communicate with quivering lips, *"I am so sorry you are in so much pain."* I knew behind that face and body holding me it wasn't Jesus and I was still alive. *It felt like how I would imagine it would feel like in the arms of God, and being held by Jesus's hands.* As if Jesus was there, cradling me ever so gently in his arms and holding my head in the palm of his hand; **his strong right hand just held me.**

I felt God was answering the prayer for me that I had prayed just a few minutes before, just like the prayer of David in the book of Psalms 62:1-4 *(ESV)*

> *Hear my cry, O God, listen to my prayer; from the end of the earth I call to you when my heart is faint. Lead me to the rock that is higher than I, for you have been my refuge, a strong tower against the enemy. Let me dwell in your tent forever! Let me take refuge under the shelter of your wings! Sela*

As I felt the comforting touch of his warm hands on the back of my cold head, and his warm arms still wrapped all around my cold and shivering body, I could see that his face looked so very familiar to me. I looked again more deeply into those big, beautiful, teary blue eyes, and then he pulled me close into his chest once again to hug me tight. He placed his cheek right next to my cheek and pressed into my face. My head was side by side with his head as he just gently hugged me cheek to cheek and held me tight for just a few more seconds.

As he lifted me close again I could see my blood was now all over his cheek and face, my blood all over his shirt, too. I was startled again, seeing so much of my blood all over him, yet I was so comforted and the pain had begun to subside. *Then the most awesome peace came rushing in like a raging fire.* The peace had now completely enveloped me!

He slowly pulled his head back a little bit once again and I could see the quivering in his lips even more. He was fighting back the tears that normally would be flowing down his face. *He could see how really devastated and badly injured my body was.* It was all destroyed! Yes my body was battered and torn; he could see what bad shape I was really in and all of my pain, too. He just held me there. After seeing everything in his face *I still felt his peace,* even through all of my pain. I knew I was dying and I knew I was going to be fine. Whether I lived or died made no difference to me anymore!

Yes, I knew I was dying, and I knew Heaven was waiting for me. **I was ready and prepared to be with Jesus**! After all, that is really what I want most of all —to see Jesus' face. I knew Jesus was standing there at the gates of Heaven, ready to swing those gates wide open and welcome me home. **I imagined it, I could see it in my mind's eye**, just like the story of Stephen in the Bible, when it says in Acts 7:55-56 *(ESV)*

> *"But he, full of the Holy Spirit, gazed into Heaven and saw the glory of God, and Jesus standing at the right hand of God. And he said, "Behold, I see the Heavens opened, and the Son of Man standing at the right hand of God."*

Yes, I could imagine and see Jesus, standing at the gate of Heaven, waiting for me to come in.

As he began to lower me back down on the pavement, he paused for a second or two one last time and I looked more deeply into his eyes. Even though I felt God's presence, I knew it was not Jesus. So I looked the man right square in his eyes and asked him.

Are you an angel?

Is this it?

Are you taking me home?

Am I on my way to Heaven now?

Are you the angel that takes us to see Jesus?

At that moment, I knew that God had sent an angel to me!

I knew, *God was there with skin on*. He sent an angel to wrap his loving, warm arms all around me, and to hold me tight. He was there to give me peace and comfort as well as assurance that God was and is in control.

Heaven was not His mission for me that night! God was not finished with me yet. He still had a plan for me to stay here a little longer.

God was transferring His love, comfort and peace by way of an angel. *That was His mission*. At that very moment on that cold November night, God sent me an angel in my deepest and darkest, most desperate time of need. He sent His messenger, reiterating His promise when He said He would never leave me or forsake me. I knew He never left me.

Yes, He kept His promise!

*God sent me a "**messenger**," and I was not alone anymore!*

From my experience, let me tell you what I think here.

"When you have entered into a tragedy or a situation like this where you have just encountered a divine appointment with the Lord God Almighty Himself, or an encounter or experience with an angel of God, eyeball to eyeball, or if you have an encounter where the Holy Spirit is working through someone, you immediately know you are entering the Holy realm of God.

It is a tragic time! Yet it is also a holy time of reverence. No matter how bad the situation is, or how bad the storm is raging all around, God is still there and in control!

Even when everything appears to be going by so fast, and time seems to move so swiftly and chaotically, or if it is moving slowly, no matter how devastating the situation may be, you know without a doubt that you have just had an encounter with God Himself.

Just Trust Him

At the instant when everything seems to be falling apart, trust in His promises! They are *true*. At that very moment you will know God Himself is reaching down from Heaven, **wrapping His Holy arms around *you*** and touching *you!*

Yes, a miracle happened right there that night in the middle of the street in Dallas, Texas. It happened in the middle of all the tragedy, trouble and pain. Even with all of the loud and weird noises all around, and even in the midst of all the chaos that was swirling all around, there came an angel that ushered in the peace of God.

Have you heard of that **peace that surpasses all understanding?** That is exactly what I am talking about here, that unexplainable peace.

It was the Heavenly peace that we dream of. But it is for real!

As my "**Trouble Grace Angel**" was leaning down and scooped me up from the ice-cold street and was holding me tight, *I felt that I was literally resting in the arms of God Himself.* At that moment, as I looked deeper into his eyes, I felt I was looking directly into the eyes of Jesus, and it seemed like Jesus was looking down from Heaven directly into my eyes. It was like Jesus, too, was holding me in His arms.

It was totally indescribable.

As my angel was still holding me in his arms that night and was gazing deep into my eyes, with tears flowing down his cheeks every few seconds and the quivering of his lips, *I was enveloped in a calming peace while I was still in a massive storm that was still raging all around me, and inside of me, too.* But all of a sudden there was an indescribable peace. Yes, the pain was still there, yes, the chaos was still raging all around, but in that tiny bit of space where I was, there was peace.

All I could think at that moment was, "JESUS! I am coming home! Am I coming to Heaven now?"

Yes, this story needs to be told, and I need to start from the very beginning and tell you all about how this story unfolds.

As Paul Harvey said, I need to tell you *"the rest of the story."* So let me take you back to the very beginning. We will come back to this point a little later so hold on; you do not want to miss the rest of this ride! There is still so much more to this story than meets the eye at the moment.

YES, God is here with us and there are angels all around us, too!

There is a love there that will never let you go!

Come on; let's go back to the beginning of this story!

<(((><

Can You Say "ROAD TRIP"?

Dallas, Texas, Here We Come

Let the fun begin

Out of here! Leaving Shreveport/Bossier City, Louisiana, Thursday evening for a fun-filled weekend in the "BIG D!" – Dallas, TEXAS. My home turf!

We are going to have ourselves a blast but first of all we have to attend a business convention, which is going to be a whole lot of fun. Then we are going to have us some real serious playtime, too! We are going to have us a party. Ahh, yes, the fun, the eats, the restaurants and shopping, then off to "Strokers" for the "Big Boy" shopping and playtime, looking at motorcycles, leather jackets, leather gloves and, oh yes, the leather chaps, too. Then come the nightlife adventures. I'm going out on the town, got to find the new late-night bars and hangouts in the West End plaza.

Yep, it is dancing time, party time! Listen to the local bands and, last but not least, check out the beautiful Texas ladies. Then we are gonna have ourselves a real party, but, first things first, business.

So off we go, fast as we can drive, headed west on I-20, straight into that western sun going to Reunion Hotel & Convention Center. You know the one;

it is the beautiful hotel with the big bling-bling ball with the restaurant at the top of the tower that signifies the Dallas skyline.

Get ready all you Texas cowboys! We are coming to play in ya'lls town. Move on over, traffic; you west-bound cars and trucks are just moving way too slowly for us! Move on over, get out of our way! Here we come. We got places to go, things to do and people to see. We are ready for a knock-down, drag-out, hard and fast, fun-filled and exciting weekend. Let's get this party started. *Yee-Haw!*

Ok, here is our plan. After the convention is over we will stay at the hotel and play until late on Sunday night. Then we will sleep a couple of hours, two maybe three, and then we will leave really early on Monday morning, say about 5:00 a.m. and drive straight back hard and fast all the way in. We should get to Shreveport/Bossier City by 7:00-7:30 a.m., run in the back door fast as we can, get to our desks, and be at work on time before all the office staff and employees arrive. What a plan, what a plan.

Ah—yes, that is the life of a single man burning the candle at both ends and pushing the envelope. Pushing the nights into the days and pushing Friday night all the way through the weekend straight into Monday morning and starting the week off seamlessly. This was our way of life. And, we did, we called ourselves "professional businessmen," too.

We really were good at business, even though we were always on the run, living life in that super fast express lane. Yep, we had a fast and furious, fun-filled life. We had a really good and very successful business going, and we were making a very good living for ourselves, too. We were awesome at taking great care of our customers and taking good care of our employees, too. See, we knew exactly where our bread was buttered! Our customers and employees are always our number-one priority in the business world.

We were clicking on all cylinders just like we were EXPENSIVE, high-performance racing machines. Just like a high-powered, foreign sports car. A silky smooth-running, well-oiled, fine-tuned, sleek-styling, *roaring machine.*

Our business was awesome. Everything was all lined up and perfectly clicking together beautifully and seamlessly. We had designed the business for maximum performance. We set it up for high-output, high-octane performance and productivity. All the checks and balances were in place. Well, most of them were in place. We did have a few glitches along the way; we will get into that later. As for now, we are on our way to get refueled and "get ready for the next round," as George Foreman, the Texas boxer, would say!

DALLAS, we have arrived!

Texas, my home, as we say here.

"We're wild and reckless, just from Texas. Steel backbone, and double breasted, baptized in a barrel of butcher knives, salted down with two forty-fives. Hold back the lightning; stop the thunder. Peace!...Well...No! Trouble is what I am hunting!"

Texas, I'm back!

We made it to Dallas; it was 195 miles in 2 hours and 15 minutes. Wow. Let's see, that is an average of about 87.5 miles an hour, food stops, gas, pit stops and all. Now that is living life in the fast lane for sure, because I know that speedometer was hitting 110 mph several times along the way.

We checked into the hotel and got started off with a big bang. The first business classes were from 6 to 9 p.m., and then it was time for a night out on the town so off we went until well after 2 a.m. We partied from one hot spot to another all night. We were checking out the girls and the bars while smoking our big, nice Cuban cigars.

It was a fun and fast night and everything was closing down at 2 a.m. So we ran into the hotel with everything just a' spinning all around in our heads. We knew we had too much fun and too much to drink and we did it way too fast this time, too. We got back to our hotel rooms and jumped right in the bed as fast as we could, and then we crashed! We were out like a light, until... The alarms went off and the wake-up call the next morning. The next morning—*oh my, ugh, NOO.*

"The next morning?"

Oh no, I don't want to get up! NO! NO. I feel miserable. I have a headache. Oh no! *Coffee, coffee, please!* Someone get me some C O F F E E.

Ok, this is the first full day of our convention and it started off with an eye-opening 6:30 a.m. breakfast meeting! OUCH! Now that was one eye-opening breakfast for sure. It had been past 2 a.m. when we finally got into bed.

The first day of the business meeting was good and a very busy day, too. I received an invitation about mid-day to a have a mix and mingle with the "big boys," the movers and the shakers. You know who I am talking about, the "BIG boys" that we all wanted to be. Plus, I will get to meet the speaker for tonight —whomever that is going to be.

There would probably be about fifty people at this after-hours mix and mingle event, and I hear this is the place to see and be seen. Now, that's my kind of place! So I am excited, I get to rub elbows with the best of the best—and I got an invitation. Woo hoo! Moving on up.

Wow, me, I'm moving on up, as the Jeffersons would say in that '70s sitcom. *"Moving on up, to the top!"* Remember the song? Come on, you can sing it. *"We finally got a piece of the p-i-e."*

See, I knew you knew that song. *"Moving on up!"* Ok, time to move on!

Convention Time

Earlier in the day we were in several really fun meetings. We had gotten lots of new sales tools and business tools for our "Business Tool Box." As a matter of fact, we now know that "information is as important to business people as fertilizer is to the farmer!" Yep. Of course, we call that fertilizer cow manure here in Texas, and some may call it by another name, BS (or bull _ _ _ _). Nope I do not use those words anymore.

Sometimes it takes some of that stinky, smelly stuff (cow manure) to get the fantastic growth and results that you want. Now, I did say fertilizer and not BS, right? But here in Texas there is a lot of that BS, too. So ya better keep your boots on, it gets DEEP here.

This was one of those power-packed, fast and fun-filled days, and it was stacked and packed with plenty of great and awesome business information. We learned what it takes to be a real executive, too!

Yep, just start playing golf! That's it! Nothing else to it.

Ya see, *if you become a golfer you graduate from being a businessman into being an "Executive."* See, I told you we were learning the real secrets of success! Time to take up golf! Move over Rodney Dangerfield, here we come.

But really, I am more like the Caddy-shack kind of golfer. FORE! As a matter of fact, do you know how to tell a good golfer? He hollers FORE, makes it in six and writes down five. Oh, this is a Christian book, sorry. That is the way it used to be, anyway!

We had all types of training classes to get to. There was my favorite, the *"Strategic Planning"* classes. Then we had the panel discussions, and mixing and mingling all day long. That is the fun part! Mixing, mingling and networking. Ya see, that is where everyone is talking and bragging on what they "can do," or what they "will do," and oh yes, what they "did do." That doesn't sound too good "did do."

Hey, in networking and bragging rights the other guy has no idea if you can do it or not! Hmm, so that is what they call networking! Networking is you just cast a broad net and catch them if you can.

Naa. Truth is, networking really is fun and building meaningful, lasting relationships. I still have friends to this very day that I met at this one mix and mingle business event. Networking is GREAT as long as you work to build relationships, then be ready when opportunity knocks at your door.

Keep a GOOD name!

Character integrity is paramount in business! Truth is that it is really like doing business in the old days when a handshake is all that was needed between men and women. But we still have to have good paper agreements, too. But your handshake is your WORD.

We were just having fun and doing business, talking and sharing with each other, information from one market segment to another market segment and from one region to another. We were learning more about sales, marketing, and advertising. Then there were products, services, communication; profit and loss statements, Dun & Bradstreet business credit report information. We had sessions on health care insurance for our employees, 401Ks, business taxes, employee taxes, record keeping, benefit packages, etc. Whew, that was exhausting!

We were busy all day long and having ourselves a blast, too! Yes, business is *fun* and *exciting*; it is always changing, every single day. Business is never boring. I just love it! Ok, I know you are getting bored here with this business talk, but hang tight a little bit—we will get there.

Business and success were natural highs for me. After all, I was the guy who could not make the grade in high school or college, but in life I could get in the trenches and make it happen! Now I am in there with the best of the best! Really....me, the guy that got INVITED by the dean, Dr. James Garner, to *"please take the rest of the semester off. Really, and you do not need to come back next semester either. Here Phillip, I have a list of some great trade schools and correspondence courses for you too."*

Yep, Dr. Garner loved me. He was always scratching his head and saying *"I wonder just what you will be one day."* So I had to leave the college because my grades were so poor. Yes, they really were pretty bad! **But today, I am one of those guys who is now beating all the odds**. I am making it happen! Yee Ha!

Business is a BLAST, It is FUN

Business has now become my drug of choice, so to speak. Increasing sales and increasing profits, making money and seeing our employees make a very good and very lucrative living, too, is a high all in itself.

My greatest joy was earning the reputation as *"The Turn-Around Guy"* in business when I took over a business and turned it into a $12,000,000.00 a year enterprise. Yes, back 20-plus years ago that was 12 million dollars a year in revenue or sales. After I learned how to do it once, it was easy and replicatable. Noy to mention putting 12%-17 % on the bottom line after all bills and taxes were paid!

Successes increase our performance like no drug could ever possibly produce!

People invigorating people. Excitement among the employees, excitement in the company, and excitement in the air. Customers get excited just walking in the door. Everyone's confidence increases, too, when you have tasted success. When the employees are happy, well, the customers are happy, too!

That is the secret to success in business. *Happy employees.* What a business model! *Employees and customers first!* Business is a PEOPLE business FIRST. Then sales and profits flow like water from a fire hydrant wide open! Wow! *Street smarts and the school of hard knocks really do work.* I could not believe I was really doing it. I was now becoming successful.

At the end of the day our customers and employees were the biggest winners of all—as for owners and managers, we had a job well done and a nice healthy bank account as a reward. We had all the FREEDOM to enjoy life to the max and buy our big-boy toys. Our team and company was awesome.

We had happy, hard-working employees; all of them were assuming their roles in the operation. They were that well-oiled high-performance machine. The sports car! Like the sweet sound of a purring Ferrari or roaring of a Formula One race car revving up to race the Grand Prix in France.

Our company was *"Moving in the Right Direction"* like the precision ticking of a clock keeping in perfect time, with all the moving gears and pieces working precisely together. I would say like a Swiss-made watch. But my Swiss watch was always in the repair shop or running slow, so maybe we were really more like a Timex. *"We took a licking and kept on ticking."* Remember that slogan? Ah-yes, there were some good old days, weren't there?

Moving & Groovin'

At 4:00 p.m. we were to be in the auditorium, getting ready for our special speaker to get us all fired up and give us one of those good-ol' swift-kicks-in-the-seat-of-the-pants get us motivated and ignited sessions. To get us inspired and all pumped up and ready so that when we got back home we were ready to do some more major big butt-kicking business, ready to make some more money, and have lots of fun doing it. What a fantastic life! Getting all "FIRED-UP."

We all entered the big, dark convention hall auditorium with the music blaring. You could feel the booming of the bass in the sound system and feel the vibration in your chest! BOOM, BOOM, BOOM. Some of that good ol' pump-you-up-and-get-you-involved music, like the song *"Y.M.C.A."* from the Village People. You know, you do the hand and body motion thing, everyone is moving around and dancing all around with hands in the air singing, *"Y.M. C.A.!"* I know, you are now singing the tune right now. *"Y.M.C.A."* Yes, it is a fun song and, well, it is really funny to watch all the people, too. *"Y.M.C.A!"* See now I've got you singing the *Y.M.C.A,* song too, ha-ha. *Gotcha!*

It was so hilariously funny to watch some of the people shake it up. You know what I am talking about. You have seen them, too. You remember how it is, watching all those people, all shapes and sizes, young and old, dancing around. Most of them were stiff as boards but they were all dancing and yes, you were right there in the mix, dancing and doing it all yourself, too! Admit it! You were shaking it up, too! *"Y.M.C.A."*

My favorite song was the *"Rocky"* theme song, *"Eye of the Tiger,"* by Survivor. You know the songs! Oh yeah, I loved that one; it really gets my fighting juices flowing, too. That was my competitive fight song. After all, I am a fighter at heart. Oh, and a lover, too, but that comes out later.

By the way, this was in 1993!

I know you are still singing that Y.M.C.A song in your head, aren't you?

The Big Boys Meeting

Rubbing elbows with them big ol' boys. Getting ready to play hot-shot businessman.

It was evening, and we were all ready to go: This is going to be *great*! These night sessions are always a lot of fun and lots of *high* energy, too! They always have fantastic programs. We had our special seats up close to the stage, a couple rows back and off to the left of center stage. We had perfect seats to see everything that was happening all around us. We could feel the sensation, that we were right smack in the middle of what was going on. Yes, one of those good ol' Texas sayings, "right smack in the middle" moments!

Wow! (And I can say that backwards, too—*wow!*) The meeting was over, and that was a powerful presentation!

Wow! Inspiring! Magical! Dynamic! Awesome! Spell-binding! I sat in awe to finally hear first-hand the author and speaker I had been reading and admiring and whose cassette tapes I had been listening to for many years now—The Man himself, Mr. Zig Ziglar. Then it happened! I received another invitation to meet him at the dinner that night with the big boys! Woo-hoo, awesome! What a day! I got to shake his hand and say, "Hello Mr. Ziglar, my name is Phillip Hatfield!" Wow, I was 34 years old and as excited as a little boy getting his first bicycle.

I waited for the dinner time to arrive when I would finally get to meet Zig Ziglar. I had been a fan for a long time, and after all these years, I would get to meet him. My heart was *pounding*, it was just a' banging inside my chest and my palms were sweating, too. This was one of my idols. I even felt the nervous quiver in my voice as I spoke. The excitement just kept on building.

The anticipation! I could hardly wait! I would get to meet and shake hands with Zig Ziglar! *Woo Hoo!*

Time had come; I was next in line! Me, I am next! I was just like a little kid waiting to get into the toy store. I just had to tell Zig that I loved his self-help books. Then, when I did, Zig said, ***"Why, thank you so much, but you see, I do not write self-help books. I write real life books on helping people. You see, it is true that you can have everything in life you want if you will just help enough other people get what they want. And it is only then that I will See You at the Top!"***

Bam, *I just stood there speechless looking at him right dead in the eye.*

Zig did not know me from Adam, yet he was telling me that it was the very core of a person that needed to change. It is not just knowing all of the mechanics of what to do and when to do it. It is not always in how you do it, either. **It is in the heart!** *It is a heart change,* it was from the inside out that had to change, not just a change from the *outside in*. At that moment, I understood precisely what he was saying. *"If I will really help others first, then I will get what I want."*

What a concept, help others first. In business, too! My mother always told me that, too. *"Do unto others as I would have them do unto me!"* Those were her exact words. Well, I thought those were her words, anyway. I found out later they belong to this Carpenter guy who lived many years ago. Yep, He was born in a barn, too. I guess I am learning that I really do need my "Edu-Ma-Cation."

All About Me

What I had been doing all these years was self-help, working from the outside in. Looking good and working on the motions and NOT the emotions! I was doing all the mechanics and "looking good." I was working to get what I wanted just like everyone else I knew in business was doing, too! I was trying to be good and do the right thing, but I also was manipulating other people, too. Oh, no! Did I just let the cat out of the bag? I wanted money, prestige, and fame. I wanted security, too, and it was all about me! I was all about getting what I wanted first and not helping others first. I was manipulating others to get what I wanted from them. I was helping others—as long as I got what I wanted! Me first. It was all about me. You know what I am talking about here, don't you? Yes, my selfishness, pride and control issues. Takes a lot of courage for me to tell you how selfish I was! But it is true! *I motivated my employees by manipulating them.* I studied them, and read them like a book. I studied the human nature, the psychology of what drives people. I studied how motives and drives can affect people's behaviors. I even had learned handwriting analysis starting back when I was 19 years old. You can learn a lot about someone by his or her handwriting, too.

Even though I was running a good and profitable business I still had some other human flaws. I looked really good from the outside in; however, I had some inner issues that no one knew all about but me. That is what I am sharing with you. My motives or methods were not always the best. My motives were not PURE. Yes, I did take some short-cuts, too.

Short-cuts?

Nope; I just whacked it right off sometimes.

I was so busy looking good and acting good. I was really great at being positive and *"seeing everything in 'my mind's eye'"* as Denis Waitley says. I was working all of the mechanics and systems that I had been studying in the self-help arena for many years to *feel good, stay positive*, and to be *optimistic*. I have always worked hard, I have always had a great work ethic, and I could see my goal and achieve it in my mind's eye. Then, after time with some application, I could really do it in life, too. I knew the routine. I had been working it for a long time now. I knew I needed more education and I was getting it everywhere I could.

Yep, I am a self-help, self-made man. Funny, when I say that now, I think of Dr. Phil on *The Dr. Phil* show when he says, *"How is that working out for you?"*

Zig Ziglar – The Real Deal

After meeting Zig and listening to him, I was totally and completely speechless that night. I was a little embarrassed and dumbfounded, too. I had finally gotten to meet and talk to him, but really, I didn't say but just a few words to him. I just stood there like a little boy who just got reprimanded by a stranger. You know what I am talking about, like I just got caught with my hand in the cookie jar. The jar of other people's hard-earned money! Yes, I was caught red-handed.

Still, I was so excited to meet Zig, even though I kinda blew it. I just smiled at Zig that night and went on to work the room. I am sure my hand was still shaking as I made all the rounds in the room. I was just thinking, "WOW! I had absolutely no reply at all to Zig. I had nothing to say." I am never at a loss for words; I can talk to anyone but, that night I just stood there like a dummy! Yes, I know, I had just been taken to school as they say. See, that is why I got back into all the business classes and seminars! I knew I still had lots to learn now that I was "all grown up."

Back then Zig was (and still is to this day) such a very gracious man! He was nicer than I had ever thought or imagined. He was genuine, *real*! He was "The real McCoy." Now with me being a "Hatfield," that is a compliment extraordinaire! Zig did not rush off that night to talk to someone else; he was patient, he waited on me to make the next move. He talked to me so calmly and politely, looking right into my eyes, speaking with that deep Zig Ziglar voice he had. He spoke with perfect voice inflection, to communicate exactly what he wanted to communicate. (You know that Zig Ziglar voice!) Then the look I saw in his eyes was a sweet but piercing look—like he could see right down into my very heart and soul. I knew he couldn't see that deep, but then again, could he? He had that soft, comforting, self-assuring look, too, and a look that caused me to begin to think and really ponder what Zig had just said to me. It was the heart that had to change!

The more I got to know Zig through the years, he always referred to the heart. He had learned some valuable information through his years and he was now sharing it. There was the heart of the matter. The heart is what the true intentions really are, and the heart is how much did you believe in what you were doing. The heart was the nucleus of your project or program, the convincing power, The UMPH in your program. He would ask, "What is the heart of the message?" This is just the scratch of the heart of the matter that I began to learn about, but primarily Zig was talking about me, my personal conviction, my character and my eternal perspective. I needed heart!

The Hotel Business

At this point in my life I had already met many famous people, so I was not easily impressed. I was the hotel general manager and vice president of

Barker Enterprises, a hotel franchise company with a total of six hotels in their organization. I had two hotels. One was in Fort Worth, Texas, and another in Shreveport, Louisiana. My first turnaround venture was the Ramada Central Beach Street in Ft. Worth Texas. I took over the hotel six weeks after a fire that killed five people and left 33 severely injured. It was a hotel NO ONE wanted to run again. After all, WHO will stay at a hotel that killed five people while they were asleep?

Before that, I was the food and beverage director for the Regency Hotel and our sister hotel, The Chateau, right across the street from the Regency in downtown Shreveport, Louisiana. We were the nicest, most elite hotels in town at the time, so we got all of the stars, actors, actresses, politicians, senators and governors and everyone from several states around, especially all the business-men who came to gamble and bet the big bucks on the race horses.

At that time all of the Texas, Arkansas and Mississippi people flocked to Shreveport. It was a mecca destination for horse races, since Louisiana Downs was close by in Bossier City. Everybody who was anybody stayed at our hotels. We served all the horse owners, presidents and CEOs of corporations, sponsors, and oh yes, those little short horse jockeys, too. I can pick on the jockeys be-cause I am not a whole lot taller than they are. Anyway, all of the other wealthy people who followed horse racing came and stayed with us at the Regency and the Chateau, too.

Ice-cold Water, Governor?

As a matter of fact, on my first day as the food and beverage director at the Regency, the hotel general manager, Dutch Ducharm, said, "Ok, I want you to serve the drinks to the head table. We have the governor, Edwin Edwards, and his host, Gus Majalis, a Shreveport native, in for a lunch banquet with TV reporters and cameras and all."

Now, there is absolutely no way to mess up serving water and iced tea to the head table, right? Are you sure? Well, as they were all having their lunch and right before the speakers were to start I was walking behind them, serving iced tea and ice water. All of a sudden, out of nowhere, "Big Gus" decided to stand up and take off his jacket. MISTAKE! Bad Idea. BIG MISTAKE! Well, let's say he and I collided, with me directly behind him and right above him, too. Yep, you guessed it. There went that whole pitcher of ICE-cold water, all over the governor. The whole stinking pitcher! It went all over him and several of the other guys at the head table, too. SPLASH, in front of all the TV cameras and the whole room of people at the banquet. Then everyone burst out in laughter at all the commotion at the head table.

It was terrible, and it was so hilariously funny, too, seeing all these guys jumping up, screaming out. The whole room burst out laughing; all the guys at the table started jumping up and running to the side. They were all getting soaked, too. It was like a circus, seeing all the politicians jumping to their feet, dancing around from the ice cold surprise. It was so funny, everyone was laughing and looking all around to see just what was going on. It looked like a new dance was going on at the head table, "The Ice Water Dance."

Thank God, Gus and the governor, Edwin Edwards, were very understanding. Oh my, what a way to meet the governor! At least, it was a very unforgettable and memorable introduction to say the least, right? They never forgot who I was, either. Oh, and yes, I did get to keep my job, too. Whew. I was sweating that one out all through the day. It was a terrible accident; however, it really was so dog-gone funny, you should have been there to see that one. Everyone laughed so hard and I learned something I never knew before. I found out that I could be an entertainer and make people laugh. I just never got paid for it.

Good Night, Mr. Ziglar

Back to meeting Zig. I was a young businessman, rocking and rolling and climbing up the ropes and the ladders of success. I was working hard and rubbing elbows with the "High Rollers." So meeting famous people by now had become a comfortable and common occurrence for me. However, meeting Zig Ziglar, that was extra special for me. It was a pinnacle in my life then and it still is to this day! Someday I will have to tell you about meeting the guys with ZZ Top, Alice Cooper and President Jimmy Carter's brother, Billy Carter. Yes, he was a nut, too. What? A peanut beer? That sounds like a peanut-head idea to me! But I really did get to meet a lot of awesome and fantastic people in the hotel business. There were lots of famous people and just common regular people like you and me, too.

Still today, I have never met a more gracious, kind, more genuine man than

Zig Ziglar—and to think this man was a boxer! (He only retired from the ring because of his hands; the referee kept stepping on them!) Poor Zig.

Zig was not in any rush at all that night we met, he was so slow, calm, cool, collected—yet he was excited and very animated, too. Zig knew he was impacting and changing lives, so he took interest in everyone that he met. It was not just me—he treated everyone exactly the same. There was no difference in race or in social status. I was just as important to him as the "REALLY" important guy. I had never seen that in anyone before! A man who was humble and had fame and fortune, yet was so down-to-earth. Zig was a genuinely good guy. He really was one of those white-hat guys, as we would say back when we watched those old cowboy westerns when I was a boy. The good guys always wore the white hats.

Zig has always shared his successes and has also shared his failures, too. He just focused on teaching us how to become winners! His son, Tom Ziglar. is just exactly like Zig is, too, *"A chip off the old block,"* and as I like to call him *"Encouragement: The Next Generation."* Tom Ziglar is now forging his way with his *"Pure and Simple"* philosophy as he serves as president and CEO of Ziglar, Inc., now.

The evening rocked on for quite awhile and I was still in the same room with Zig. He was talking to one person after another and I had hoped I would get the chance to talk to him again. After all, I really did not get to talk to him earlier: But I was still a happy camper that I had gotten the opportunity to meet him and to be in the same room with him. I was tickled to death, as we say here in Texas, just to be around the man.

Awhile later, in the evening, I kept looking over, hoping for the opportunity to talk to Zig again, but it never came. I had finally given up. The night was almost over; a lot of people had already left. The evening was winding down. I looked over one more time, hoping that just maybe…but Zig was still busy talking! So it was time for me to head on back to my hotel room and get ready for the next day of convention activities. Plus, I was completely exhausted. After all, I had been out partying, drinking and dancing 'til 2 a.m. with the senoritas, then to be at a breakfast meeting at 6 a.m. that morning. I was dead tired. It had been a very long day for me.

As I was leaving the room, I heard that deep, resonating, soft voice right behind me say to me, "Now, just where are you off to, young man?" It was Zig Ziglar.

"I am calling it a night, Mr. Ziglar, heading up to my room," I said to him.

Then Zig said, *"It really is way down deep inside where the change happens. Self-help is self-less help; it is really no help at all, only a temporary solution to a permanent problem. A change of the heart will change the outcome of your circumstances. You have to help other people become successful. You have a great evening young man, and I will see you at the top!"*

See you at the top?

As I look back today, that was the whole lesson in just a few short words.

Everything was all wrapped up in a few well-chosen and well-spoken words! The master communicator had said it without mincing any words. *"It really is way down deep inside where the change happens. Self-help is self-less help; it is really no help at all, only a temporary solution to a permanent problem! A change of the heart will change the outcome of your circumstances."*

Wow, how profound! I discovered my real problem that night. I found out I had a heart problem!

Yes, *I really had no real heart, no real conviction.*

The next day I was so happy that I bought even more books and cassette tapes and more of those packaged tape programs. After all, I had met the man himself, so now I was all into getting to the TOP! I read all the books, listened to all of the tapes, and I learned a tremendous amount. I was really into reading and listening. I still bought other books from other authors who offered "self-help." But I did not connect with the other authors like I did with Zig's stuff.

I had spent several years on my "self-improvement" now. I was a young professional, a real go-getter. All of my mentors were professionals 20 to 30 years older than I was, and all of them were very successful in their business field and I was doing pretty well for myself, too. I was smart enough to get around wise men who had already proven themselves and glean from the nuggets they left under the table.

Temper, Temper Young Man

I was a pretty good guy overall; however, I had some character issues to deal with. I had a terrible temper, which I kept under control 98% of the time. But that other 2%, well, how do I explain it? Occasionally, I would get frustrated with people who did not see things my way. There you simply have it. I had all the answers, so I thought. I knew I had a temper problem so I kept reading and listening to Zig's material to try to get help with my temper, too, as well as learn how to be a better businessman. There were always some golden nuggets that I would glean from him, no matter how many times I read or re-read the book or re-listened to his cassette tapes. Things would always just pop out from nowhere.

One of my major flaws was that I could not understand people who did not want to be the *best* they could be in their field. Complacency and selfishness were all around and it drove me bananas for people not to try hard to be successful. I did not understand people who did not commit and give 100% to their projects or to their goals. Not to mention not giving 100% to their career. It seemed to me that most people were just so stinking selfish.

The truth is, I had the same old stinking selfishness problem, too, but I could not see my own selfishness. I was looking at the sawdust in their eye when I had a plank in my own eye. You've heard of that one before, I am sure. I got that from the Carpenter who was born in the barn. (No disrespect)

But I had another problem, too. I had a huge, massive, four-letter vocabulary worse than any sailor you had ever heard. I had some real whoppers I liked to use, too. And yes, I did—I even used them in business situations! The f-word was part of my daily frustration vocabulary. Yes, I knew them all and used them all when I got really upset.

I can remember when my mother worked for me in the office. She would get really upset with me and tell me, "I did not raise you to say any of those words," then she would ask where I got them. But I was the big man on campus now, so I made the rules. She was my mom and I knew she was right, so I listened to her. I would settle down. Then a few days later I would belt out the f-bomb again right there in front of my mom. Seemed I could always justify my temper tantrums, but then again I had all the answers to my problems, too, right?

I remember when I was doing it with all of my "self-help system." I knew how to fix it all…The Power of *Positive* Thinking. That will fix everything for me, right? But I did not do power of positive thinking like it was supposed to be done. I just heard the expression and never read the book; well, not until years later.

I would ignore the negative situations and concentrate on the positive and be optimistic. Stick to my plan, stick to the agenda, stick to my goal. Other people would fix the problems for me. I would just delegate it. Yep, I did just that, I delegated for someone else to fix the problem and then I would never follow up on the solution or the result. And here I called myself a professional! Just look good and be positive, do the best you can do and stay upbeat! Delegate the problems. Everything will work out. Somehow the problems will just fix themselves and go away! Right? Wrong! When I could not escape those tough situations that needed my attention, I always wound up going back to Zig's books and tapes. They were like a Bible for me, even though I did not read the Bible. I went right back to the one place I knew I could find help. There was just something special in Zig's message and in his delivery that resonated with me. I felt a connection; after all, I did meet the man himself!

I know you are wondering what in the world this rambling has to do with being *"Carried by Angels."*

Hold on—we will get there, I promise!

The Gambler

The next few years I was in denial, ignoring some of the minor negative situations and problems in my business and personal life.

Usually they were from my own selfish decision-making. But for some reason, the problems did not just go away! Wow, what a surprise, right? I was not working on the real problem. All of the issues would just get bigger and bigger, then I would sweep them under the rug and keep on trucking with my positive, optimistic thinking. Until the rug I had been sweeping it all under looked like a huge hill that could not be ignored any longer. I had hills under the rugs at home and at work now, too! I had some big ol' mounds of trash under those pretty antique rugs.

Usually my problems did not center on running the business directly. There were personal conflict issues where I had to prove my point that I was right and someone else was wrong!

It was my pride!

The "I" Problem

I was cocked and loaded, ready to fire and determined to prove my point!

I was very competitive and I was going to win, no matter what. After all, I was running a successful company. I knew how to run a business. I was the professional in my industry. However, I seemed to forget all that I had been learning from Zig. I would forget things like helping others, listening, thinking before speaking, being humble, always responding instead of reacting. I forgot that "if I helped enough other people get what they wanted, I would get what I wanted."

Sometimes I would have an issue with the general contractor or a sub-contractor. Sometimes it was the project manager, sometimes inspectors, or even "The State Fire Marshall." Most of the time it was on technical issues where I knew that I was *right*! And I was going to prove it, too. Yes, I would win! Yes, I was *right*! I would win the battle! But I would lose the war! I knew my stuff, so to speak, but my methods were not the best. It was my *pride*. I would then win another construction bid and go to the construction site and *there they were!* Same building superintendent and building inspector, and, you guessed it, the same state fire marshal, too. Needless to say, I had not *"earned"* their respect.

Ok, so I have a surprise for you now. Are you ready? I was not always ethical in my business dealings, either. What? I did not surprise you? I projected professional and ethical mannerisms and I "tried" to always do the right thing; however, I was always looking out for me, my best interest and my money. I wanted the win-win situation—as long as I came out the winner and on top. Hmm, I do not think this was the "see you at the top" Zig was talking about! Ok, so I really was not a winner—I was a wiener! A bonehead! A doofus-brain, whatever you want to call it. But at least I can now admit it, so that is good, right?

WIN/WIN. Well, I now knew all about *ethics*! Finally, I learned it through all of those tough years of pounding in from Zig's courses and remembering what my mother taught me all those years. It was all now sinking into this thick, hardheaded skull of mine. I really did have a "heart" issue! And I knew it. The real problem was that I could not fix it myself. I did not know why. I tried to be ethical. I tried to be honest. I tried to do what was right. But, like that old comedian of the '70s, Flip Wilson, used to say, "The devil got into me," the devil made me do it!

Most of the time I was really doing *great*, 98% of the time I was an awesome businessman. But those occasional lapses of judgment, when I had them, were severe! But as long as I looked really good on the outside, all was *great*. I was still the king of my own hill.

As you see, I had a terrible "I" problem!

Did you count all the I's in that segment? Ok, email the answer; I do not want to count them all; I am too embarrassed to try. I know it is pretty bad!

Add it up! Count the Cost!

Early one Sunday morning in September 1995, I went to the grocery store with my friend, Janet. That was the only time I would go to a store, early on Sunday morning, when no one else was anywhere in sight. I did not want to deal with all the people in my way. I was too busy and too important for all that. Besides, I had to go get all of my Sunday newspapers, chips, dips and, oh yes, my cigars and beer for the guys, too.

On Sunday morning all of the partiers from Saturday night were still asleep, and all the church people were at church. So Sunday morning was the best time in the world to go grocery shopping! The store was empty! No people in my way. Yes, it was all about me, so off we went to one of those new, self-bagging grocery places my friend, Janet, liked—Super One Foods. (There we go back to that SELF-thing again!) Man, I sure do hate bagging my own groceries! I don't like this self–help thing so much anymore!

We got to the grocery store and were about to go in when it hit me just how special I was! Those grocery store doors just opened right up for me automatically when I strolled on up to the entry! Yep, they did! But then my bubble burst when all I could find was a shopping cart with one of those loud squealing wobbly wheels, and there we went off making all kinds of embarrassing noise. Down the aisle we went. Eek-eek-eeek, wobble-wobble-wobble. Squeeeek. Yes, my happy camper "self-help" face went south really fast. Eek, eek, eek from that shopping cart wheel as we strolled down the grocery store aisles. Eeek.

I learned something new today!

I learned that going to the grocery store is like going to church!

I stopped and loaded up the cart with my Sunday beer when Janet said, "You know, you will never get into Heaven with all those twelve-packs of beer." Duh. What? I was startled and I answered back quickly.

I said, "Well, Jesus drank wine." She said, "NO, read your Bible, Jesus turned the water into wine, so there!"

I told her, "Look, I have no intentions of going through the gates of Heaven with all this beer, I am going home!" She said, "I know! He won't let you in!" Then she asked, "What if you die before you get home?"

"*What?* Janet, are you out of your ever-loving, stinking mind or what? Are you planning to help me out on this getting-to-Heaven-quicker thing or something?" After a few seconds I told her, "Well the Bible says thou shalt not kill, too!" Then she asked, "How do *you* know what the Bible says? You have never even read one." After a few seconds I asked her, "What in the world are we doing talking about the Bible on Sunday morning in a grocery store? We do not even go to church!" Jeez. Then she said, "Did you say Jesus?" I abruptly answered, "NO, I said *JEEZ*!"

I always tried her patience when I went grocery shopping, I would take my calculator and try to get the exact total of how much we were spending. It was a game to me, it was fun, and it kept my mind sharp. I was always calculating numbers. In business, I was crunching numbers all week long, and my football statistics and gambling numbers all weekend long! I was becoming a math machine. I finally understood numbers; it just took some real life application.

You see, I failed algebra four times in high school, and math did not make any sense to me at all! Well, not until I got into the business world! Then I was working margins, percentages, cost analyses, profit and loss, balance sheets, productivity and profits, job costings, payroll percentages, employee benefits—and yes, taxes, too!

Taxes, whew!

There is the inventory tax, franchise tax, sales tax, income tax, payroll taxes and taxes, taxes, taxes. Oh, I forgot—and all of the audits, too. Insurance audits, worker's comp audits, sales tax audits—whew! (I know I left off something in this entire list.) Business is complicated nowadays and a profitable business is hard to achieve, but it is fun! So math—yes, you had better be very good and very sharp or you had better be getting sharp, no matter how good your advisors and your CPA are. You had better know what they are talking about or you are going to be in really big trouble really fast.

Math is fun! As long as I am winning! And I LOVE to win!

Sunday FOOTBALL!

Math had now become fun, and I learned more every day. So, with my calculator, Sunday morning shopping was a perfect time to work and hone my skill set. But we had to be done shopping and I had to be home by 10:00 a.m. because…. Today is SUNDAY FOOTBALL…all day long! (Ahh, Heaven!) I had to get back home to watch all of the sports shows. I had to complete my last-minute details so I could place my noontime game bets. Yes, I was a gambler, too. I had to see what the Vegas line was for that day, and what had changed in the Vegas line since the night before. The "Vegas line" rules the football gambling world!

Even though gambling is illegal, the Vegas line is listed in EVERY NEWS-PAPER! Now, that really makes a lot of sense, doesn't it? Oh, yes, remember, this was back in the '90s before on-line betting, and most of all these casinos we have now. This was 17-20 years ago.

I had to decide who I was going to bet on.

How much am I going to bet?

Will I take the spread?

What will I do on the overs or the unders?

What teams am I betting on?

How much do I put on each game?

What is the Vegas line spread now?

Who is out of the game?

Who is on the injured reserve list?

Who will be playing in the game?

Who is probable to be playing?

Decisions, decisions, decisions. A mind game! Then I had to figure out my total budget for gambling that day. $500.00? $1,000.00? $5,000.00? Or more? By now I am sure you have figured out what I had not figured out!

Positive thinking and gambling/illegal betting is a recipe for disaster! Or a huge success! And yes, there were some huge successes and yes, there were disastrous failures, too!

My BOOKIE!

At this time, gambling and betting on sports was completely illegal except for horse race betting. That is why the horse-racing track in Shreveport/ Bossier City was so successful. So in order to bet on football I needed to have a "bookie." Eewe. Yuck. Even the term "bookie" should have told me something! It just sounds nasty!

B O O K I E! Go ahead, say it out loud! BOOKIE. Chicken, say it! "B O O K I E!" There ya go.

Yes, I did make an awful lot of money and I lost a lot of money betting football, too. The football-betting week ran from Tuesday morning until the end of the Monday night football game the next week. So, if I lost, then all of the bets had to be paid to the bookie on Tuesday for the entire past week.

If I won, I got paid on Wednesday! YA-HOO!!! Then the next round of football betting started all over again on Thursday night before the first football game of the week. "Thursday night football." Da-da-da-daaaaaa ! "Are ya ready for some football?"

So you can win a lot of money or you can lose a lot of real cold, hard cash, especially if you are betting college football games and professional games, too! College game scores tend to run much higher. The players are really fighting hard for success and to get entry to pro football in addition to supporting their school pride. College players seem to always give 100%, no matter what.

Now let's get to the "professional players."

In my "opinion," and remember, I am a gambler so I have to have my own strategy and opinion…

Professional games are lower scoring games, in general. Most of the professional football players seem to get hurt a whole lot more frequently. Then they will stay out of the game for a much longer time too when they are hurt. However, I do have to give them credit, they do play much harder during the playoffs! They start to give a lot more of what they have starting around the first of December. By the time the end of December hits, they all are giving 100%. That is the fun time to bet on football! Remember, that is my opinion, now.

Gambling on the Coach

Now, the coach in pro ball makes all the difference in the world.

A coach with character and integrity has the guys always giving 100% and they seem to have much fewer injuries, too. They have a better team spirit and better team morale. So the coach is very important when deciding which team and how much money to bet.

Now, I may not have had great integrity myself at the time, but I really admired the coaches and the players who did live with purpose and pride, character and integrity. As a matter of fact, I could bet on those coaches, teams, and their players because I always knew they were in it to win it. As I said, they were always giving all they had. They would leave everything on the field every time. From game one to the last game they would play in the season, it was all heart. I admired and respected those coaches and players! I required character and integrity, even though I would let mine slip pretty big sometimes. I had that double standard thing going on.

The worst night of my life!

The most memorable game I remember betting on was a Monday night football game, September 11, 1995, the Packers and the Bears.

I had a very bad week. I was winning some and losing some, but I was losing way more than I was winning! It was the end of the day on a Sunday night, almost 10 p.m., and I was down over $12,000.00. What am I going to do? Twelve thousand dollars was a lot of money in 1995 and I had to pay on Tuesday when the bookie would call and tell me where and when to meet him. I know the rules for gambling in Louisiana—PAY UP! There are no special favors; everyone pays on time, NO EXCEPTIONS! The only deal you will get is a brother-in-law deal, if you know what I mean. Twelve thousand dollars back then is like $25,000 today.

Okay, so what could I do? Hmmm, okay, I thought to myself, I can make some of it up on the Monday night football game, Packers against the Bears. How much do I want to make up? There, you see it? The power of positive thinking and gambling! The thinking without the doing! Yes, Zig was right. It is a matter of the heart, and I definitely had a heart problem.

I thought, positive…*be* positive. I can do it, I can do it, I can do it! Okay, let's do this, as Larry the Cable Guy would say—" git 'er done."

To solve this problem, I would need to take off work the next day. I would need to listen to all the radio sports shows and all the sports shows on cable TV. I would need to get my newspaper, look at the Vegas line. I would need to go to the newsstand and get all of the major newspapers in the country and read the sports sections and see what all the analysts said about that night's game!

I HAVE to WIN. I am a WINNER! I am a WINNER! I HAVE to win this game! Gotta read, study, be positive, do not worry, be confident, WIN! Okay, this is simple…I've got this in the bag…it is all mine.

Now, how much do I want to bet?

Should I bet the overs? The unders? Should I bet the spread of the Vegas line? Straight bets? Should I bet on a player's performance? Who did I want to bet on? What? How many receptions a receiver would make, or how many touchdowns a running back would make? Which one? Which team? How many ways could I hedge my bet?

It was Monday night, and I was trying to wait 'til the very last minute to call my bookie, Vernon. I had to be sure I had it all together, plus I needed to listen to the pre-game show on TV. I had to see what last-minute changes would affect all my betting scenarios. Ok, I had it all together!

Yes, there were some changes, so I totally reworked all of the day's work. However, I was very confident. I thought I knew everything! I knew as much as all of the pro-analysts did at that very second.

So I placed the call to Vernon, my bookie. Okay, no answer and it is three minutes to game time!

I called again…still, no answer. Two minutes and 50 seconds 'til the game time…busy signal again!

Two minutes and 30 seconds 'til game time; still I got a busy signal over and over and over. I was getting nervous and sweating. I could not get through and it was almost game time. I called back, over and over and over. I wondered if I was getting a busy signal from interference of my own calls. Finally, Vernon answered; 45 seconds left to place all my bets! Vernon said, *"We do not have time; the game is about to start. Let's just go double or nothing, and go straight Vegas-line.*

Which way do you want to go?"

Oooohhhh, wow! I had a twelve thousand dollar debt now, times two for double or nothing payout, so $24,000.00 if I lost, or zero to pay out if I win. I knew what I was doing. I had this one down!

I said, "OK, Vernon, great! Let's do it. Book it, Danno."

Now, if I lost? Ooohhh nooooo…I was not thinking straight! I am so STU-PID! If I lost I would have to pay DOUBLE—$24,000.00!! Ooohhhnoo! *&%#$&*.

*Vernon *&%#!$^*)*&%#@$ me, I can tell I just)(#%&!(@#%^&(_)*^!..........*

Mmmmmmmm…ok, it is DONE!

Me: I am POSITIVE! OK, we can do it; focus and stay positive.

After a long night of sweat, worry and fear of not having all the monies to pay my bookie the $24,000.00—and yes, my mind started rolling and I was really thinking about paying out on Tuesday! I had most of the money but not all of it. Like I said earlier, in Louisiana in 1995 you had BETTER pay your bookie! You had NO OPTION! There were no IOU's in betting football il-legally with a bookie! It was pay and be paid! That is it! I thought, "Who can I borrow a few thousand dollars from?" There was no one!

I thought "I know. I can take it out of my company account!" No, that would cause some major accounting and tax issues and I would really get in a lot of legal trouble. I was all on my own! I dug my own hole, now I had to find a way to climb out of it.

I walked the floor the whole time, all night long I paced. I would get ex-tremely happy and holler and scream for joy. Then I would get extremely de-pressed, worried and scared to death. Ordered a pizza for delivery, and Dr. Pepper. NO BEER tonight! It was the highest of highs and the lowest of lows; all night long I was sweating. I shouted, I screamed, I hollered. I watched the game all alone. I did not want any interruptions. I would get scared and call a friend. I would get happy and call another friend, back and forth, all night long. I knew as soon as the game was over, if I lost, the phone at home would ring and I knew it would be Vernon, my bookie. I had never missed a payment, but I was never down so much money before, either. I had not done anything like this—then going double or nothing, either. I was really scared to death but I would never, ever admit it to anyone at all back then. That is why I watched the game all alone in an empty house.

After a long, long night I had the most draining, tiring, exhausting win ever in my life!

Well, I do not believe in luck—not then or now. But somehow I made it through. I won. It was not fun, it was not enthusiastic, and it was an awful experience. That was the worst night of my life! I can look back and just be thankful in all my ignorance and stupidity, somehow there was a grace given to me. The score: Packers 27, Bears 24. It was very early in the game and Brett Favre threw a 99-yard touchdown pass to Robert Brooks in the second quarter that seemed to really be the winning play, even though it was early in the game. That play seemed to be the game maker.

After being raised in a good home, being taught not to gamble (as well as the many other wrong things I was doing), I am totally embarrassed and ashamed to write these accounts of who I was and what I did. However, my family and friends are all aware of my gambling and other activities, so if my experiences can help anyone else, then great! I'm all in! Share this story with anyone who will listen to you. Hey, listen-up guys!

Hey, Guys, DO NOT GAMBLE! YOU CAN'T WIN!

Gambling is always a losing proposition! Have fun! Enjoy the fun of the football game! There is a reason betting on football is illegal! I lost the fun of the game. The game had now changed. It was now all numbers and statistics and not a fun, exciting football game with favorite teams and favorite players and pulling for your guy to win.

Remember this! They did not build those big casinos with their money. They used your money, they knew you would come so they got a loan and built a building so you would show up and play black jack, roulette, slot machines, cards, and Texas Hold 'em. So guess what, they are the ones saying, GOTCHA! They go laughing all the way to the bank.

But as for me, at this point, I still had not learned my own gambling lesson. Yet.

Bragging Rights of The Gambler

I was now invincible; bullet-proof! I was a WINNER! My biggest win EVER! BRAGGIN' RIGHTS! Even my bookie Vernon was using my story to drum up business! "See, Phillip beat me out! He won $24,000.00 in one game!" Even though no cash changed hands, I won over $24,000.00 by betting on one football game. I was a betting machine, or so my stupidity told me.

Yes, I was gambling and betting out of control thousands and thousands of dollars a week. Yes, I had the money to bet with, it was all my money; I had it, I earned it, and I chose to gamble with it. I lost some but mostly I was winning lots of under-the-table cash each year. Yes, I did make money gambling. However, I was gambling with my life, career, reputation, my family and my future.

I was breaking the law! I could have gone to prison. How stupid I was, to be such a good businessman. I could have lost just one or two weekends of gambling and really gotten myself in a big, huge mess that I could not get myself out of. I could have even lost everything—and I mean *everything*.

I know you are still thinking, "Ok, so just what does all of this stuff have to do with being *Carried by Angels*?" Everything! You have to see that I was not a deserving man at all! I deserved nothing. No grace, no mercy and certainly no angels. But just hold tight. You will soon see God giving grace where it was not deserved and angels coming from all around. Like I said earlier, this is about God and His story through my story. He will forgive anyone who asks and He will give us things we do not deserve.

Oh, No, Here we go!

On the very next Sunday, September 17th, I still had to hurry home. I had not learned my lesson. The Sunday morning ritual you know—if I needed groceries and chips, dips and drinks, that was the time to go to the store!

Janet was all excited and ready for Football Sunday. I popped a cigar in my mouth and headed out the door. I hollered out, "Come on, Janet, let's go! Hurry up! Got to get the *New York Times* at the newsstand, the *Chicago Tribune*, the *Dallas Morning News*, and see what they say about today's games. I have lots to do! Let's get to the store early. I have to get back for the sports shows!"

We shot out the door and flew down the street to the Super One Foods, and then we hit the newsstand downtown and the cigar shop, too. We got back home close to 10:00 a.m. We brought all of the groceries in. Janet was stuffing the cabinets and refrigerator; I was getting my coffee, pens and papers. I turned the TV on when all of a sudden I had the weirdest feeling come over me. I had never felt anything like it ever before; everything seemed to swirl around in my head. I was dizzy and felt weak, my chest started hurting, then my arms were tingling. I was weak at the knees, they became like rubber. I started sweating profusely from my forehead. I told Janet, "Call the ambulance! I am dying!"

At that moment I instantly fell, listless, to the couch and was just lying there. The fire department and paramedics arrived pretty quickly. I lived only a mile away from the fire station. They rushed in, slapped an oxygen mask on my face, and started checking my pulse and blood pressure. Then they threw me on the stretcher and hauled me out the door of the house and down the steps, then they loaded me in the ambulance. They fired up the siren and off we were flying down the bumpy, curvy country roads headed to LSU hospital in Shreveport. As we were driving down the road I heard the paramedic from Keithville Volunteer Fire Department tell the hospital on the ambulance phone system that he thought it was a gallbladder attack.

WHAT? You gotta be kidding me, I thought.

Wow…what a misdiagnosis that turned out to be! But thank you guys for the quick response and the ride to LSU hospital anyway.

Is She an Angel?

We arrived at the hospital. I was limp and could hardly even breathe. All of the nurses and doctors were frantically working on me. They were thinking I'd had a heart attack or a panic attack; my oxygen level was so low. I was told my oxygen was below a level that sustains life. They were taking blood for blood gases and immediately hooked me up to the EKG machine as they were running all kinds of tests. They were all busy working on me when I saw a young female intern who was passing by in the hallway. Something got her attention and then she stopped, right in her tracks! She overheard the main doctor discussing my information with back and forth dialogue to the nurses. Everyone was busy and scrambling all around while they were working on me. The young intern came to the doorway and leaned on the door frame. She was listening intently to the conversations and was watching the procedures and everything that they were doing. She was deciphering all of the information and getting it all straight in her head as she heard all the specifics. Then she said, "*Stop*, wait a minute, he didn't have a heart attack; he has sleep apnea, look how low his oxygen is." Immediately the doctor stopped and started re-evaluating all their data and processes. Then in a couple of minutes the main emergency room doctor changed all of the procedures. After several hours there in the emergency room, I was finally on my way up to the 7th floor of the hospital to the sleep clinic department.

Sure enough, after a day or two we found out I had sleep apnea and not a heart attack, and certainly I did not have a gall bladder issue, either. They told me that I stop breathing while I am asleep 78 times an hour. There was no damage to my heart or to me at all; however, I was going to be admitted and confined to the hospital for the next several days for them to continue running all kinds of tests. So, needless to say, I couldn't care less about football and gambling or betting! I was going to have some relax time, and get room service for the next few days, and have people waiting on me hand and foot. Well, so I thought anyway. I found out when you are in the hospital it seems like every 20-30 minutes, day and night, someone is coming in for one reason or another to stick you, poke on you, take blood pressure or your temperature.

Wheeew! What a day! That surely was a close one. I had never been in an ambulance before. It was a whole lot different than I would have imagined. That was the roughest bouncing ride I had ever had. Someone needs to invent a Rolls Royce smooth riding ambulance.

There is still a question that I have to this day. The intern, who was she? Where did she come from?

They tell me this intern possibly saved my life! But who was she? I never saw her again after that day. She never came to my room to check on me, she was not one of my main doctors or intern doctors. I even asked about her. No one knew who she was or what I was talking about. But I saw her! I knew without a doubt that she was there and they were all listening to her. I saw the response from the main ER doctor and everyone else when she spoke to them.

She was a young Asian lady, short with long, straight black hair, she was wearing a black skirt and that white doctor's smock coat and had that stethoscope wrapped around her neck. I still can see her so plainly and clearly to this very day. Who was she? Was she an angel? Did God send an angel to save my life? Hmmm. What a thought! I do not know! While I was in the hospital the next few days one of the other doctors came to my room with three or four of the interns. They all wanted to talk with me; they had a few questions for me.

"Mr. Hatfield, you were pretty close to death, your oxygen was way below a level to sustain life, you did not die but you came pretty close to it. What did you see? Did you see a bright light or a tunnel with light at the end?"

"No," I replied, "I did not see a light, a tunnel, not anything like that at all, I just saw the doctor and all the nurses all around the room working on me, and the intern who stopped by and helped them."

"So, Mr. Hatfield, was that an out-of-body experience?"

"No, just normal lying there, looking side to side, watching everyone as I looked up from my bed!"

"Was it dark?"

"No, I did not see anything at all other than doctors and nurses."

"What did you feel? Any special sensations?"

"No, I felt everyone working on me, sticking me like a pin cushion with all those needles, and poking and prodding on me, just all of the normal hospital stuff."

Well, I did not have any of the answers they were looking for so they all packed up and left the room about as fast as they came in. Now that was a pretty short doctor's visit. I like those. No sticks, no stabbing, and no poking around. But what about my little Asian intern doctor? Who was she?

I do not know if she was an angel or not. However, she surely seemed to have all the characteristics. No matter what, I do know that God was at work doing something that day! The funny thing is I can remember her so vividly and I could not tell you about any of the other doctors. After I think about it she was kind of cute, too.

Thank you, Lord, for that young lady!

<((><

5

Who is Gideon?

Up, up, up, to the 7th floor we go. I lay there in my new hospital room, completely bored out of my ever-loving, stinking mind!

There was no TV! No telephone. No cell phone. No computer. There was no radio. No radio talk shows. No music, no iPod, and there were no people to talk to, either! It was just me. I was all alone, having myself one of those pity parties. Ever had one of those? Poor, poor, pitiful me!

I have always been a very busy and active person and I am a people person too; I need social interaction. I am always on the go, always on the move. My favorite saying back then was, "I got things to do and people to screw and I don't have time to fool with you!" Yep, that was my motto back then. I always had to be on the go. Some might even say I was ADD or ADHD times two. There I was, lying there flat on my back, feeling good and frisky, too. You know how it is, once they give you some of those meds—you're feeling good and everything seems fine and you begin to think you are Superman. I thought, *it's time to get outta here. Get home and get back to work, time to get on with my life. It is the middle of the workweek and I got to get outta here. I am missing the excitement of doing business.*

There were about a hundred (at least it seemed like a hundred!) wires hooked up to me still. There were wires to my chest, wires to my head, wires on my forehead and temple, wires on my neck, on my abdomen, wires on my legs, on my ankles; a loudly beeping monitor for my heart and pulse, an oxygen sensor meter keeping track of my oxygen level, an automatic blood pressure cuff on my arm. Who knows what all that stuff is?

I had been diagnosed with sleep apnea and given a prescription for my newest friend, my new companion, a C-pap machine! I just put this mask on over my nose to sleep at night and I look and sound like "Darth Vader" from Star Wars! Yes, I had that cool-sounding, deep-voiced, air-sucking muffled sound. Well it is cool only until you try to go to sleep. Then all that noise will flat drive you bonkers.

The doctors told me that I would always have to sleep with my C-pap machine every night. So I gave her a name. I named my C-pap machine...yep, I did...I named it "My Wife." No, I was not married, but she (my C-pap) went everywhere I went. So if I was leaving home for the night, she went, too. She was right there with me—every trip I went on, everywhere I went, and every time that I was away from home at night she went with me. I now had a new "best friend." I never go to sleep without "My Wife."

I was getting ready to go out of town one day for a last-minute business trip and I told my friends and business associates, "Hey, I need to go home and get my wife, see ya in a few!" I came back a little while later with my little black zipper bag slung over my shoulder and they asked me, "Hey, where is your wife?" I patted my little black bag on my side with my C-pap machine tucked away inside. "I've got 'er right here, fellas. (Tap, tap, tap.) She is right by my side."

Ok. Back up to the 7th floor of the hospital with absolutely nothing to do, and no one to talk to. I could only have a few visitors so I read magazines and newspapers. I could not really concentrate on a book, so short magazine articles were perfect for me. After reading and re-reading the same magazines over a couple of times, I was pretty bored. I needed something to do and everyone I knew was at work; they all had their own responsibilities. Business everywhere was going on and it was happening without me participating. There I was, stuck in the hospital, and I kept wondering what was going on at my business, too.

I owned a company at that time and typical me, I thought to myself, "How can they survive without ME?" I am "The Grand Master of Business!" They cannot survive without me. "Will I be broke when I get back?" Of course not! I had *great* people; they all were very well trained and cross-trained. They were all more than capable. I was very fortunate. Each one had all the tools in their business toolbox they needed, plus they were all great communicators, too. After all, I had taught them! (I know, I just have to do something about his ego of mine!) I was truly blessed. I had a team that worked like a well-oiled machine; yes, they were silky smooth, too! All of that team building and training really does pay off. Thank you, Zig Ziglar!

So, who is this Gideon guy anyway?

Back to my hospital room (I should say, my prison cell). I felt stuck and trapped and I had now been there for a few days and I was still bored to tears! I needed something to occupy my mind! I needed more reading material! So I opened up that drawer of the nightstand by my bed to see if someone had left some business magazines, newspapers or anything at all. Uh–oh, *Big Mistake!* The only thing in the drawer was an ugly light blue book. Aww, shucks! No, no, no, not that! I knew what it was. It was a Bible...a *"Gideon's Bible."*

Now, just who is this Gideon guy, anyway? Why would Gideon leave his Bible here? There it was, an ugly, light blue Gideon's Bible, and it was right there in my hospital room.

That ugly blue book was all that was in that drawer and that was it! There was nothing else there to read at all. I thought, *"Really,* did someone read this #$%^&@ thing and then accidently leave it here or what? After all, these stupid things *(Gideon's Bibles)* only go in hotel rooms, not hospital rooms!"

Now, I knew all about the Bible. After all, I had gone to church when I was a little boy and on up and into my teenage years. I grew up going to church. But I had gotten away from church and from God. I left the church when I was about 19 years old. There was a series of events—and more events after the events of the events—that led to me leaving church and turning my back on God. Now after 20 years I had become a "Christian Hate Machine!" Let me give you just a little insight.

Murder

First, there was a tragedy in my family when I was 19 years old. I have a little brother one year younger than I am who has been in the Tennessee State Prison system for over 32 years now.

Harris was arrested October 5, 1979.

From that day on, he and my family were all ostracized from "The Church." What my brother and our whole family experienced in this time was not a pretty sight at all! It was a pretty terrible time in our lives.

Harris was in the Cleveland, Tennessee, city jail waiting for his trial. He was left there and confined to a jail cell all alone. Yes, all of his friends had left him, too. It was just us, the family. Everyone else had vanished! Well, not only did his friends vanish, but our family friends left us, too. Everyone was gone except my old college friend from Canada, Bruce Doroshuck from Winnipeg, Manitoba, and his family, and oh, yes, there was the church pianist, Sonny Sample. At the very time when we needed the church the most, they were nowhere to be found! We were left all alone. No one wanted to even acknowledge they knew any of us.

We were attending a local church in the city with the world headquarters for the denomination that we attended and we thought we were well-connected church members. Now that is really what surprised and hurt us to the max, being left all alone, without our church or friends. It was an unreal experience for us. We had no support at all. I am sure the church was afraid of more publicity of the murder. Even the city people were angry, too. The whole city of Cleveland was upset at the situation, and rightfully so!

But that is the way life is sometimes. We all have our disappointments and there is no perfect church or no perfect person or organization. We are all walking on the same road and we are all on the same journey. There are times none of us knows what to do. I guess they were in that same boat as well as not knowing what to do. So all is forgiven. We harbor no ill feelings. Somehow it all has worked out in the past 32-plus years. Not a pretty sight but sometimes that is how survival is.

The Burglary Plan

Let me share a few details about his incarceration. Harris did not actually commit the murder for which he was convicted; however, he was there and he did have a part in the crime, so he is not 100% innocent. Things did not go quite as they had been planned out. It was supposed to be a quick and easy burglary, and, as always, things get turned upside down and go terribly wrong. Harris had tried to stop the murder as it was happening, but he was not able to make a difference. He was so small in stature and had just turned 18 years old three weeks earlier. He was about 5'4" tall (or short, I should say) and weighed about 130 pounds soaking wet. He looked like a small seventh grade junior high student; he was so little for his age.

The guy who actually committed the murder was Paul. He was about 5'9," 175 pounds of solid muscle, and a very good athlete, too. Harris could not do much at all physically to stop it, and there was no real dialogue in the midst of the moment, either. However, he did try the best he knew how to stop it. His effort just was not good enough.

Harris stood trial there in Cleveland, Tennessee, and was convicted of murder. He received a life in prison sentence with no possibility of parole, a class X crime in the state of Tennessee at the time.

Now if you put a good-looking, small, young, 18-year-old boy in a men's maximum security adult prison, well, you can only begin to imagine all of the difficulties he had to face all those years. I will spare you the details! Justice here on this earth is sometimes an injustice!

Yes, he had made some pretty bad choices and was trying to correct them when the incident came about. He was trying to get away from the circumstances he had gotten himself into. Harris had asked for my help the night of the murder. He came to the house late that afternoon, about 5-6 p.m. and asked me to help him. He wanted to move out from living with Paul. I said, "OK, let's go!" "Tomorrow," he said. "I am afraid you and Paul will get into it tonight, you will get into a bad fight."

I said, "Harris, let's go now. I will take care of the problem. You know I can take care of it. I will take care of Paul and you know it."

Harris was very emphatic, he said, "I know you and Paul will have a really bad fight—you both have really bad tempers, so tomorrow is better and I will have everything all packed up and ready to go. Please. Let's do it tomorrow, ok? Please!" I said, "Ok, we will wait until tomorrow."

I stood in the driveway that evening and watched him as he drove away! That was the last time I saw him, free, outside of a jail cell until his release.

<(((><

6

The Murder

It was on that very same night, October 5, 1979, three hours later, when Paul approached Harris and told him, "Get up, we're going!"

"Going where?" Harris asked.

Paul said, *"We need to get some money. I'm going to get it from the arcade."*

Harris said, *"No I am not going!"*

Paul said, *"Yes, you are, get up! NOW!"*

Paul was working at the arcade inside of the Cleveland Mall. He had a plan to break in and burglarize the place where he was working!

Harris was afraid of Paul by that time. I do not know all of the reasons, but Harris had a real fear of him. So he got up, not wanting to go with him but thinking, *I have to do this! I have no other choice, but tomorrow I will be out of this mess!*

As the burglary was in progress he saw the security guard coming and hollered out to Paul, "Security!" The security guard and Paul had had major words and problems many times before that night. The security guard was a very big, older man and had a very bad reputation in the community as being a mean man. Almost all of the police officers in the community were even afraid of this man, too.

I am not sure how it all came about, but the guard came in, saw something suspicious and went to check it out. He and Paul had a confrontation of words and then it was on! A scuffle started. Paul, being a young, strong and very physically fit man approximately 21 years old, began to fight with the security guard with all his might. They started slugging each other with their fists, and then they wrestled down to the floor. They got back up with fists-a-flying again, **bam, bam, bam,** when the security guard finally pulled out his long black nightstick, his baton, and was beating Paul down with it pretty severely. Paul was on the ground as the man continued beating without any mercy; he was beating him over and over. Then Paul finally reached out and grabbed hold of the baton. He took the stick away from the security guard as he snatched it right out of his hands. Paul then began to use the long black baton to hit the guard! He was beating the guard with his own nightstick as mercilessly as he had been being beaten.

As the scuffle, fighting, and beating went on for awhile, the guard was down completely on the ground and Paul kept beating him. The security guard was begging for Paul to stop but the rage was still on for Paul. Harris finally *screamed* out as loudly as he could, *"Stop, Paul! Stop!"* But Paul, in his rage, screamed back *"No!"*

So Harris was stepping in and going to try to stop the beating. Paul was still beating the man over and over and over with the stick. Paul was a strong guy and a tough fighter, and Harris had never even had a single fight in his whole life. Paul turned to Harris and then he screamed to him, *"Stop!"* Paul had pulled out a knife and was stabbing the man as he told Harris, *"Stop, I will kill you, too!"*

Yes, you know what happened.

Paul killed the guard. He died from the severe beating and being stabbed.

It was all over now! All the fighting was done! There was nothing left but the hard breathing, and now it was time to run.

The news on the TV early the next morning and the announcement on radio and all of the TV stations in Chattanooga told of a murder at the Cleveland Mall during the night! The whole community was scared to death. In 1979 there were no murders in Cleveland, Tennessee. Panic set in and fear covered the whole community. What happened in the night in our quiet, peaceful city?

My brother Harris was definitely wrong. Yes, he deserved punishment, but not the punishment he received. He did not deserve life in a men's maximum-security prison. He was a young, scared, naive and slow-thinking 18-year-old boy. He had suffered a serious head trauma in a car accident that occurred while he was driving a couple of years prior and was a little slow in processing information. Even his high school put him in special classes.

During the trial, Paul told the jury and the court the same thing he had been telling the police from day one: "Harris had nothing to do with it, I made him go!" The police would not listen to Paul in this respect and no one was listening in the courtroom that day, either. Thank you, Paul, for telling the truth and trying to do the right thing!

The trial time had come and we had never heard of such a concept of two trials in one, especially for a capital offense. They were tried together. The prosecutor for the State of Tennessee was seeking the death penalty! The prosecutor tried Paul and Harris in the same courtroom at the same time. Each one had his own defense attorney, all of them sitting at the same defendant's table. There was one trial for two defendants, one of them being the confessed murderer and the other the accomplice. "Aiding and abetting" was how they charged Harris.

From the very beginning Harris confessed. He took the police to the site out in the country where Paul drove them that night following the murder; where they took their clothes off and burned them, along with the nightstick and knife Paul used to kill the guard. Harris was telling the police everything and crying and sobbing in great remorse. The police had all the evidence they needed.

Harris had a lot of guilt from the minute the murder happened. He was terribly shaken and couldn't sleep. He was in a jail cell re-living the moments over and over in his mind. He would lie on the floor of the jail, curled into a ball, and cry and wail for hours and hours on end. The sheriff would call my mom; he didn't know what to do with Harris. The sheriff was pretty smart, and he knew what was happening with Harris and all the remorse he was feeling. They even took him to the hospital for treatment a time or two; Harris would get back to his cell and do the same thing for days and days and days. He would just lie on the floor of his jail cell in the basement of that old musty police station and just cry for hours and days at a time. Finally, the sheriff and the city officials just left him all alone to deal with it.

Harris was there and he participated in a murder. It was like a slow-motion movie to him, playing over and over in his mind. He heard the man's screams and cries for help as he was being beaten and stabbed unmercifully. Harris kept hearing the nightstick as it struck the man's body—thud, thud, thud—he could hear the screams of the man and the moans and groans of the man at the very end of his life, begging for Paul to stop and begging for his life. Harris would re-live the night over and over again. He would just wail and cry. Seeing and hearing the stabbing of the knife as it was plunged into the man's body over and over, the smells of the incident as it was happening. Harris could still feel and hear Paul's rage at the scene, recalling everything he saw and everything that he heard and witnessed. He also recounted his own actions as he, too, had participated in the taking of another man's life! He was guilt-ridden.

Being involved in a murder at 18 years old, he was still in shock from what he had just seen a few hours earlier and was still traumatized even several years later. He was terrified and all alone in that cell. He did not know what to do, but he was telling the police everything each time they came to get him out of the cell and questioned him over and over again as they continued building their case! He was feeling the shame and the guilt for his own actions. He was so ashamed that he participated in taking the life of someone's father, brother, son, and someone's husband. He was overwhelmed.

I do know that Harris never asked for any mercy at all for himself; he never asked for a lighter sentence, either. He was in such remorse he didn't care whether he lived or died. We, his family, were the ones fighting for his life. The death penalty was on the table and that is what the prosecution was going for; either death penalty for both or life in prison for both. Each one was going to have the same sentence. Harris wanted to give up. He was so ashamed he couldn't lift his head; he couldn't look anyone at all in the eyes. He knew that he deserved whatever punishment was given to him! I, on the other hand, totally disagreed and I still do! He deserved punishment yes, but not the punishment he got.

Harris never had a fair trial or any counseling for the trauma he went through. Yes, he was guilty. Yes, he did deserve punishment. I myself don't know what would have been fair. But I never believed that he deserved to grow up in a men's maximum security prison, suffering years of abuse and trying to defend himself from all the attacks of the older, more seasoned, rough, tough convicts there in the prison.

From here I will spare you all of the horrible details of his 32-year prison life. I know you can only begin to imagine it all for yourself. It is way more horrid than you could ever think possible, and I do not even know the half of it myself —I could not stand to hear the stories when my mother would call to tell us what was going on. I felt responsible, I was not the brother I should have been, and I have carried that guilt with me all my life!

While Harris was in prison he did have to protect himself! He had to protect his life and his honor. In prison your "honor and respect" are all you have to defend yourself from vicious attacks. In the process of Harris defending himself, he had to take another man's life while he was in prison. The man had threatened Harris to do severe bodily harm; he had even set the place, the date, and the time. He had broadcast and made it known all throughout the whole prison system what all he and all his buddies were going to do. The guards all looked the other way, knowing what was about to happen.

Murder #2 Inside "The Walls"

The time and date had now come! This was it! The date of the most horrid, abominable, abhorrently hatched plan had now arrived!

The man and his group of men were boasting and telling everything that they were all planning to do to Harris later that day. The whole prison knew what was coming; they were all watching to see what the entertainment of the day would be! All of the men in his group were boasting the whole day about the details of what was going to happen. So Harris had to go out into "the yard" as they called it. He had to confront the situation head-on and right out in the open, in front of everyone. Harris knew he had to make a stand and then to stand firm in it. Harris knew it was better for just the two of them to settle up all by themselves, and this was the best time and place, out in the open in front of everyone and in front of the guards, too. Now was the best time to try to talk to the man. Better now than to have to deal with the whole group of men later, in the dark, confined room, and then to endure all that they had threatened to do to him.

There was no turning back. He walked out of the main prison to the yard.

He walked right up to the man who was the entire gang leader and who was the author of the threats. The man was lifting weights while lying on the bench press. Harris walked right up and started talking and trying to work it out. But the threat by now was magnified and it was inevitable. There was *NO* way *OUT*! At that time Harris lunged at the man and they were fighting one-on-one. The little young man was fighting for his life with a grown man. It was a tough fight between them, and Harris knew if he lost what all was going to happen later that day, so he fought with all of his might.

During the squabble Harris had to kill the man with a shank (homemade knife). He had no choice. The man was older, bigger, and had a large following. Harris was all by himself, and was just trying to talk and settle the issue if there was any possible way. This was the only option he had to protect himself. The man insisted on a massive abuse session that would inflict tremendous bodily harm to him.

Yes,—we call this "rehabilitation," putting a young boy in a men's maximum-security penitentiary with the worst of the worst criminals and expecting him to grow up and survive and protect himself all on his own!

Our prison system had now made a killer out of him!

A young man now had become a murderer by protecting himself from yet another vicious attack and more physical abuse! Then we, the people, blamed him for becoming a murderer.

We blamed him for protecting himself! Our justice system required him to stand trial again in a court of law, and he was convicted of murder again, for a second time. But this time he did have to kill another man, to protect himself! With all the evidence they reduced the charge to manslaughter because he went out to confront the man instead of waiting for the man to attack him first. They added several more years to his "life-with no-parole" prison sentence.

So he was left there again! A young, naive boy left all on his own to survive and fend for himself in a HARDCORE men's maximum security prison in Nashville, Tennessee, called "The Walls"!

So I have a very TOUGH question for you.

What would you have done in this situation?

Breaking out of Jail

We had a joke when we were kids and Harris still loves to tell it today. *"You can put a man in jail, but you can't keep his face from breaking out!"*

That is what he had done! He "broke out" of jail. Well, not like you think! He was still there; however, his heart and his mind had broken out years ago when he completely surrendered his life to Christ. Yes, Harris did survive and he is alive and well. Today he is a solid Christian man for over 22 years now. He is genuine, real, and sold out for Christ.

The "convicted murderer" is now a Christian MAN, living the Christian life in the absolutely worst of conditions and circumstances.

He lives in the roughest, toughest environment anyone could possibly live in here in the United States. But no one messes with Harris in prison today; he is now 51 years old. They all know he can and he will defend himself, but only if he is placed in the situation where he has no other option. So, as they say in the walls of the prison system there in Nashville, Tennessee, he has *"RESPECT."*

However, the greatest thing is all of the other prisoners know that Harris will do anything at all to help any one of them! He will have a Bible study with them and pray with them, too. He has earned the reputation of being known as genuine, not perfect, but devout Christian man who is living his life trying to make a difference in as many lives as he can inside a tough prison system! He is trying to leave a legacy. But he also knows he is laying up treasure in Heaven. He is making a difference in men's lives, not only teaching Christ and salvation, but self-responsibility and accountability!

He is getting ready for one of those mansions that Jesus said He was going away to prepare. For him, any one of those rooms in the corner of Heaven will be just fine with him. But there are not any of those corner rooms that I know of. He will be living and standing right there beside you and me, praising and worshiping with us.

Harris really is a lover of people and not a fighter. He is a giver and a forgiver. He will turn the other cheek, yes. Now, that does not mean he can be taken advantage of. It means he will forgive and forget and try to help anyone at all for any wrong they have done to him or anyone else. But! Do NOT mistake his

Christianity for weakness! If you confront him, he will try to reason with you! But make no mistake! He will protect himself if he has to, just the same as you and I would do to protect our families and ourselves.

You see, he knows he has a mission to serve Christ and to serve others, and he protects that mission and calling by protecting himself!

Forgiving "The Church"

Yes, all is forgiven! I know that the people and the church just really didn't know what to say or do. I understand all of that now. There is no perfect church, the same as there is no perfect family. It was a very tough life experience for Harris and my family, my mom and dad especially.

I had to drop out of my college classes in Cleveland. The things that went on even at a Christian college in this situation were still horrible. Sometimes it was almost impossible to endure! So, I found myself at an impasse. I had a big temper problem in those years. I had been working on it and I thought that I had it under control, but I had difficulty dealing with how our family was being perceived, talked about and treated at such a horrendous time in our lives. So yes, I did make a few big, big mistakes during that time. I was asked to leave the school at the end of my sophomore year, which was the right thing for them to do, anyway. My grades were very bad and the school was right and justified in their response by asking me to leave.

My brother Harris was released from prison after almost 33 years in a maximum security facility called Riverbend in Nashville, Tennessee. He became a FREE man on July 2, 2012. THANK YOU LORD! His release alone was a MIRACLE. July 2, what an independence day that was for him. Two days before we celebrate our independence as a country on the 4th of July.

Harris was imprisoned 33 years simply for being in the wrong place at the wrong time with the wrong person. That is it. Bad choices placed him in that situation. So choose your friends wisely at every age and stage in life.

Share this story with your kids and grandkids, anyone who you think needs to hear it.

<((><

Back to that Gideon Guy!

I hated God. I hated church and I hated Christians.

Back in the hospital room I picked up the Bible out of that nightstand drawer. I did not know where to start reading. It had been 20 years since I had even held a Bible in my hands. Through all the years I had grown so cold. I hated God. I hated church and I hated Christians. In my mind, every wrong thing that had ever happened to me, and the worst things that had ever happened to me were always by *"The Christians."* I was not living for God, so I blamed whoever I could for my own lack of understanding and knowledge, and yes, I am sure I blew things way out of proportion in my mind about how bad Christians were.

I had been thinking about God and spiritual things when He brought a man in my life and I saw him change right before my very eyes. I was amazed.

Bill Ebarb from Shreveport, Louisiana, accepted Christ. He also owned a motel up in Montana with his new wife, Cindy. They would come back to visit his kids and family from time to time in Shreveport and I saw Bill was a changed man!

I watched his life and everything he did. I watched him like a hawk. I looked for the hypocrite, but it never came. He had genuinely changed. By the way, just so you know, Bill is the older brother of the girl who introduced me to gambling on football! So, as you see, God was at work the whole time.

Where are Those Stinking Bible Stories?

There I was in that boring hospital room on the seventh floor. I needed something to do, anything at all. I looked at that Bible in the drawer and I thought, "A good story will do," and so I picked up that Gideon Bible and I did not know where to start reading or what to even do with it. I did not want to read any of those boring Scriptures that I would not understand very well. All I wanted was to find a story to read like, David and Goliath, or the story of Samson and Delilah, even Moses and the burning bush or the Red Sea. I wanted to read about the walls of Jericho that came tumbling down. I wanted to read about that guy who won a battle after God kept dividing his army down to 300 men, and his name was Gideon, too. I wanted to read about the three fish and five loaves of bread. I just wanted to read the stories I remembered from my early years of going to church.

So, I picked up the Bible. Then I just stared at it; I looked at it for a long, long time! Then I opened it up. I looked for the stories but they were not listed in the front of the Bible in the table of contents. So I looked in the back of the Bible and they were not listed there, either. I knew there were Scriptures in the Bible but I knew there were Bible stories somewhere, too.

So I flipped through the pages some but I could not find any stories at all. I was totally lost. I had no idea where to even begin to read or where to turn.

"Where are those stinking stories?" I thought.

So I took that Bible and I decided I would use my own system to find something to read. I flipped that Bible over. Then I flipped it back over again. After a few minutes I closed my eyes and I began to flip it over and over and end over end, then I flipped it some more over and over and over again. I turned it backward and forward, upside down then right side up. I opened the pages and flipped through them like they were cards. I would continue to turn and flip that Bible every direction possible, flipping from page to page, front to back and back to front. I was shuffling and riffling through the pages as fast as I could, now front to back and back to front again. I was going to take a chance and let my fingers do the walking. Then finally, ***Bam!*** I stopped.

I took a chance and finally landed on the two open pages of the book, then I took my right index finger and circled all over the pages, around and around I went. From the left page to the right page and back again and again, from the top of the page to the bottom of the page, over and over again. I would go all around and around, and up and down with my eyes still tightly closed. Then I decided it was time to Stop...Bam!

I opened my eyes, and then I looked at where my finger had landed. I started reading,

> *"Seek ye first the Kingdom of God and His righteousness, and all these things will be added unto you."*– (Matthew 6:33 KJV of the Gideon's Bible.)

I was shocked and stunned. I was baffled and amazed and frustrated, I was not happy at all.

In the recent past I had been searching for some answers for issues in my life at that time, and I had begun to think about God and religion some, too. It had been on my mind for quite some time. I did not have any problems, just no real fulfillment to my life. Yes, I had a very good life, just no real happiness, no purpose or peace to my life. Something was missing. I was happy, but I had no joy. Happiness came as long as everything was good.

As soon as I read the Scripture, it scared me!

I was so stunned and aggravated and I was shocked because I was searching for my own reason to be alive. I was searching for my purpose in life and now the Bible had just answered a question I had been asking, but I was not looking for an answer at that particular time. I was not even thinking about God and purpose. I wanted all the answers, just like it said. But NOT today. I just wanted to read some stories and pass the time away, that's all. I just wanted to read a simple Bible story or two. I was bored. I just needed some reading material! I just wanted to read a story. That was it!

I read those words from the Scripture in the Bible and it hit me right between the eyes and I knew it.

I very quickly threw the Bible about five or six feet away from me as fast and hard as I could! *Slam-Bam!*

I threw that Bible

I threw that Bible hard and fast off to my right-hand side over to the wall that was by my bed, Splat! That was the same wall that created a walkway to my bedside where the nurses would come in to check on me.

The Bible hit the wall with a big, *loud thud, bang* and a splat about bed height. Then it slid down the wall and fell to the floor. The Gideon's Bible was lying there on the floor with all of the pages sprawled out all over and lying face down on the tile floor with that ugly blue Bible cover now facing upward. It was a complete pile of mess.

I laid there disgusted, looking at that Gideon's Bible lying on the floor all mangled up; I just wanted that Bible out of my sight! I was now aggravated and I just wanted it gone! *GONE!*

The Angel Nurse

The Angel Nurse

***About an hour or two later, a nurse came in; she was a very nice
and sweet older black lady.***

She came in a' hummin' a tune and said in her Louisiana-southern-drawl
black singing-toned dialect, *"Awwww, Honey-child! You dropped yo' Bible! Let
me pick it up fo' ya'. I'll jest set it right here fer ya', so it will be reght-cheer on yo'
nightstand when ya' need it."*

I still to this day do not know what she came in for that day, that is, if she
really was my nurse. She did not do anything for me...all she did was pick the
Bible up off the floor.

Who was she? *She was NOT one of my nurses!*

I had never even seen her before that day, yet she came right in my room like
she was one of my nurses. She picked the Bible up, straightened it all out, and
unfolded all of the wrinkled up and crinkled pages. She precisely, meticulously
and methodically unfolded each sheet of paper. It took her a good 3 or 4 minu-
ets, then she closed it up. It was all so nice and neat when she finished, **just like
it was a brand new book.**

I watched her as she bent over to pick the Bible up with both hands, and she
gently held it like she was about to present it to someone. She handled it with

such care, like each page was made of thin sheets of pure gold paper! Each crease and fold in the pages had to be straightened, smoothed and ironed out with her hands, ever so gently.

Then she placed the Bible on top of the nightstand with such care. She placed it so carefully where I could see it if I looked anywhere in that general direction. She placed it by my head on the nightstand, not back in the drawer "where it belonged" *(that is where I wanted it)*, back in the drawer out of my sight.

Then she slowly turned toward the door as she smiled and looked at me one last time as if to say good-bye. She looked me right in the eye and continued humming that pretty melody, then, she slowly walked away and left the room! *I never saw her again.*

There was a nice, sweet spirit about her and it was like she humbly commanded respect just by her sweet presence. But all she did was show me respect.

Who was she?

Who was this lady? Was she really a nurse? She did not do anything for me. She just came in and picked up the Bible and that was it!

Ahhh-Yes! Not a doubt in my mind. **She was an angel!**

But I was still frustrated; the *Gideon's Bible belonged back in that dadgum drawer!* I thought to myself, but I did not dare say it out loud to her. But I wanted to holler it out loud enough to get her back in the room. "Please, lady! Come back here, please! Put it where it goes! Put that Bible back where it was in that drawer! Please, lady! Please come back and put it where it belongs, in the nightstand! I don't want to touch it and I do not want to see it at all!" But she did not come back.

She was an angel! No doubt. She was one of those angels that we entertain unaware!

I was there in that hospital for a whole week and I knew all of my nurses. I never saw her before that day and I never saw her again! But I remember her so vividly to this very day and I cannot remember anything at all about all the other nurses. I cannot remember anything about them. But my black nurse I remember so well, just like it was yesterday.

She had that presence all about her; I remember her walking into the hospital room on the seventh floor humming a tune. There was such sweetness in the aura that was all around her. She had an objective and a mission to accomplish. It did not take her long to do what she came to do. Then her mission was finished. She left the room that day and never returned. Her job was completed. The impact was made! An indelible imprint placed in my mind that plays like a slow-motion movie sometimes when I just sit and think about that wonderful and frustrating day.

God sent her that day to make an impression that would last for all eternity, not only in my life but also in the lives that I have had the privilege to touch.

I did not know she was an angel at the time, but all through the years I have thought about that lady. She was only there for a few minutes, but I can still see her as clearly and as vividly today as I did that day in 1995! Her personality and the countenance that was all about her were *indescribable*.

Yes, I believe God sent an angel to point me to the cross of Jesus. Just like it says in Hebrews 1:14 *(ESV)*:

> **"Are they not all ministering spirits sent out to serve for the sake of those who are to inherit salvation?"**

Possibly this Scripture is for those already saved who are to inherit eternal salvation in Heaven, or does it mean for those who do not know Christ and are to inherit salvation and come to know and accept Jesus as their Savior here on this earth?

For me, I can see it both ways. As I said, I am not a Biblical scholar. I believe God sent someone to make an impression on me that day! I believe this Scripture in Hebrews came alive for me!

Hebrews 13:2 *(ESV)*

> **"Do not neglect to show hospitality to strangers, for thereby some have entertained angels unaware."**

She had a mission to accomplish and as soon as it was accomplished she was gone. Yes, she was an angel.

That Ugly Blue Bible, Again!

The cover on the Gideon's Bible was a significant blue color. I saw it as such an ugly, annoying color, especially since I did not want to see it at all. It definitely was a color that could not be ignored. The Bible sat there where she had placed it on the nightstand all of that day and all through the night. I ignored it. I consciously looked the other direction to ignore it! Okay! Believe me. I tried to ignore it!

The next day I was all alone again. Everyone I knew was working—again. In my opinion there was really nothing wrong with me at all. I felt great and I was ready to go home. The doctors were still running tests, but I felt fine. I was ready to go.

It was afternoon, approximately 1:00 p.m., and I was bored stiff again. I had re-read all my magazines again and tried to read a book. I was so stinking bored. There was no window in my room; it was just four barren, ugly hospital walls and yes, me. I looked over and there it was! I stared at the Bible on that nightstand for a long, long time. Then after several minutes I slowly reached over and picked up that Gideon's Bible once again.

"What in the world am I doing?"

Am I out of my ever-loving mind? I held it in my hand for quite a long time, just looking and staring at it. I just lay there, gazing at it, thinking; *maybe, just maybe this time I can find a story in there today, but where?*

It was not very long before I did the exact same thing with that Bible all over again! I had not learned my lesson yet.

Once again I put my brilliant plan into action. I closed my eyes as tightly as I could and I took that Bible and started flipping it over and over again; I turned that Bible every which way I possibly could. This time I wanted to be sure my plan worked, so I flipped it some more and kept shuffling and riffling through the pages again, over and over and over. Then I finally opened it up, found a page and, again with my eyes still closed, I circled around and around, all over the page with my finger, up and down, over and over. Then it happened again. **Bam,** I stopped.

I opened my eyes and read,

"My Spirit does not always strive with man" – (Genesis 6:3 Gideon's KJV).

I threw that Bible again! *Bam!*

It hit the side of that wall HARD. I threw it as fast as I could throw it with a nice quick fling and snap of my wrist, then splat on that same wall. Once again it fell to the floor where it stayed for quite a long time. This time no one came in to pick it up! It just lay there for hours.

I remembered enough about the Bible from my earlier days and my teenage years about that specific passage, so this time that ugly blue Bible had really gotten my attention. I also remembered a song from that Scripture that my Uncle Judge Bates in Jackson, Mississippi, would sing. He would sing this song for awhile, as he was playing his old stand-up bass guitar. When he would come to these Scripture words he would *stop*. He paused. He would not sing them! He would speak them in a quiet, yet firm, authoritative voice, *"My Spirit does not always strive with man."* I knew immediately what that Scripture meant. There was no doubt at all. I knew that "I" was to seek God first to find Him, and second, He would not always be there to wait for me! I would have to make a decision!

Those words lived with me. They never left my mind. **"The Lord said, my spirit does not always strive with man."**

There I was with my stupid, selfish pride! Playing games with God! I was so stubborn; I just knew I was going to do it all my way, no matter what. This time I was taking a different gamble. A gamble of time. I was not really thinking about the fact that I could lose my life at any minute. I was young, strong successful and invincible. I was in control of my own destiny, so, I was doing my life, my way.

I would like to be able to tell you that I accepted Christ that day! But, I didn't!

Back to my way of life

After being released from the hospital, I very quickly got back to living my life and doing business! Everything was really good for me. Money was coming in, business was really good, and I had lots of "friends"—it was life as usual. I was back to gambling and betting my football. Life was good. All except...I lived with that nagging. There was a nagging, pulling and tugging way down deep in my heart; the Scriptures from the blue Gideon Bible stayed in my mind. It was that missing link. Then, knowing that I was not really happy with my life, there was still something missing, I began to start searching. Quietly.

I was working more on changing myself on the inside. I was trying my best to do better business and still I was having that occasional lapse of judgment. It was not too often, but still I would have that "I" problem. I was still doing what was best for me, what was in my best interests. I really was diligently reading on how to get that feeling down and change my character, change my heart. I was trying my very best to live with integrity. I did everything I knew to do from all my books and tapes; I did everything I was committed to do with all of my heart. But it was not working.

9

The Music, It Got Me

I dug back in. I turned off the talk shows on my radio as I drove in my 4-Runner to the job sites.

I started listening to my Zig Ziglar cassettes again as I would drive down the road. **"Automobile University,"** as Zig calls it. I would still get up early on Sunday mornings and get my coffee, walk down my long, winding driveway out in the country to get my local paper, and read the sports section. You know what I was looking for—the **Vegas line.** Then back to the same ol' system I had been using before.

I started reading my newspapers and watching TV again. I was going to find a station to watch and keep me occupied until the sports shows came on. As I flipped through, changing the channels, one of those TV preachers came on. I thought, "Oh crap, nope, he is fake, everything about him looks and sounds fake. I am not listening to that stupid junk or any TV preacher for that matter! Been there—done that."

I changed the channel again, and there was another TV preacher. This one had his hair and beard all dyed jet black and his silver roots were shining through like a bright light in the darkness from needing another black hair dye job. He was there on the TV wanting people to, "Send your money! Send your money to plant a seed! Plant a seed?" Right! Plant a seed with money? You gotta' be kidding me! Now, that was just plain stupid, in my opinion. Everyone knows you cannot plant a money tree. Send money to this guy, to plant a seed?

Come on, gimme a stinking break! What a doof. Needless to say, I changed that TV channel again, as fast as I could.

Plant a seed with money; show me that one in the Bible! He said if I would "come to Jesus" I could have all the success in the world I wanted. God would answer all of my prayers. I could get all the money and wealth I wanted, if I would surrender my life to Jesus. I could even pray and have a Mercedes; I could have a jet, too. Just like his. All I needed to do was come to Christ, and plant a seed (send him money), pray, have faith and *WAIT*! What a blooming idiot, I thought! Did he think I just fell off the turnip truck or something?

Finally, I found a station that had nice, relaxing, pretty music. I loved it. Now, this was way before music channels on cable TV, so I thought, *I love this station.* I listened to the beautiful music and then an awesome choir came on. It was so beautiful! I learned later they were right there in the city where I lived; it was all local, there in Shreveport/Bossier City, Louisiana.

As the music played, I would drink my coffee and read my local newspaper, and work on my betting budget for the day, and then it happened! Another preacher came on! So, I turned the TV volume way down. It was so low that I could not make out one word of what he was saying. However, I could still hear him mumbling. "Perfect," I thought, "Perfect."

Usually, after the preacher talked, the music would come back on again and I would turn the volume of the TV right back up to listen to that beautiful singing and music while I was figuring out what teams I wanted to bet on. After the program was over, I would load up in the truck and off I would go to Super One Foods store, then the newsstand, and let's not forget the cigar shop downtown, too. I had to hurry up and get back home so I could get all of my bets figured out and my noon-time game bets placed.

Friends, Football and the Sunday Party

I was getting ready for the guys and gals to come over and have our Sunday football fun day. Grilling out, watching the game, laughing, talking, drinking, smoking our cigars outside and having a fun time. This was the every Sunday fall program at my house.

All of a sudden I began to sit and really watch all of *"my friends."* I looked hard to see who was really happy with their life, because I was missing something in my life! I had lots of friends, a great family, a mom and dad who I loved and was close to, and my son Jeremy, whom I loved dearly. Those relationships seemed to be the only things in my life that had any significance to me. The funny thing was today and most Sundays I was around a lot of people, yet I was still alone. Not lonely, but alone! I did not feel like anyone really loved me. I wanted to love someone and be loved by someone, too.

As I watched my friends interact with their spouses and with their boyfriends and girlfriends, I saw what I already knew: they really were all unhappy in their own situations in life as well. The husbands knew that occasionally their wives would have a little indiscretion and the wives knew that their husbands would have an occasional fling. They all seemed to be okay with that. They would have their spats and knock down, drag out fights and somehow they would still work through it all. It was a constant revolving door, every few months or every year or two another major problem would arise. But when everyone was together on football Sunday, it was *PARTY TIME!*

I was beginning to get mixed messages. I wanted to change who I was and the two Scriptures from that Gideon's Bible now lived with me and seemed to haunt me continually.

While my high-rolling friends were not living the way I wanted to live, I would just continue in the same direction they were going. I was changing but they were not. It was a weekly role and I watched every weekend the drama — or the results of the lifestyle. I simply stayed now because of the peer pressure of losing my *"friends."*

I began to feel more and more that "I did not really love anyone and that no one really loved me, either!"

I loved my mom, dad, and son Jeremy (who I call "Mr. Magoo," that is the nickname I gave him). The first time I saw Jeremy after he was born, I looked at him and he was so cute—and yet, he had an ugly, big red nose! Truth was, he was sort of ugly! Jeremy looked to me like Mr. Magoo, so in a few seconds I named him Mr. Magoo. Now, today, 29 years later, he is still my Mr. Magoo. But he looks just like his dad, me, so I think he is the best looking thing God created. But the only people I really loved were Mom, Dad and Jeremy—Mr. Magoo.

I forgot to turn the TV volume down!

As life went on, I would get up every Sunday morning and turn the TV on, find the channel with the nice music, and yes, I turned the preacher down every time when he came on to preach, too. Yes, that was my every Sunday routine. However, I would occasionally forget to turn the volume down when the preaching started.

Well, this one particular preacher at least had a good, sincere speaking voice! He made a little bit of sense from what little I heard from him. Nonetheless, I would turn him down anyway, as soon as I realized he was preaching. Well, as it turns out, one Sunday I forgot to turn him down quickly enough! I heard him say, **"God is love. If you don't know God, you don't know love."** Then the beautiful music came back on.

Bam!…He Got Me!

Now the TV preacher had my attention! Remember, I did not feel like I really loved anyone or that anyone really loved me. So now he had my full attention, now I was turning up the volume instead of turning it down.

I heard a message that made a little bit of sense to me. I listened intently, glued to the screen, watching every movement of the pastor. I was reading his body language and his voice inflection; I watched his eye movement as I listened to his content. I observed how he moved on the stage. I watched every nod of his head and blink of his eye. I came to the conclusion that this preacher really believed what he was saying, and the delivery was absolutely amazing. Remember, I love speakers and seminars. This preacher spoke in tones of love and compassion, as well as in tones of accountability. He spoke with confidence and assurance, yet matter of fact. He seemed nice but he "pulled no punches, "as they say in the boxing world.

Now, if only everything the preacher was saying were true!

I wanted it all to be true.

I wanted what he was talking about! When the message ended, I was off again on my usual Sunday morning adventure; yep, you know where I was headed. However, this time I was thinking all the way about what that preacher said. I recounted every single word. It was imprinted in my head just as he had said it all. I replayed every word over and over again in my mind. I could still see him in my mind, delivering that message over and over again! I could even remember his voice inflections and his mannerisms. I loved it! But I *hated* it, too.

I wrapped up my morning adventure and got back to the house pretty quickly. I placed only a couple of bets that day, which was very unusual for me. My passion for gambling was diminishing. My mind was preoccupied with those words I'd heard that morning, "God is Love."

I really, really wanted what that preacher talked about!

The name of the program I was watching was *"First Word"* with Dr. Fred Lowery at First Bossier!

Now, I liked that he was not one of those "Baptist churches" or one of those hard-nosed-rules churches. They were simply *"First Bossier."* They were just a local church. I knew exactly where they were. After all, I worked right down the street on East Texas Street in Bossier City.

As I found out later, they really were a Southern Baptist church. Now, if I had known that they were a Southern Baptist church, I would never have driven on the parking lot or even opened the door! I wanted no more rules!

Sunday was over and it was back to work. Monday morning came and I was in my 4-Runner, getting around, checking on my crews, starting off the week, getting material on the construction sites. As I drove down the road I grew tired of talk radio and had listened to all of the Ziglar and other cassette tapes, too. I had been listening to the same ones several times over and I just wanted to hear something a little different. That preacher was still on my mind the next day, all day long.

I do have a confession I need to make at this point.

Number one: *I hated TV preachers.*

Number two: *I hated radio preachers, too!*

After all, I had seen scandal after scandal of TV and radio preachers play out in the media. I had seen the big, rich and famous preachers fall from their ivory towers and the failure of church empires and the criminal charges filed against TV preachers. I'd even seen some of them going to prison. So I had no love at all for TV or radio preachers. None. Zero. Especially after my family's previous experience when we really needed our church family and we were deserted. I felt like everyone in religion was a hypocrite. The only one I even liked just a little was Billy Graham. I even began to watch him every now and then. I liked the music and I loved the way he said "Come to JEEzus."

My Funny African-American Radio Preacher

As I turned the radio on and ran through the stations, I came across a black radio preacher.

Now, this guy was absolutely funny. He was hilariously funny. This guy had me laughing out loud and I was in the truck all by myself. He had me laughing so hard I was in tears! Truth is, I almost peed in my pants, I was laughing so hard, because he was so funny.

This guy was a way-back country preacher, a black man. I never knew that Bible stories could be so funny and told in a comedic way. Now, I am not prejudiced at all today, but back then I did have my prejudices. But this guy and his dialect and the people of his congregation were so funny to listen to. He had that thick, black, country dialect thing going on with his Eddie Murphy humor-twisted Bible stories.

The things he would say and the way he would say them were an art that he had to have personally developed himself. It was all him! He was not just telling funny stories; he was preaching with all he had. He had the old-time Louisiana Pentecostal hacking and a' hollering, shouting preaching style. Then in his deep voice he would say, "Shout amen fer-me! Com'on now, somebody give me a shout out! Is there anyone in this house gonna help me preach this thang?"

Not only was he keeping me in stitches with my big ol' belly laughs, the preacher did say a few things that I understood and I really liked him, too. He kept me laughing. Then I would hear the congregation, "Come-on now, preach! Yes, L'od we hear ya L'od." It went on and on and I was cracking up laughing out loud.

I would drive on to the construction site after listening to this guy and get out of my truck. I remember the first day I called my crew chief/foreman over to tell him what I just heard while I was driving to the job site. My foreman would say, "Oh, yesssss, brother! I can preach just like him!" Sure enough, he could put on a show like I have never seen white men do before and there I was, cracking up all over again! He sounded just like the guy I was listening to on the radio. We were laughing so hard we were doubled over. I had to go find that porta-potty as fast as I could or I would have peed in my pants right there in the driveway.

Now my construction guys were not Christians either, so we all really hammed it up pretty good. My foreman would imitate the preaching and they would all chime right in as the congregation. This went on for at least 20-30 minutes. From then on I would drive onto the sites, get out of my 4-Runner and start preaching myself, like my new friend, the black radio preacher man. Then all of my guys would join in and be the congregation again. "Come on, now, preach it! Yes...yeessss...come on down now, Lo'd, come on down..." Well, you get the idea. We had a blast. We would laugh so hard we would be bent over, laughing at ourselves.

As time went by, I had some of those days when I was working hard and stressing out. I would start searching and looking for my new radio friend. I would turn the country black preacher on my radio just so I could have myself a good laugh. But you know what? Something happened! The things he was saying were sinking in. I was beginning to understand his dialect and the words he was saying. Little by little my heart and mind were opening up. I was listening intently to what he was saying while I was being entertained with his preaching and the congregation. This guy was now talking to me. He was ministering to me.

I always got my big laugh I needed from my radio preacher. He and the congregation were providing a ministry to me and I am sure they had no idea of what it was or whom it was they were affecting and impacting! Their ministry was affecting me in an untraditional way from what I am sure they had designed the ministry to do. However, they were changing the life of their white prejudiced mocker. I loved that little black church and congregation and that preacher even though I had never met any of them, I was connecting to them. I, the white control freak, know-it-all businessman who had all the answers, was listening to this message from the people who I used to look down on, and I did not like them simply because of the color of their skin. I now understood some of his Bible stories like never before. The characters were coming alive. They were jumping off the pages and leaping through the radio airwaves and piercing my heart. All of a sudden this guy now had a special gift of communicating.

I was enjoying his sermons but I had lots and lots of fun and laughs with him, too. He just never knew he had a white guy out here who was always look-ing for him and listening to him and his church congregation.

Oh, how I would have loved to know who this man was, I would have loved to let him know what that ministry did for me.

I was on my way home one night after a really bad day. It was late at night and I knew my new friend, the black preacher man, would come on again late at night as well as in the morning, too. Sometimes I would listen to him on the way home; he would come on about 9:00 p.m. So, I located the station where he was and all of a sudden, he was gone! My favorite new friend was gone!

There was now a new preacher voice on the radio in his place. I think he was black, too. Yes, he's pretty funny, too, but not like that first guy. It was a differ-ent kind of humor, and after listening a few minutes I determined that yes, for sure, he was a black preacher and I liked him, too. He was really a great and dynamic speaker and an awesome communicator, too. He had a sermon that night that I needed, even though I was looking more for a laugh. I got a good light-hearted message that hit me right between my eyes. He had a unique way of telling his stories too and he was a little humorous as well. He had more of those stories I was looking for back in the hospital. He also had a different spin on those stories, and he would tell some funny modern-day Bible stories and analogies to boot. I really liked this new radio preacher guy. Oh, I did say that I hated radio preachers earlier, didn't I?

This new guy made sense. He was articulate, concise, had analogies that made sense. He was very intelligent and quoted his facts and figures in a very unique way. I loved what he was saying. My old friend, the entertaining preacher, had now been replaced by Dr. Tony Evans of Oak Cliff, Texas.

I really liked this guy, Tony Evans. There were so many times that I would get home from work and I would spend the evening at home. I knew he would come on the radio at 9:00 p.m., so I would make up some excuse; I would get up and in my 4-Runner, pop a cigar in my mouth and light'er up, then drive to the store 10 miles away just so I could listen to him on my radio for 30 minutes. I loved this Tony Evans guy! I would drive around for an hour sometimes, and just park and listen to him, and then I would drive back home.

Funny, how God will use the very things we do not like to get our attention! I hated TV preachers, yet God used TV preachers. I hated radio preachers, yet God was now using radio preachers. And the Bible! I did not believe in God and He sent me an ugly, light blue Gideon's Bible!

GOD really does have a huge sense of humor! And I say, "I did it my way"? *Riiiiggghhhhttt.* Yeah, I think God did it all His way! That ugly blue Gideon's Bible was not really ugly! It was just the convicting of what was within its cover!

It was a Gideon's Bible that was in the right place at the right time and started the stirring of my mind and heart. No, it wasn't a "warm, fuzzy feeling" at the time. It was "in your face "conviction because I knew and I remembered the Scriptures from all those years of going to church as a teenager.

Hey, Gideon! Thank you for leaving your Bible in that hospital room at Louisiana State Medical Center in Shreveport, Louisiana, back in 1995!

As for the Gideon's Bible, let me tell you a story. I know The Gideon's is a professional Christian men's organization that distributes Bibles. But I love the fact it was the Gideon's organization that made sure there was a Bible in my hospital room, and that there are Bibles everywhere all over the world. Thank you guys so very much!

Another Gideon story.

My wife Erika, and daughter, Emma, were going on a mission trip to the barrio in South Texas, on the border by Mexico in the Rio Grande Valley. The youth mission group needed Spanish Bibles to distribute. A Gideon member's son, John Kimmel, Jr. (he was about 16 years old), was sitting in a meeting room and getting ready to go on that same trip. As soon as the meeting was over, in a matter of seconds and with a sense of urgency, he bolted out of the room. Just a couple of minutes later, also with a sense of urgency, in hobbled his dad, a Gideon, Big John Kimmel, Sr. (in pain as he awaited double knee replacement surgery). Big John went directly up to meet with the mission trip organizer.

The Gideon's and Big John Kimmel supplied over 100 Spanish language Bibles to the kids on the mission trip to distribute to the Spanish-speaking people of South Texas. Wow! From out of seemingly nowhere, God supplied another Gideon! God and His Gideon's were providing over 100 Spanish Bibles in a moment of need. I did not know much about the Gideon's and I really needed to check them out. They are actively involved in reaching the world for Christ and we usually never know their names or the sacrifice of what they do to distribute all those Bibles. Where does the money come from? How do they do it? Who are they? Their Bibles are everywhere. Well, it was now time for me to find out who they were.

The teen youth mission group at Lake Pointe Church in Rockwall, Texas, got real-life lessons in giving from the Gideon's, as well as in supplying their own personal effort to spread the Word. While they were working and helping people and distributing those Gideon Bibles, they also were experiencing the need of so many people who wanted the Scriptures in their own language so they could learn of God. But they did not have them.

The 100 Bibles were not nearly enough for all of who wanted them. However, I believe God supplied the perfect number of Bibles to be placed in the right hands and possibly another Gideon Bible to be left "accidentally" in another hospital room!

Stu Schlackman's Gideon Story

Another friend of mine, Stu Schlackman—a Jewish man from Yonkers, New York, now living in Dallas, Texas—tells his story as a Messianic Jew who came to know Christ while sitting in a hotel room in 1983 at 31 years of age in Hoover, Alabama. Here's the story from page 80 of his book, *From the Star to the Cross.*

"When I curiously opened the drawer to the nightstand, a Gideon's Bible

stared up at me, I pulled it out of hiding. I thumbed through the book..."
Wow! What can I say? My friend and I both came to Christ from a Gideon's
Bible, mine in a hospital room and his in a hotel room. You have to read his
amazing story. If you cannot find it, look me up and I will get you a copy from
him. It is only $15.00 and a great story of a Jewish man coming to Christ.

But I still have a question for you.

Who was that first black preacher man?

Was he an angel on the airwaves?

God was using him in a very special way. I do not know if he was an angel
or not. I do know that God was working through his radio ministry.

I don't think that either of these two men on the radio were angels, but who
knows?

**I often wonder about the funny black preacher man if he was for real
—or an angel?**

Hey, Gideon!

Thanks for leaving your Bible!

<(((><

11

The First Word

Early fall and it was that time of year again. Football season was starting back up!

Yes, I was back to my Sunday morning TV time. Throughout the year I would get up and sometimes I would turn on the local church TV program, Dr. Fred Lowery, and listen. Wow, what is going on? *I was listening to and looking for a TV preacher?* Hey, I am the guy who hates TV preachers, just like the radio preacher!

I was doing much better at changing my heart, so I thought! At this point in time I decided I would place only two or three bets. My dollar volume was still the same, just a whole lot less work; so I convinced myself I was not betting as much. More every day I really was losing my passion for gambling and betting. However, I wanted to find that pretty music and preacher on the TV and I wanted to work on my game plan. But somehow I couldn't remember the time the preacher and the music came on...or the station. I didn't remember the name of the program, either. The TV guide in the newspaper just had a whole listing of "paid programming," so I couldn't find it for a week or two. I was up looking either too early or too late.

When I finally found it, I started watching "First Word" every week. I *loved* it!

I was connecting. Only one problem: I just wanted everything that he was saying to really be true. This man, this TV preacher was REAL!

Now for me, being a Hatfield, I would say, "That Dr. Fred Lowery...he is "The Real McCoy" too, like Zig Ziglar.

I had finally decided that I would go to his church. WOW. Me, going to church after 20 years! I wanted to check it out. I loved the music and the preaching, it all sounded pretty good to me. He was funny and he had some good stories, too. He would read from the Bible, he would tell the story, then explain how it fit today; then tell another story and a funny joke or two along the way. This guy, Dr. Fred, was an awesome communicator! I wanted to see him in person; I needed to see if it all was for real. I wanted to look in his eyes and see what was there. I thought if I could see him and look in his eyes and read his body language and his passion, I could tell if it was all real or not.

I worked up the courage to go to that *big* church with the big white columns outside, and the pretty, tall, white steeple you could see from a mile or two away. It was the church with those BIG doors. So, with all my courage, I called my friend (chicken me!) Everett Phillips and said, "Lets go to this church next Sunday." Yep, I was a "chicken!" But I strutted like a rooster. Chicken me had to have a security blanket, so I called a friend for support.

The next Sunday Everett came by and picked me up. We went to the church and the parking lot was full, so Everett and I decided to go down the street to another church. We walked in the door, went into the sanctuary where they were singing with no musical instruments, and they started taking communion. This was my first church visit in 20 years. It was different from what I expected. We sat there all of five minutes and then...we *bolted*! Outta there! *Let's go as fast as we can. Hurry up before that silver plate comes to me.* So, needless to say, these two courageous men really were big chickens! I bet we left a feather trail with all the feathers flying off our backs, we were flying outta there so fast!

Chicken!

We were afraid of some crackers and a little bit of grape juice!

Now, I love communion today, but walking into church for the first time in 20 years I was wearing my feelings on my sleeve pretty well. I guess I really was looking for a reason to leave and that was as good as any. After all, first time in a church building where a service was going on, plus the churches I was used to typically had attendance of anywhere from 30 to 100 people, maximum. There were 500 to 4,000 people in these two churches, and everyone was in the sanctuary all at once!

NEXT Sunday

The next Sunday was coming and I was itching to go. I still had my courage and it was building; I really wanted to go. This time I planned to go alone. I arrived fashionably late; I didn't want anyone who might know me to see me going to the church! So, I dressed down a little, hoping not to see anyone I knew. I really doubted I would see anyone I knew, anyway—*Wrong.*

I parked close to the building and those big ol' doors. I watched and waited until I thought everyone had gone inside. All was still and it was so quiet you could hear the church mouse. Okay, now...I could sneak in! I got to those big ol' doors and pulled one open and a very nice lady was right there. *"Welcome! Come on in,"* she said in her sweet, sincere, southern-drawl singing voice.

I said, "Ohhh, noooo! That is all right! I'm late! I'll come back another time!"

Angel in the Foyer

Well, from approximately 30 to 40 feet away, inside the foyer area, an acquaintance of mine came running over just as I was turning to walk away. "Hey...Phillip...Phillip! Good to see you!" Even though he spoke quietly, the foyer had a little echo in it. He said, "I am so glad you're here!" He was so animated and excited. "Come on in, it is so good to see you here!"

I said, *"Oh, I'll come back. I'm too late."*

He said, **"Oh, no, no! I have just the place for you! I know what you want! You are looking for a seat in the back of the church, dimly lit, where you can see and not be seen by everyone!"**

Wow! How did he know that? I thought, *that is exactly what I want but how could he possibly know that?*

"Ohhh, come on in, right through these doors," he said as he reached out and shook my hand. I think he was really pulling me along inside the door, too (very smart man!). As I followed him we went into the sanctuary from the foyer and he said, ***"The back row seat is right here, close to the door so you can leave any time you like!"***

I settled in the seat and all of the people were standing and singing, but I had my spot now and he went back to the foyer. All was good! Perfect seat! I was happy as a lark. It all worked out so easily. I sat there through the whole service and Wow! (And I can say that backwards, too. Wow!!!) It was even better live than it was on TV!

The music and singers were MAGNIFICENT!

The choir was more beautiful and powerful than I had seen on TV. Wow! The preacher, Dr. Fred Lowery, was fantastic. *I loved It!* He was so far away from me, but it seemed like he was standing right there in front of me talking to me in person, face-to-face, eyeball-to-eyeball. It was like his words were meant just for me! I could see it in his face and in his eyes. I was reading all of his body language, facial expressions, and his eye contact. I could see it was all in him, that he was for real. He had a great presence about him, he walked with a confidence and yet a humility. Not like the other TV preacher guys I had seen in the past, where every hair was perfectly in place, the suit was high-dollar and they had a strut to their walk, like they were the "cock of the walk," as the old-timers would say about the strutting rooster being the only rooster in the yard with all the hens.

Dr. Fred was different and I was nowhere close to him at all. But I could see it in his eyes. I could feel it in his voice and in his words. He was dynamic.

The altar call came and I bolted! I was outa there as fast as greased lightning! Ohhhhhh, but I loved it so much!

I loved being in church. It was better than I had imagined!

All week long I thought of what I had just experienced. As I drove through the week I listened to Dr. Tony Evans every day and every night on the radio in my 4-Runner. I was looking forward in anticipation to the next week; I wanted to go back to Dr. Fred's church! I was so excited. I *wanted* to go to church! *ME!* I wanted to go to church and I could not wait 'till the next time I could go back. But nobody had any idea how excited I really was. I just pretended all week to be the same ol' me, but something was different.

Finally, Sunday came. When the time came, I got a little nervous but did exactly the same thing I had done the prior week. After all, if it ain't broke, then don't fix it, as we say down here in Texas. (I may have been in Louisiana at the time, but I was still a Texan and knew that someday I would be going back to God's Promised Land of Texas.) So I did the same thing—I parked close to the front door and watched all of the people as they were going in. When all the movement stopped outside and people quit going in, when everything was quiet and still outside, it was time!

I opened the door to my 4-Runner and jumped out. I walked as fast as I could, but I was trying to walk as calmly and normally as I possibly could, too, so no one could see how excited I was. Up the steps I went, hurrying to the big white doors. I grabbed hold of the handle and began to pull the big church door open, All of a sudden once again it swung wide open just like someone was pushing it open for me. This time it was the "acquaintance," the same man who had helped me the week before.

He said, *"Phillip, it is so good to see you again!"*

He said *"I was waiting for you; I have just the place for you! I know just what you want."*

I know I looked at him like he was crazy but I looked him right square in the eyes still as if to question him, and then he said, *"You want to be in the same area as last week, but you want to be able to see the stage a little better."*

I said, *"Yes, but how did you know that?"* He did not answer my question! But how did he know what I wanted?

He said, "Follow me," at the same time he was shaking my hand and gave me a tug and pulled me on inside the door a little bit just like he had the week before. As I came in the door from that little tug he had going on, he dropped my hand and turned and walked on ahead of me, giving me no time for any rebuttal. I just fell in right behind him and I followed him all the way through the big double doors separating the foyer from the sanctuary. I was as comfortable in my surroundings as I could be. As he opened the door it felt like an arctic blast, not of cold air but of the music and the atmosphere that was in the air. We went on into the sanctuary and he took me a couple of seats up from the back row, just a little closer and off to the left, slightly under the stairwell that led up to the balcony with a support column for me to hide behind.

"Perfect," I thought to myself. The music was playing and people were beginning to sing and no one even noticed me come in. Cool!

It was almost over. The singing was so awesome, it was powerful. You could feel the stories as they sang them in the songs. They would sing their praise and worship songs and you could see it all over every choir member's face, as they would look up toward Heaven as they were singing. Some of them would cry a tear or two, even the men. Some would raise a hand every now and again. It was like they were watching the congregation and were looking at us eyeball-to-eyeball. You could feel way back where I was that they really were worshiping a living God. *"This has to be real!"* I thought to myself. **It just has to be true.** Oh, the music, the preaching, and all of the nice people! Wow. I was just in awe. The altar call came and this time, I snuck out not in quite as big a rush as the week before. I just slid quietly right out the door, but I did not want it to be over yet. There had to be more of this feeling. It was over and I did not want to leave. It was amazing!

The work week was a good week for me. I thought about what Dr. Fred had said on Sunday. Then I would listen to Dr. Tony Evans every night. My heart began to soften and I felt it finally begin to change. *Is this what Zig Ziglar was explaining to me back in the early '90s? Is this what he was telling me? Is this it? I am feeling things in my heart that I have never felt before!* But I knew I had a special feeling in my heart.

Each week I would go back and I would slowly move closer and closer to the front of the church. I noticed that the closer I could get, the better the music sounded and there were no distractions. I could not see all the distractions of all the people walking in and out of the sanctuary while services were going on. I could really listen and watch and pay attention. I was enjoying church! The closer I got to the front, the better it was. I absolutely loved going to church, it was so much fun.

Now I am sitting up 20 plus rows from where I started. I am six rows from the preacher now.

Me! I was enjoying church!

As I kept going back to the church I would arrive on time or even early. I began to look for my "acquaintance" who was in the lobby. I knew that I knew him from somewhere, but where? He knew my name from the first time I opened the door to the church, but I could not remember his name. I searched for him but I could not find him. I knew he worked every week on Sunday morning in the lobby; however, I never saw him again. I do not know where he went.

Where did he go?

Who is he?

What is his name?

How do I know him?

Was he an angel?

Ahh, it has to be! There is no other explanation. How could he know all that he knew of what I wanted?

Yes, I believe he was an angel.

Another one of those angels we entertain unaware. He had that nice, sweet, yet not a pushover personality. He had a wonderful welcoming and comforting smile and a sparkle in his eye; he was dressed so nicely and neatly and spoke with confidence and assurance. He was very strong with a very firm handshake, but not overpowering. When he answered me and said he knew what I wanted, there was no doubt or question in his voice. It was fact, like he was reading my mind.

I kept going back to First Bossier and I was waiting for the other shoe to drop. Yep, another one of those Texas sayings.   I was waiting to hear all of "The Rules" come out. I was waiting for all of the do's and don'ts. But you know what? I never heard them. Dr. Fred taught about the Ten Commandments and the two commands that Jesus gave to the Scribes and the Pharisees when they tried to trap him. When they asked Jesus what was the greatest commandment of all, He answered, "To love the Lord your God with all your heart, mind and soul, and to love your neighbor as yourself." Now I think I could live with those rules.

Wow that sounds kind of like Zig Ziglar a little, *"You can have everything in life you want, if you will just help enough other people get what they want."*

I learned it was not the rules; it was the love, the grace, the mercy…and when you do mess up with someone, because we all do, then fix it fast. Talk to God, then talk to the other person, ask forgiveness and try not to repeat the same mistake. I learned it was living in grace and letting God help you to help yourself.

Throughout that year I would go to church at First Church Bossier, read and re-read Zig Ziglar books and listen to his tapes. I could hear the same message in Zig's tapes and read it in his books, but there were no Scriptures! **Zig**

was teaching the Bible without using the Bible! Then he was applying it to his everyday business and personal relationships and teaching us to do the same.

I would continue listening to Tony Evans during the week. Then I went to a couple of Sunday school classes at First Bossier and—get this—I even put a few bucks in the offering plate as it passed by! Now, for me, that was an accomplishment! God was working on my heart. It was softened and ready to listen, finally!

I watched everyone and I watched everything. I surveyed, I calculated, I watched how the people at this church treated each other, how they helped each other. *These guys are like bikers. These church people are real! Not perfect people, but genuine and authentic people.* I watched Eddie Faith—yes, that is his real name. He was genuine. I watched Ray Raney, a volunteer part-time singles pastor, how he served the people as well as ran a business. He helped everyone. Ray always had a big smile and a big heart for a small 5'4," 130 pound man.

I went to a men's group on a weeknight and built some great relationships with men who mentored me—Robert Finley, Willie Buffington and Ron Lewis. These guys were all professionals and became like my brothers and I love them dearly to this day. Then there were other men in the church like Pat Worley and Lee Phipps, who were great servant leaders who provided leadership to me as well. I loved the early morning meetings at Shoney's before going to work with Lee. There were many more men, like Carlos Meza, who mentored me and spent hours at his kitchen table teaching me the Scriptures. I still remember being at Carlos' home and his mother-in-law saying, *"Carlos, how can so many tears come from one man?"*

Thank you so much, men of First Bossier!

DJ-Angel, on the Airwaves?

After some time had passed I was having a super difficult week at work. It was payday, a Friday, and I had to drive two hours south to Alexandria to inspect a job and be sure the customer was happy, and then pay all of the guys. After that I had to drive back to Shreveport/Bossier and bid on another job later in the day. Things were not going well at all for me that day. Problems on job sites, employees calling in sick, I had overbooked my day with my promised responsibilities and with all these new problems popping up.

As I was driving down I-49, I was listening to some easy listening music to calm myself down. Then I turned to that Christian music station on the radio as I drove. I was also talking on my cell phone from the cab of my 4-Runner, handling one situation after another. So I decided I needed to take a break from the phone and turned the radio up. I just needed to relax, chill out, and think. As I was driving and trying to calm myself down and think, I heard a couple of nice songs that made me feel a whole lot better and helped me relax some. As I listened to the radio I heard a little dead air. There was no one talking and no music for a few seconds. Then the DJ came on and said, *"I have a very special song I just feel like playing right now. Would you please listen to this song?"* I listened to the song; it was called *"One Drop of Blood."*

The song goes like this:

> Standing in the courtroom
> When I heard, how do you plead?
> The accuser of the brethren
> Was staring at me
> He said, we got your number
> There is no escape
> For here are your transgressions,
> Your failures and mistakes
>
> He pointed to the corner
> Where the scales of justice stood
> I saw so many failures there
> There was nothing good
> And in that very moment
> When it seemed all hope was lost
> I said, I plead the blood of Jesus
> And his death upon the cross

CHORUS:

One drop of blood

Fell to the scales

It covered my transgressions

And all the times I failed

The enemy was mighty

He came in like a flood

He was defeated by one drop of blood

I stood and watched in silence

As others were brought in

I saw them start to tremble

When they turned and faced their sin

They offered no excuses

They offered no alibis

The truth was overwhelming

And it would not be denied

Their righteousness like filthy rags

And nothing they could say

They bowed their heads in silence

As they were led away

But for the true believers

Each time it was the same

His glory shown around them

As they called upon his name

No greater sacrifice has any other made

Oh yes he paid the price

With every drop he gave

Oh, wow, what a story! It sounded so real and so much like a true courtroom scene, about Satan is a liar accusing me of all my failures and Jesus defends me before the judge who is God. The scales of justice turned with one drop of blood from Jesus that fell to the scales. All my sins were so heavy on my side of the scales of justice, but one drop of blood on the other side immediately tipped the scale. My debt was paid with that one drop of blood. Satan was defeated by one drop of blood!

Wow. This song really made sense to me about Jesus' crucifixion.

I began to really listen to the story in the song. I was engulfed in the story and the music. The song ended and I was in awe, I was amazed yet I was very humbled.

The song had gripped my heart and would not let go. My heart was really softened and began to melt away. I felt a serene feeling.

I desperately wanted to hear that song again, just one more time.

I wanted to hear that song so badly because it spoke to my heart like no song ever had before! It was so real, it sounded like it was me standing there in that courtroom. I could see Satan standing there accusing me of all my failures, my arrogant pride, foul mouth, selfishness, deceitfulness, lust, gambling and many more chains of sin and bondage that had engulfed my once happy life. Yes, once I was so happy until all of those "fun" things I was doing and the destructive consequences of my actions all came falling down on top of me. They were crushing the very life and soul out of me. The "fun" of the sin had become an albatross tied around my neck! It was no longer fun.

As I was driving I really wished that he would play that song, just one more time, please, for me. There were a few seconds of silence when the song had ended, it was just seconds of that dead air-space again, a few seconds passed when the DJ came back on the air and said, *"I am not supposed to do this, but I just want to play this song one more time. Listen closely to these words."*

Wow, is that not a God thing or what?

God had sent a DJ to my rescue!

The song came back on and I listened intently. As I was listening I could see even more vividly than before a scenario playing out in me. I began to feel all types of emotion and my eyes began to well up with tears. I was moved in my heart more than ever. My soul felt restless, and I was so stirred to the very core of my heart and soul. I cannot begin to explain all that I was feeling.

Tears began to well up in my eyes for the first time in many years and I began to cry. The tears flowed down my cheeks, and then it was just like the floodgates of a huge dam were slung wide open. Tears were now flowing like a swiftly moving stream down my cheeks and on down into my lap. I felt things that I had never felt before in my life!

Now, I am not a crybaby. It had been so many years since I'd had tears in my eyes or since I had cried! As I listened to the song playing on the radio again, I felt chill bumps all over my arms, and a slight quivering in my body. I felt a peace, and yet I felt a fear and a reverence for that *"One drop of blood that flowed down for me and fell to the scales just for me."* As the song was playing I had a different picture running through my mind. I had already seen that one drop that fell to the scales. But this time I saw that one drop of blood completely differently.

This time I could see the pool of blood at the foot of the cross in my mind's eye. I could see the dripping of the blood as it fell from each of the arms of that cross, and there was Jesus hanging on it.

I did not see a pretty Jesus on that cross but a beaten, battered, torn and ragged man hanging on that cross looking down at me. But I knew it was Him. I could see each drop of blood as it slowly dripped out of His hand and rolled down from His hand onto the wooden beam of the cross. Then it would drop from the wooden beam onto the ground and splatter into that small pool under His hand. I saw two pools one on each side of the cross where His hands were nailed. Then I could see in the center at the foot of the cross the pool of blood right there in front of my eyes. This pool was in the center where He wore that crown on His head, and His feet where they were nailed to that huge, old, brown wooden cross.

Then I saw myself standing there at the foot of the cross as a drop, one single drop of blood, fell down and splattered into the pool of blood that was there on the ground in front of me. It was pooled at my feet. Some of it splattered and hit me as I was standing there.

It all played out like a movie in my head. It was so vivid, like I was right there 2000 years ago, all alone, watching Him. There was no one there but just Him and me, we were all alone as I stood there looking up at Him and He was looking down at me. It was almost like I could see a glimmer of a smile on His face.

What is going on inside of me?

As I sat there still driving in my truck, I felt warmth come over me. It was almost like I was being held, being hugged in a way that I had needed for many years. I was getting a Holy Hug. But I sat there, driving all alone in my truck; there was no one around but me. The Holy Spirit had just wrapped me up in a huge ol' holy hug! I felt like someone was right there beside me, holding me tight like they would never let go.

I was still driving down I-49 south of Shreveport, but now I couldn't see the road with all the tears in my eyes. The tears were flowing; I could not wipe them out of my eyes fast enough. I literally could not see the road ahead of me very well. About that time I saw a sign on the side of the road that said Powhatten Exit, so I pulled over to the side of the Interstate and finished listening to the song. I was filled with so much emotion, and there was just a holy quietness in the cab of my truck. The song had ended and there was a complete, utter silence for about five to ten seconds, but to me it felt like ten minutes of complete silence!

I didn't understand what was happening to me at that moment.

The Prayer

I cannot tell you what the DJ said after that. I turned the radio off and after sitting there all alone on the side of the road for awhile I said, "OK., God! I do not know if you are real or not! But I am going to pray this prayer now. If you are God you are going to..."

Ok, God, I am going to pray this prayer now!

There was silence in the truck for a few moments. I sat there, gripping the steering wheel with tears still streaming down my face. I was looking down at the floor then up to the windshield, and I tried to pray. I did not know what to say; I was waiting for the words to come to me. After a minute or two I said it again,

"OK, God, I am going to pray now."

I was still sitting there in awe and in silence, crying and shaking, wanting to say the right words and searching my entire mind for them to come to me. Then I said it again, one last time, "Ok, God...I am going to pray now!" I gripped the steering wheel so tightly I could see the white knuckles from such a firm grip. I was crying, waiting, and still not knowing what to say. After a few seconds I prayed this awful, terrible sounding irreverent prayer:

"OK! If you are God, this is what you are going to do!"

So I told God my long list of what He was going to do!

Then I told God what I was going to do in return! (Here I am, telling God what He is going to do!) I have to tell you now; this was the most irreverent prayer that you or anyone would have ever heard prayed. Yet God knew my heart. I was genuinely convicted and at a loss for what to say. I did not know how to pray at this point, so I was barking out my marching orders to God.

After I finished telling God all of His marching orders, I remembered Dr. Fred saying from the pulpit many times, *"If you want to accept Christ, pray this prayer anywhere you are at any time."* So I ended my irreverent prayer with these words from Dr. Fred.

"I believe Jesus was born of a virgin and lived a sinless life. I (sniffle, sniffle), I believe Jesus died and rose again. Forgive me of my sins! Amen."

In an instant! At that very moment! I felt all of the weight I had been carrying, the weight of the whole world, lifted from my shoulders. Now I really began to cry! But it was a different cry. Tears of relief, of a fight that I finally had given up!

I felt relief from all my chains of bondage. I felt my heart change in an instant; in a split second everything was different! There were tears rolling down my cheeks, tears on my shirt, tears dripping off my steering wheel, and tears dripping on my pants as I sat there for quite a long while.

I knew right then that **"Jesus was real!"**

I was overcome with peace. I felt every muscle in my face lift. I felt an encouraging empowerment to help me overcome my failures in life. I knew I was forgiven. I finally had a heart change. The change I had been looking for now for over five years, since my first meeting with the first messenger "Zig," in 1993, and now I knew I could be a better man and businessman, a better father, son, and brother, as well as a better friend.

I had just experienced a new birth. I was changed. I literally felt the old me leave, and a whole new man had come in!

My heart was finally changed!

It was literally indescribable!

I am a Life that was "Changed"

In that moment, I became a Christian, a believer, a follower of Christ.

The Date:

Friday, September 11, 1998, at approximately 10:00 to 10:30 a.m., sitting on the side of the road on I-49 at the Powhatten Exit sign, in my red Toyota 4-Runner!

God kept knocking on the door of my heart from the first meeting with Zig Ziglar. God kept knocking on the door of my heart through the reading of those two Scriptures from that Gideon's Bible while I was in the hospital, and through listening to *"First Word"* on TV with Dr. Fred Lowery, then through the radio with Dr. Tony Evans.

And yes, God used that country black preacher man—and his congregation. God used the music of the church called First Bossier.

But let me ask you a question: this funny black preacher man on the radio, was he an angel? Was he sent to deliver a message and to lead me towards Christ?

The Bible says in Isaiah 55:11

"God's Word will not return void."

Amen!

Those verses from that Gideon's Bible planted a seed that three years later finally sprouted from fertile soil. It once was hard, red clay where nothing good would grow.

Isaiah 55:11 *(ESV)*

"So shall my word be that goes out from my mouth; it shall not return to me empty, but it shall accomplish that which I purpose, and shall succeed in the thing for which I sent it."

My personal testimony is verification of that! As for me in my life, I have been greatly blessed by the successes and failures in my own personal salvation journey. No, I am not a perfect man today, either, I have made many mistakes along the way. I am still a sinner, just forgiven. I am a man trying to live a Christian life and fighting the spiritual warfare of Satan, who is always there to damage my witness of declaring the Gospel of Christ! So no, I am not perfect at all, I am just like you. I am just *forgiven*!

Then there was the black nurse, and the young female intern doctor at the hospital and there was the *"acquaintance"* (my foyer angel) who was in the lobby of the church. I have never seen him again; I do not even know his name.

Who was he?

How did I know him? I do not remember.

Was he an angel? *Who was he?*

Yes, absolutely, yes, he was "My Foyer Angel."

He had that countenance about him and in his voice, and the sweetness yet directness that we discussed earlier. He was a nice man yet he had a matter-of-factness about him. He knew his direction and he knew the mission he was on. He was zeroed in; then when he achieved his mission, he was gone! So yes, I believe he was an angel sent just for me. But I could be wrong. It doesn't matter whether he was an angel or a man used by God or the Holy Spirit. I am so thankful God opened up His toolbox and found an instrument to use.

Then there was the radio DJ who I cannot identify. He broke all of the station's rules to play the same song two times in a row. Wow! Another "God Encounter" that caused me to come to the cross and finally accept Christ as my Lord and Savior!

There it is again, see it? Verse 14 in Hebrews, chapter one, answers so many questions for me about the angels. It says,

> *"Are they all not ministering spirits sent forth to minister to those who will inherit salvation?"*

Yes, there are angels and there are people who are used by God and the Holy Spirit, too.

The DJ, the *"acquaintance"* friend I never saw again, the black country preacher on the radio, the intern doctor and the black nurse lady were all tools

God used. Some were angels, in my opinion, and some were following the Holy Spirit. No matter what you think, they were all available to be used by God. There were angels and there were just regular ordinary people like you, who God used to do extraordinary things.

Think about Elisha again, just for a minute, and the servant who was afraid! Then Elisha prayed that God would open his eyes that he could see the protection all around him. Let's look at it again in chapter 6 of II Kings *(ESV)*.

> *"When the servant of the man of God rose early in the morning and went out, behold, an army with horses and chariots were all around the city. And the servant said, 'Alas, my master! What shall we do?' He said, 'Do not be afraid, for those who are with us are more than those who are with them.' Then Elisha prayed and said, 'O LORD, please open his eyes that he may see.' So the LORD opened the eyes of the young man, and he saw, and behold, the mountain was full of horses and chariots of fire all around Elisha."*

Yes, these are God's mighty angels of protection in action. Can you see those angels all around you when you are in time of need? Pray that God opens your eyes, not that you necessarily can see angels, but that you can see God at work through whatever tool He has chosen to use for you at the time. See, Elisha did not ask God to show up. God had already supplied the need. Elisha knew God was on the scene. All Elisha did was pray that God would open the eyes of the servant that he could see. That is why God gives us leaders to follow. They already have the vision. They see with a clarity that sometimes we do not have. Pray that God opens your eyes.

Do you think you can see angels in your life, or can you see where a divine intervention has come your way sometime in the past?

It could possibly be someone being used by the Holy Spirit or an angel encounter. Either way, God is at work. You see, God opens "His Holy Tool Box" and the instrument is already there, ready to be used. It is not all rusty and crusty from not being ready for the job at hand. This time God used angels for me. Other times he used people. How about *you*, are you ready and able and available to be used? Remember, "If we will do the possible, God will do the impossible."

Who do you think all of these people in my life are? What are your thoughts?

I would love to know. And Gideon, you played a part the same as all the others in changing a life. What if you had never had that Bible placed in my hospital room? Where would I be today?

YES, I am a life that was changed!

But hold onto your seat. We are about to get caught up to the accident in the first chapter, and you will be blessed in what you are about to see!

Oh yes, we are Carried by Angels.

Phillip on Loudmouth Betty two hours before accident.

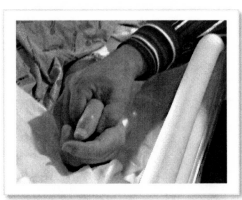

Zig & I, a couple of days before he went to his Celebration in Heaven.

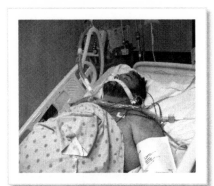

Phillip in hospital.

Phillip with first posthetic leg.

Look Mom! No hands!

Taking first steps.

Harris (Phillip's brother) and Phillip on Harris' release from prison.

At The Harbor our first date, and my FAVORITE picture of Erika and me.

Phillip and Erika.

Phillip and Zig Ziglar. Zig was literally holding me up.

Phillip, Zig Ziglar and my daughter, Emma.

Dad, Dan, and Moher, Rosa. Dad is like Jesus to me because he chose to love me when our biological father left us.

My sister, Sharon Rose and my niece, Heather Rose.

My granddaughter, Lilly, daugher-in-law, Stine, grandsons Cameron and Matthew, and son Jeremy.

Rock 'n Roll, Baby!

10 years later!

I have been up and awake since about five o'clock this morning. I always get up early when I am going to teach a Sunday school class...

I got up very early that Sunday morning. It was about 6:30 a.m., the sun was coming up and it was a beautiful day! "Rise 'n shine," as my mother would say.

It was nice and cool outside. Aahh, that nice crisp fall air felt so good! The dew was still on the ground and you could still see the mist and tiny water droplets on the petals of the flowers. You could hear the little birds chirping as they flew about; feel the breeze as it rustled through the leaves. It was a nice, relaxing morning! Aahh.... Just to sit and listen to the sound of the waterfall as it flowed over the top of the spillway and splashed down on each rock, all the way down to the rocks at the bottom, then into the pool below.

And oh, yes...the aroma of my hot, steaming cup of hazelnut coffee with a hint of cinnamon, cream and sugar. Can ya' smell it? Nice! I love to come out here in the morning and sit here on the back patio, sipping my hot cup of coffee before I start the day. Yes, it is ten years later, November 9, 2008.

My sister Sharon is in her room, sleeping. I am tip-toeing quietly around the house, being as quiet as I possibly can, trying my best not to wake her up. Well...I did say I was trying not to wake her up, right? Here I go into the

kitchen and, as always—yes, I did; I know it was wrong. I really was just clean-
ing up after myself when Crash! Bang! Splash! Squeak! Rumble! Cling-clang!
Got 'er all done—the kitchen is all cleaned up! Now off to the bathroom I go to
get ready. Got things to do, places to go. I turn the shower on, brush my teeth,
and….well, it seems I'm not quite as quiet as I think I am!

Ugh. Oh-oh! There she is, as I open the bedroom door, ready to head out for
the day. Oh, no! I did it! She is sitting there with her cup of coffee.

I get *"the look"*—you know the one, like "Why did you wake me up? I want
to sleep!"

Oh, my! Boy, am I in big trouble now! It's that quiet, silent look! Okay, so
you didn't know there was such a thing as a "quiet, silent look," didya? Well,
yep, there is here in Texas!

I have been up and awake since about five o'clock this morning. I always get
up early when I am going to teach a Sunday school class, and, well, you probably know how it is when you've been up for awhile. It's like, why isn't everyone
else up? What's wrong with the world? Get up! Let's get going! Rise 'n shine! If
I'm up and at'em, then everyone else should be up and at'em, too! (Okay, at'em
is another one of those Texas words, for your information.) And nope, everyone
else is not up just because I am!

I always look over the week's preparation for the Bible study class I am teaching. I will re-read and re-write the lesson. If you are a Bible study teacher in any
capacity at all, then you know all too well what I am talking about. We always
want to be sure we are prepared and usually we will change something at the last
minute.

I now live in Dallas and I am a member of Prestonwood Baptist Church in
Plano, Texas, for the past five years. It is only 15 minutes away from my home,
so I get dressed and ready to go. I start the car and backing out of the driveway
it hits me, ohhh! We are going riding this afternoon and I don't have time to
come back to get my bike, so I had better go back inside and change my clothes.

Ok, all changed now, I'm done and ready to go, so let's ride the Harley to
church today. Rock-n-roll, baby! It's a Harley-riding Sunday.

Today's destination after church is a place called "Strokers." This is a biker
hangout and that's a pretty cool name for a biker place if you ask me, "Strokers."

It's down on Harry Hines Boulevard here in Dallas. Now, a little disclaimer here, we all know that if you are going to a "biker hangout," anything at all can happen, right? So keep close by and keep an eye out and have fun with us on the ride! Yep, you are coming along for this ride too, so buckle up.

This is going to be fun. There will be anywhere from 500 to 1500 bikers there all throughout the day, and my friend Rob and his buddy Kenny from Dallas Christian Singles will be playing in the band from 2–5 p.m. They will be playing all types of music with some nicely placed sprinkles of Christian music in the mix (wink, wink). After all, so many of the secular songs do talk about Jesus or God. Really—have you ever listened closely to the lyrics of the songs you sing along with on the radio? There are some good lyrics and there are some not so good lyrics about God! So today, Rob and Kenny will be doing songs about Jesus in a whole new context for these hard-nosed bikers all day long.

Yes, we are going to have fun and join in. The bikers, the band, and DCS Singles, all of us there are going to be like Christ, mixing and mingling in the group and seeing just what God may have for us to do today! The neat thing is we can have fun, ride our motorcycles, and do ministry all at the same time!

Yep, we are all good committed Christian men and women and yes, we are going to go to a biker hangout. We are going to have some fun and talk about Jesus anytime the door opens for us. We are here just to plant a seed or maybe we are here to build relationships so that when the time does come and they are comfortable, they can ask us about Christ. Hey. We're just here to do what we do and let God do what He does!

As we know "if we do the possible, God will do the impossible!"

God has used us and many bikers like us many times to lead other people to Him. We get to be "Jesus with skin on...Biker Style." We get to do what we enjoy, ride motorcycles and witness to others! Now, that is the ultimate calling! Being a "Biker for Christ" is an awesome calling. It can be fun and exciting and definitely adventurous, too!

Bikers!

Let me tell you a little about bikers. Are you ready? Bikers really are "a different breed." In many ways they are just like regular people, too; they act like they have it all together. No problems, everything is under control, just cocky, cool and laid back bikers.

It is always so neat, when one of the biker guys comes up to you later in the day and asks, "Hey man, can I ask you a question?" (Duh.... hook-set!) Then they want you to walk off to the side, way away from everyone else so no one can see them talking to "the Christian biker guy." You know, the dude with all those Christian patches on his leather biker jacket. The only way they can tell a difference is by the jackets and by the actions of Christian bikers. We blend in just like Jesus did.

At this point, you are looking them right dead in the eye, and they are looking right back at you eyeball-to-eyeball (even if it is for just a second or two), they know! *They know* that you know! Yes, they know you have been exactly where they are right now!

So many bikers are just like me and possibly like you, too. They grew up in church, having a relationship with Christ, and got away from their walk, or as some put it they are "The Backsliders" (ouch) who became discouraged for some reason. Maybe they weren't plugged in. Who knows? But they got away from their walk with God or backslid. No matter the verbiage you choose. Some of them knew of Christ before and some knew Christ before! Yep, better go back and reread that sentence again. Each story is so different. But God uses us Christian bikers to let them see they can have fun, be happy and live for Christ. We can still have a blast and be a Christian, too.

We are just demonstrating that they can have that same relationship with God that we have. They do not have to give up the biker lifestyle. No matter whether you are a business executive who is a weekend warrior biker, or just a deadhead, hard-nosed, hard-core biker, God wants to save you right where you are, then usually do work right there where you are, too. God will save and use a "Hell's Angel" the same as he will use any of us! What if God leaves him right there in that biker gang?

Leading Bikers to Christ

The greatest experience for us is to have a biker start the day off rough and tough, four-letter words rolling off their tongue, talking to you and having fun at your expense all day long, picking on you and pushing your buttons all throughout the day. Then, by the end of the day that rough tough biker is crying like a baby just like you did when you were saved. You know exactly what

I am talking about. When God gets hold of them, their heart is convicted and they are tired of all the drama in their life. Finally, after many years of *"doing it my way,"* just like I did, they are ready to surrender to God and bow on their knees before the cross.

They give up! They give up having all the answers and they accept the gift of grace and they accept Jesus! Oh, to be there and experience this you just have to see it for yourself! WOW, what a feeling. It is so awesome to see God work, especially when we least expect it. This experience will give you chill bumps, to be there to see the difference in a biker's eyes when he bows his head and accepts Christ, then looks up and you see a whole new facial expression and see a new person in just a matter of a second or two. It is *amazing*.

Sometimes a biker will come to you in broad daylight, right out there in front of everyone. Because that is how they are, just out in the open, bold, loud and boisterous. They have to let everyone know exactly what they are thinking, and what they are doing, as well as what they are saying, too. They are bold, crass and genuine in who they are. They have a reputation and a fol-lowing. There may be only one person or several people in their group or gang. Maybe they are trying to gain respect from the other bikers in their group, or gain respect from other bikers in the other groups around them. So they have a tell-it-like-it-is attitude. Ok, so just what kind of Christian will that make? A tell-it-like-it-is biker Christian.

Then there is the secretive kind of biker. There are times when we are way away from everyone else and they will come up and start a conversation. Some-times they come to you in the shadows of the dark, nighttime (Nicodemus). It is still the same when you can look them right in the eye, they know, too. No matter how they come or when they come or if they never come to us, the key is that we be as genuine in our stance of who we are as they are in their stance of who they are.

They all want the same thing—the assurance that you "respect" them and then they will respect you. I did not say you approve of them, but you respect them as a person. All that matters for us is that they accept Jesus Christ as their Lord and Savior! If not today, fine! But we have planted a seed or watered a seed that will allow them to continue exploring their belief and continue looking for the God they are searching for. You see, we all know that if they truly look and search and read any part of the Scriptures, they will see Who God is and who Jesus is. Our prayer is that at that moment, whenever or wherever it is, they accept Christ. So we want them to see that we live a life that is true to our belief, too. This is the kind of seed I like to plant, not the one where *"send me your money and plant a seed"* like that TV preacher with the jet black dyed hair and beard I saw that Sunday morning! This is planting seeds! We are out in the richest soil of sin and redemption, just like Jesus was in His ministry.

After all, that is what we are all here for, isn't it? To be Christ living among them! We are just regular people who are not perfect. We enjoy the same things in life they do, except we believe in Jesus! They just need to know that we are genuine and totally committed followers of Christ! It is just like sales, you have to be sold on your product and a user of your product. You have to believe in it before you can sell it. No, we are not "selling" Jesus! He is free! We just present Him. That is all we can do.

Now, when you get to see a biker accept Christ, most of the time you will find a man on a mission! Unstoppable! You will see a modern-day passion like the Apostle Paul most of the time, but with a body like you would imagine of rough, tough, old-time fisherman like the Apostle Peter. You see, when "much is forgiven," there is tremendous gratitude toward God. Once the peace and love and joy come in with all the other fruits of the Spirit, you will find a person who wants to share what they have found with all those who are close to them. There is no shame because you believe! Also, they will have a passion to learn and to share with everyone! **They automatically fall into an existing network of biker believers! Us!**

They have their support group, life group, already in operation. How cool is that!

When you have lived way on the other side of the sin line, so hard and for so long, and have picked up so much baggage that you can no longer drag it along, then experience that Amazing Grace, just think about it for a second. For the rest of their life they will be doing the same thing that we do, sharing Christ and riding their motorcycle! The new biker Christian is now *"joining in to see where God is working and joining Him there,"* to once again quote Mr. Henry Blackaby. It is so true! *"God is always at work!"*

The question for us is, will we join Him where He is?

Strokers

Let me tell you a little more about what to expect when going to a biker hangout, especially one like we are going to today. "Strokers" really is a one-of-a kind neat place if you like motorcycles and other bikers, especially if you like to do the good ol' American people-watching thing! Have you ever done that? Just sat for awhile and watched all the people as they go by? It is so much fun to watch all the strutting bikers go by, everyone has a different kind of strutting thing going on. It is so funny to see all those banty roosters doing their own unique strut. Strokers and people-watching is a great free entertainment venue here in Dallas, If you want to try something new and different then give it a try. It is a blast, it's hilarious and super-funny. You will see literally anything and everything. As I said earlier, you never know what is going to happen at a biker hang out/bar.

Remember, at a biker hangout you have a lot of big egos. Oh, yes, bikers are definitely in an ego league of their own.

(Oh, no! I am so sorry, ladies! I forgot! I know you are not interested in motorcycles, but just hold on tight and let me tell the guys about Strokers and bikers, Oh, yes, I have to tell them about my bike too, okay? Hang with me here, ladies, for just a few more lines. We'll be right back; this really is not a book about bikers! I promise. However, there are a lot of female bikers out there. Some are bikers; and some are biker babes!)

Okay, guys, as you probably know, 90% of us out here are everyday bikers. We are your neighbors and co-workers. However, there are the groups and there are some real biker gangs, too, as you already know. By now everyone knows of *"The Hell's Angels"* biker gang. I want to be very careful here, because there are lines here that I do not want to cross! However, I want to give you a true and accurate picture.

There are just regular bikers like me; then there are rougher bikers; and the real rough, tough biker gangs, like *The Scorpions, The Warlocks, The Banditos, The Booze Fighters*, and many others. No, I did not forget about "The Hell's Angels." Hmm, now that you mention it, yes, Hell does have angels, too. Remember the first "Hell's Angel"? *Lucifer!* That is who hell was really made for! Not for you or me. However, we do get to have a choice which angels we want to surround ourselves with! So you have all the rough, tough bikers; then you also have us regular guys, we are the 90% who have been riding motorcycles for years. We are just regular ol' people like you who like to ride motorcycles.

There are the millionaire bikers, the doctors, lawyers, plumbers, electricians, businessmen, salesmen and yes, preachers, too. There are bikers who are nasty, filthy, rich and very successful, and there are the low-class poor bikers, too. But there is no distinction in the biker world! Bikers are from all professions, from the working-class and just the common, regular guys next door, too.

Now you can see why biker ministries are one of the biggest ministries of our time! There is a vast world and great number of bikers from all over the world bringing their own bike from continent to continent and riding all the scenic roads of the world.

The biker world can be very dangerous at times, especially when one of those Scorpions, or Hell's Angels wants to discredit you, demean you, or challenge you. Yes, Satan can try to intimidate you and he will get you if you are not prayed up and filled with the Holy Spirit and surrounded by other Christian bikers. Just as the Bible says, *"Where two or more are gathered in His name, He will be there also!"* So no worries! We always are there in His name. That is the mission. One thing is for sure: you had better know your firm foundation before you get too entrenched in conversation with the big bad boys, especially if you are making a stand for Christ. They are *big* and *bad* too, and they do not play by the same rules that we play by. That is why they are called "The Hell's Angels." *Lucifer* is still recruiting his own angels, from bikers to the business world and yes, even in your own neighborhood, too. Satan has powers too, but Jesus has overcome him. But do not ever underestimate the powers of Satan.

There are some great biker organizations, too, like the Christian Biker Associations, the CMA (Christian Motorcycle Association out of Hatfield, Arkansas) and Bikers for Christ. There are groups that even require classes, like the CMA, on witnessing to bikers, evangelism, and prayer teams, prison ministry, biker rally ministry, etc. It is about living life and doing what you like to do, riding motorcycles and reaching other bikers for Christ. Yes, it is fun but it also is a calling for some bikers, too. We just blend in with them and just "Be Christ on two wheels." We have learned that if you will just be available where you are, God will use you!

There are bikers for children's needs like the very well-respected

"BACA"(Bikers Against Child Abuse). BACA has all classes of bikers, from the Hell's Angels to the rest of us regular Joe's. This is one cause everyone from the entire biker world joins in.

Here is the gist of it,

"If you are a child abuser or if you know a child abuser, you may want to introduce them to Jesus, real *quick*, because the bad boys here show no mercy."

However, there are police officers who are bikers and attorneys who are bikers and many other professional bikers in BACA who get involved to help the victims of child abuse. They will get the child out of the situation, get them to safety, and prosecute the abuser. There also are the Bikers for Christ who are in BACA, too. We are there in the whole process; we help get children to safety, also. Then we share Christ with the abuser and try to share Christ with the families of the victims as well.

Then there are the "Patriot Guard" riders. It has been a privilege and an honor to ride with these guys. The Patriot Guard welcomes fallen soldiers home with a biker escort in the front and rear of the procession with American flags waving big on their bikes. They will meet at the airport and escort the casket with the fallen soldier to wherever they are going. They escort the funeral procession front and rear, even stay at the funeral home and show respect for the soldier and their family, then guard to be sure no one disrupts the service and family in the process (especially in Kansas when we rode and there were protesters against the fallen hero).

Thank you to our heroes who died to protect our freedom!

There are the Toys for Tots runs, Teddy Bear runs, March of Dimes "Bikers for Babies," and on and on it goes. Millions of biker men and women getting involved and raising millions of dollars to help mankind, too!

That was just a spotlight look at who bikers are. You will never find anywhere people who bind together for the love of anything, much less the passion for riding motorcycles and helping each other and strangers, like "bikers." Biker community sounds like the church, doesn't it? Bikers already have the concepts and programs; we just need to connect them to Jesus and disciple them. I just love it, bikers and Jesus. Ok, so now it is time to connect on a deeper, more intimate level. Let me tell you about my beautiful Betty.

Loudmouth "Betty"

Bikers really are one with their bike. Each person makes a statement by how they customize their motorcycle. Everyone is decking out their ride from the day they buy it, so there really are no two motorcycles exactly same. So let me tell you about my bike, yes—beautiful Betty. A beauty she is! That is what I call her, Betty. Let me tell you all about my special girl. Oooh la la, what a babe!

Betty is a black 2007 fuel-injected Heritage Classic with saddle bags, seven-inch chubby chrome ape hangers, and lots of chrome—and oh, yes...she is a Harley...and a Harley is not a Harley if it is not loud and proud, right? Right! I knew you would agree. Yes, that's my loudmouth Betty! Now, Betty can talk up a storm and she can brag a bit...because she can back it up!

Yep, she is very loud and very proud. She's all souped up with 103 rubber burning horsepower to the rear tire. She has a Stage 2 kit and Stage 2 Download, with some other tweaks to her as well. She has Vance & Hines chrome shotgun pipes and—yes, I did, I pulled her baffles out, so she can really SCREAM! Betty is one loud screaming machine! Black and chrome spit-shined and polished. Everything I could chrome and add onto her, I did! Betty is an awesome, one-of-a-kind, absolutely gorgeous and beautiful girl.

Oh, I forgot to tell you, sorry—Betty has a family all her own, too. Three weeks earlier, my friend Ray Hackman and I went back to Kansas City. I bought two more brand new Harleys for my collection, so I have four new Harleys in my garage. A fully customized Deluxe, a Heritage Classic and an Orange County Custom Chopper. Lastly, a pearl white Harley 1200 Custom Deluxe.

Getting Ready to Roll

Okay, back to the story about our ride. As our Bible study class ended this morning, we made our way to the church sanctuary. Not long after we sat down the music started, and everyone was ready to worship. The music was so awesome today! Every song today was a special song with a special meaning for me. The message was on Joseph and the choices he made. It just seemed to be a special day of worship. As we wrapped up a wonderful praise and worship time with a fantastic message, it was time to head to the parking lot, climb on Loudmouth Betty and fire her up!

As I was walking through the parking lot to where my bike was parked, I began to think and reflect. It was such a great morning; I just felt sweetness in the air. It was as if today I received an extra special blessing. The music today seemed to be just for me. The message seemed to be just for me. Even the prayer at offering time seemed to be just for me.

Today as I sit here and write this book, looking back at that afternoon, I see it like this:

A Conversation with God

(Hypothetically speaking, not a real conversation, only in my mind.)

God says,

Okay, Phillip, I see what a fantastic fun-filled and exciting day you have all planned out for yourself today.

Change of plans!

I have another plan! I am going to use you today, Phillip! Ok? I need your assistance.

Phillip, I have heard you many times sing your songs of prayer and praise. I have heard you so many times sing that song; "I Am Yours, and I Surrender All."

Phillip, I especially love to hear you when you are singing "How Great Thou Art."

When you sing that song, "How Great Thou Art," I feel your heart, I see your gratitude and how great you really think I am. You always tear up and I feel your worshipful and grateful heart. I see you completely opening up and worshiping Me, and I can see those crocodile tears of gratitude every time as they roll down your cheeks. I just love how you worship Me with all your heart and appreciate all that I have made for you. And Phillip, I love so much to hear you sing "Amazing Grace," too.

I love it! You sing it with such passion because you have now experienced that grace, and now you know!

Yes, you are truly so thankful. I love especially when you sing that praise and prayer song to me, "Take My Life and Use It."

Today, Phillip, I have to call your note due! Phillip, I accept all of your offers!

I have a very special mission for you, Phillip. Will you trust Me?

Will you join in with Me today? It is your choice!

Remember this; I am here with you always. You are etched and engraved in the palm of My hands and I will never let you go!

Ok?

So are you are ready?

Now, let's go ride!

Know what to expect?

As you read this you know what to expect, right? Are you ready to go on this ride with me? Are you ready to go on this special journey? Take a deep breath and say a prayer, this is going to be a rough ride.

Okay...come on; time to mount up with me. Let's get ready to ride. I am going to need all of my friends along for this one.

Hang onto your seat and say hellooooo to my Loudmouth Bettttyyyy!!!

Let's get ready to rumble! Fire it up—let's ride!

Rock 'n roll!

<(((><

The Ride of Your Life!

Today, a very special day!

Today it seemed I was so alert and attentive to everything that was all around me, my senses were all on heightened alert.

I was focused; yet I was relaxed, too. It was a perfect day; everything was good. But why was this morning's church service so special? I was so wrapped up in every worship song today and literally every word, even the offering song and the prayer. I remember tears coming to my eyes while I was singing and worshipping God. It was a great day of worship and praise. I remember singing these words that morning: "You are my Deliverer, my Very Present Help in time of need!" I do not remember much more of that song but that was enough for me.

Even Pastor Jack Graham's prayer for dealing with the circumstances of life, all of the struggles that life has sometimes, everything seemed to settle in with me. As I thought about that, I thought, *"But everything in my life is great! No problems at all. My life is almost perfect and I could not ask for anything to be any better. I am so blessed. I have a great job, good friends, and a super family. I have peace in my heart and my quiet time is great. I stay in the Scriptures. I have real, true joy, happiness and peace. Everything is GOOD."*

I listened to the 500-member angelic choir that morning at Prestonwood. It was powerful. They sound so amazing! Especially when the Praise Team kicks in and cranks it up! You can just close your eyes and feel you are in the presence of God.

Wow. Todd Bell, our minister of music! I just can't say enough about Todd, who hails from Cleveland, Tennessee. Todd's commitment is to always have the choir, and whoever sings, to sing every song as if God is standing right there! Thank you, Todd Bell. You have blessed us with your devotion and the passion you bring. God uses you, Todd, to bring us to authentic worship and I thank you so much. You have taught me even more to make every song we sing a prayer and a true praise from all that is within us. You have greatly added to my life, Todd Bell.

Christian music and songs

I remember a topic covered at the Men's Conference at Prestonwood Baptist Church just a few months before, when Alistair Begg was teaching us about Christian music. He discussed the theology of songs, and how some songs sound good with great lyrics, and they have a good beat and melody. They also have a good Christian message; however, they are not songs that really bring honor to God, or bring us into worship with Him!

Some of our Christian songs, as Alistair pointed out, actually are just songs. They really put more emphasis on the singer of the song. Lots of times the emphasis is on us, me, my, and I, instead of focusing on God and Jesus. Songs need to focus on the attributes of God and worshiping Him, and giving Him thanks, singing praise or prayers in song to God Almighty. What about entering His (God's) courts with praise and thanksgiving? What a thought for a real worship song.

Todd has really done a wonderful job (in my opinion), having great theologically-based songs of worship and praise, bringing honor and glory to God from us.

Yes, God inhabits the praises of His people, as Scripture tells us. As for me, when I sing I always sing as if it is my prayer to Him or an offering of my praise to God or to Jesus for His wondrous sacrificial gift. We sing to welcome the Holy Spirit and thank Him for His leading, guiding us and comforting us. We always should be careful to worship God and Jesus, and not get the Holy Spirit ahead of the Father and the Son. Yes, the three are one with three separate personalities, just as I am a father, a son and a brother. Each one is still me; however, I communicate and act differently in each role. I do not talk to my sons as I would my dad, nor do I talk to my dad like I do my brother.

So music to me is so vitally important. Look at all of the songs written in the Scriptures. It is so wonderful how a song can say exactly what I want to say when I do not even know what to say or how to say it! My heart sings out and the Holy Spirit is delivering the message of my heart to the Father (God) and to His Son (Jesus). Yes, music, praise and worship songs and the old hymns are all so important to me.

The Songs of the Day

I have to tell you this, so you get an understanding of where I was and who I am. The first song we sang on this day was "Blessed be Your Name!" It says,

"Every blessing You pour out I'll turn back to praise—Blessed be the Name of the Lord!"

I am not sure of the title or all of the words, but it says,

"Every blessing you pour out I'll turn back to praise. Blessed be the Name of the Lord! You give and take away—You give and take away; blessed be Your Holy Name."

Now I really like that song. Then we sang another song that morning

"Holy is the Lord God Almighty. The earth is filled with His glory! Together we sing, Holy is the Lord God Almighty!"

Then Leona Rupert sang a hymn I love, too: Praise the Lord

"Oh, Lord, You are my Shield, My Shelter, my Strong Tower, my very present help in time of need."

Wow, this song says everything to me and especially today! I will need that strong tower by the end of the day. I will need my very present help in time of need today, too.

Then the offering song by Michael Chenoweth—wow again,

"You are worthy, oh Lord, of all honor. You are worthy of all praise!"

Oh, wow. I get chills thinking of this song.

Yes, the songs today at church were awesome! And each one spoke to me in a very special way. I had no idea what the rest of my day had in store for me, but God knew I would be leaning on Him later like I never had before.

The Sermon this Morning

The awesome sermon today was on "the choices that made Joseph" by Pastor Jack Graham. Did you catch that? The choices that made Joseph, not the choices Joseph made. That is a concept I'd never considered, have you? Joseph's choices made him who he was. Joseph's choices also showed his character and integrity. His choices kept laying out a path that would show he really did trust God, and God did take care of him.

Today this sermon was delivered to the whole church, but it seemed it was sent just for me!

So, how about you? What choices have you made? As my friend Zig Ziglar says, it's time for *"a check-up from the neck up"* and that is what the Holy Spirit does. He convicts us of the sin or the wrong we have done. He helps us to reflect when we have messed up, so we can quickly correct our path and keep our fellowship with God and not continue sweeping stuff under the rug. Kind of sounds like Mom doing a room check when we were kids or just keeping us on the straight and narrow as the young boys that we were.

The Holy Spirit is Kind-a-like Mom

For some of us the Holy Spirit is like our mother. Have you ever thought of that? The Holy Spirit is like our mothers here on earth.

I remember so many times hearing my mom say, "Hey, boy! You'd better straighten up, right now! Do you hear me? I said, do you hear me, young man? Now, you go apologize, kiss and make up, say you are sorry and you'd better mean it, too!" Yes, I am sure you have heard the same things from your mother, too, haven't you? And what did we say? Okay, now it's your turn to answer this question this time. I have already answered it a million times or more. The answer is..."Yes, Ma'am!" Then we go make up and then we can go on our merry way and live like nothing ever happened at all.

Yes, the Holy Spirit is sometimes like our mom! Maybe that is why God gave us moms. Thank you, Mom! (But I call my mom mother, so thank you, Mother.)

The Ride to Strokers after Church

Talking about our choices, I had made some choices myself. I had decided to go on that motorcycle ride to Strokers as soon as the concert was announced. Then I received a call from Stephanie Novack, asking if I was going to go to the DCS concert at Strokers.

"Of course," I said.

"Great," she replied, *"can I ride with you? I was going to ride with JC Cantu, but he is spending time with his daughter, Cheyenne."*

"Okay," I replied, *"only if you can meet me at Prestonwood after church about 12:30 p.m. You can leave your car and I will bring you back to the church when we are finished."*

"Great," Stephanie said, *"it's a deal. I have not been on a motorcycle in years!"*

Stephanie met me at my bike. We decided to get to know each other a little better, so we ate lunch at McAlister's Deli across the street. (I had the huge loaded baked potato with cheddar cheese, bacon and who-knows-what-all-else ...mmmm, delicious!) After we talked a bit, we loaded up, ready to ride. I had a helmet in my saddlebags, which I pulled out for Stephanie to wear. But I did not wear a helmet today! I did not want to get my hair all mashed down and hot and sweaty. I did not like "helmet hair." I wanted to ride cool, with the wind in my hair and the sun on my face. You know, just being a cool, easy rider.

I got on my bike, swinging one leg over the seat, and fired 'er up. Loud-mouth Betty was just a rumbling. Ohhhh, the rumble of the engine and the vibration as I gunned it, revving the engine up...ohhh, the sound of a Harley, there is nothing like it! Steph got on behind me and off we went.

We took the long, scenic route and rode for awhile. Oh yes, the ride...the leaning into the curves, up the hills, down hills, over the cresting top of the ridge as we go over the hill, taking in the beautiful view. You know, what you see when you reach the summit of a hilltop, the pinnacle and then riding over as you are now gliding down the other side.

When riding a motorcycle you really have to look fast, it all goes by so quickly. One second it is a breathtaking view at the top, then the exhilarating feeling of swooping down a swift, steep hill, feeling the coolness of the air as it changes temperatures when going down into the bottom of the hill or into the valley between the two hills. Oh, yes, how nice as you ride and smell the aromas of the countryside..ahhhh, the sweet smells...taking that country road, passing by all the fields, smelling the honeysuckle vines and the flowers. But let's not forget all the BBQ grills going or fireplaces burning. Smell the nice fresh air and, oh yes, you get a whiff of the pig farms, too. Hey, it takes the entire ride to enjoy it all. Ok, there are some tiny little parts of the ride that may not be so much fun, like the road kill, or passing a dead skunk in the road. Skunks leave a somewhat distinctive trail or odor I should say. Seems most of the ladies are not impressed with that part of being a biker babe.

As Steph and I were taking in all the scenery on a beautiful day, the sun beaming brightly through those puffy clouds above, we rode back into town slowly on the side streets so we could still talk and ride. We got back into Dallas pretty quickly, then we took the highway so we could get there faster. Our time was running out, we needed to end our joy ride and get to Strokers where all our friends were there waiting.

As we rode we came to a nice, long, easy curve and I let the bike follow the road as we leaned way on over, laying into the curve. The floorboards of the bike were almost scraping the concrete pavement, we were leaning over so far, but it felt wonderful.

We took the wide and long connecting "S" curves on the Dallas North Tollway as we headed south from Frankford down to Arapaho, leaning hard into each curve, feeling the power of the bike as it hunkered down and bit into the concrete, gaining traction on each of the curves as we accelerated more and more each time. The bike would hook and grasp the road as it anchored in, each time biting down harder and harder as it gripped the road more and more on each turn. We would swing left, right, then left, right, then swing left into the curve again, swoosh, swoosh, swoosh is how it felt each time. Wow. What an awesome and exhilarating feeling as you take the curves on a bike! It is a feeling you can only get while riding a motorcycle.

The Strokers Biker Parade

We arrive at Strokers and, as usual, it's like a parade. Each bike comes in, one at a time. Sometimes they are all in a long procession line of other bikers, a line of 15-20, and sometimes up to 40 or 50 bikes file in one by one. You hear the loud roar and the deep rumbling of the pipes as you feel the vibration of the engines of each bike as they come slowly creeping in.

Yes, we all put on a little show so everyone knows, "Hey, I am here! I have arrived! Hey, everybody, look at me! Look at my bike! Listen to this "Hoss" of a machine! Ayyyy, guys...now take a look at me with the pretty blonde on the back of my ride! Look at my pretty seat cover, she looks good!" Yes, we are still good Christian men on a human ego trip! It is fun as long as we remember not to take ourselves too seriously.

I parked my loudmouth Betty (my bike) in a highly visible spot for all to see. Oh, yes, a very strategic placement. Stephanie got off the bike as I dropped the kickstand down and leaned it over at a nice, cool looking leaning angle, making sure I had a cool look going on and all eyes were on us. My bike was as nice as the coolest bike there. Well, at least that is the attitude all bikers have, me included. And, yes, you know it, we do have a little attitude and confidence thing going on, even a little bit of being a tad cocky. We've got the strut down, too!

We stroll around, looking at all the bikes, saying hello to all our biker friends, making sure they see my pretty lady rider. You know, even though we are Christian men, we still love the thought of being the envy of the other guys and having the prettiest, nicest lady with the best personality.

Yep, we still like our arm candy, too. A nice, smart, beautiful, classy Christian lady works for me.

The band was striking up now, starting to play some songs. Everyone from DCS was gathering around. DCS (Dallas Christian Singles) is a meet-up group started by Fred Pascarelli, an ecumenical group of over 2,700 good Christian single adults, all doing life and ministry together.

Bikers and Leathers

We met up with our entire group from DCS. We listened to the music, talked with everyone as bikers do, watched the people and looked at all the bikes as they paraded in and out of Strokers. The bikers roll in and bikers roll out, all day long. It's an all-day parade!

Inside at Strokers there is a really nice motorcycle store where they sell custom-built bikes, choppers and all kinds of jackets and t-shirts. And they sell the #1 thing we all love and need, leathers. Yes, bikers love leathers! Leather jackets, leather vests, leather gloves, chaps, etc. I wonder if some of them have leather underwear, too.

People who are not bikers often do not know that a good quality leather outfit protects you in case you have an accident. Leathers also block the wind, rain and all of the outdoor elements. See, God knew what He was doing when He made cows! After we eat the hamburger and the steak, then we get to wear the protective coating! Most of all, leather looks cool!

Have you ever noticed that 95% plus of all the famous actors on TV, and the cool singers and the bands, men and women alike, all wear "Biker Jackets"? What's with that? Most of them have never even ridden a motorcycle! Ya' see, everybody knows when you wear a biker's leather jacket you look cool! Or you ARE cool. I'd even bet you might have a leather biker jacket or two in your closet, too. Go ahead, take a look and see, I dare ya! Ok, how many did you find in that closet? We all love a nice leather jacket and we all like to look cool, too.

Stephanie went in the store at Strokers and boy, did she drop some major big bucks! She bought some really nice leather chaps and a nice leather vest, too, and I could not tell you what all else she bought. So, Stephanie got the "Biker Babe Fever" that day.

Another Biker Hang-out, Duke's Roadhouse

We were leaving Strokers, going to ride up to Duke's Roadhouse on Beltline in Addison. It was November, and evening was coming on. It was about 5:00 p.m., so it was cooling down pretty well as the sun was slowly going down. We suited up, got all our leathers on and were calling it a day.

We arrived at Duke's and hung out on the deck and in the parking lot for awhile. There were about 300 bikes and 400 bikers there. Yes, the bikers here do the same thing as at Strokers. We all parade in, same show; different place. But Duke's has a totally different atmosphere and a whole different personality. Some of the same guys will ride and hang out here but they will not go to Strokers at all, and vice versa.

We listened to the ride stories and any other story that might be told, true or untrue. We talked for awhile and then decided to get a good steak, so we went inside and had a nice dinner. After dinner the sun was about to go down; we had about 20 minutes of daylight left. And it surely was getting cool outside now.

That November air was getting downright chilly. We suited back up and put on our leathers—well, Stephanie had never taken her leathers off; she liked how she looked. She had the attitude like, "I look good, I am a hot biker babe; all eyes turn on me." I am sure that was in her head, because she had the walk down! "I'm cool. I'm bad. I'm hot." Yep, and she was right, too!

Steph and I went back out on the huge deck where all our friends were and said our good-byes. I specifically remember waving across the way, telling my good acquaintance at the time, Chris Bogard, good-bye. We were heading back to Prestonwood to drop Stephanie off and I was going home. "See ya next week, maybe?" That's how bikers are; you never know just where the ride will take you next weekend, or when you may see them again.

I got on loudmouth Betty, fired her up, racking out the pipes a little as if to announce, "Hey everyone. Look at us. We are leaving. Watch us ride on outta here into the sunset." Hmmmm...as I am deciding, *Let me see, am I going to make a cool fast exit or....am I going to just cruise outta here nice, slow and laid back?* Stephanie climbed on behind me, held on tight as we cruised on out slowly and in a very cool style. Off we went, calling it a weekend. We had a great, fun weekend and now it was over.

North-bound on Midway Road we go, straight from Addison to Plano. We had about a seven-minute ride left. As we left I revved up the motor and racked out the pipes one more time, bellowing out the loud rumble of that Harley motor as we pulled onto the street as if to say "Good-bye all, have a great week ahead, see ya later." A-chugging we went as the engine dug down in that nice, deep sound, like the engine is bogging down. That is just one of those neat Harley HOG sounds, chug-chug, chugging, down the road we went.

Sunday night was all wrapped up and it was time to get ready to get back into the real world on Monday. Yes, we are professionals in real life, real professionals, running businesses, making those second-by-second business decisions. But now it was back to the weekly grind of life, getting that competitive business professional fighting spirit ready for the week. We are as aggressive during the week in our respective professions as we are on the weekends. However, on Friday after work we get to strap on our leathers and put on our alter-egos and ride again until the next Sunday night. Riding our iron horse!

Ride 'em, Cowboy!

<(((><

14

My Greatest Tragedy

I quickly assessed the situation around me. There were three lanes going north and three lanes going south with a turning lane on each side to cross traffic. I was in the center lane going north, and the girl in the red car was in the center lane headed south.

Stephanie and I headed north on Midway Road as we left Duke's Roadhouse. We were discussing the nice day it had been. It wasn't too far now, only a short drive to our destination at Prestonwood or, as some call it Preston World, because it is a huge mega church. As a matter of fact, I wonder if it even has its own ZIP code! With approximately 30,000 members, that makes Prestonwood one of the largest churches in the United States.

OH NO! NO! NO!

As Stephanie and I were riding north up Midway Road, heading to the intersection of Midway and Park, we were traveling about 20 to 25 miles an hour, talking, looking at the cars as they passed going south. We rode through the intersection at Frankford. My buddy Ron Mumford was there at a traffic light. He waved at us but we never saw him; he was in the traffic somewhere at the cross street. We kept on cruising slowly, looking around, talking; taking it all in, plus it was now getting downright cold! We were almost there, cruising toward the overpass at the George Bush Turnpike (or Texas 190).

We had just passed the traffic light at Midway Road and Rosemead Parkway.

My friends Rick and Astrid were riding right behind us on their Harley and a Honda Shadow. They turned off to the left at the light, going to a place called Shuck 'N Jive. We waved them off. I looked up and saw a red car coming south under the overpass of the George Bush Turnpike. The car swerved to the right outside of its lane a little bit, so I looked at the driver, trying to be sure what her intentions were, to see if she was sleepy or was it just a momentary lapse in judgment.

A biker is trained to always look a driver right square in the eye to get a good read of what their intentions are and what they are doing. When I looked at her, all I saw was a young blonde with her hair swinging in the air as she slung it to the right. I told Steph, "Hold on tight and stay with me. Do not lean in any direction, just stay with me and the bike. Do not move." I didn't know what she was about to do!

I quickly assessed the situation around me. There were three lanes going north and three lanes going south with a turning lane on each side to cross traffic. I was in the center lane going north, and the girl in the red car was in the center lane headed south. Great, I thought, there should be no problem. Then I looked in my rearview mirror. There was a big Ford F-350 pickup truck right behind us and cars were coming up beside us on both sides. The red car with the young blonde driver was coming toward us and there was no one else going south at all but her.

At that moment I looked back at the driver in the red car. She slung her hair the other direction now, to the left, as her car swerved a little again out of her lane, to the left this time. She then slipped the cell phone up to her ear. She was having a conversation. She glanced, looking back over her left shoulder to see if traffic was behind her, since she was in the center lane. But she really wasn't paying any attention at all. It was all clear on her side, no traffic behind her or beside her or in front of her. All of a sudden I could see it coming! I pulled Steph up close behind me and said, "Hold on to me! Stay with me!" She slid up as close as she possibly could and held on as tight as she could, squeezing the air out of my lungs she was squeezing so hard. I told her we needed to be as if we were one person on the bike because I think we have a big problem. She could see it, too, before I could finish telling her.

The driver of the red Pontiac was talking on her cell phone and it looked like she might decide to turn to her left across our lane of traffic to get on the George

Bush Turnpike. She did not even look at us at all, the oncoming traffic. She did a 90-degree instant turn to the left, heading straight across our northbound traffic. We were in the center lane and I had to be sure we were not boxed in! If it was a close call and we were not trapped, we could swerve right or left or whatever we needed to do. If it were close, we could slide by and avoid an accident.

The young blonde driver now had made a firm decision to cut hard and fast across all of the lanes of traffic. She was committed to getting on the George Bush Turnpike entrance ramp. It appeared that she made a split-second decision based on the cell phone call she had just received. **It turned out she answered the phone while she was texting; that was why she was swerving in the road.** She was too busy talking on the phone and looking behind her, in her mirror and back over her shoulder, and never once looked at all in our direction at any of us, all the cars, trucks and motorcycles, coming head-on straight toward her in the oncoming traffic lane. She never even looked at the traffic light to see she had a RED light.

Steph and I were out a little in front of the traffic. The red car literally turned on a dime! It was the fastest spin turn I had ever seen in traffic.

After this, refer back to Chapter 1

BAM!

This is where the accident happened. Go back and re-read Chapter 1 if you'd like to get caught back up to this point! I think it will help you see the full picture of where we are and what all is about to happen.

Trouble Grace

I remembered another saying from Dr. Fred Lowery. He preaches a sermon on "Trouble Grace."

When we get in trouble, God is there with **"Trouble Grace,"** just for the trouble we are in at that moment. No, there is no mention of trouble grace in the Bible, but Dr. Fred surely cloned a thought that will forever live with me, and I want to share it with you, Trouble Grace.

I remember several times that night, as I lay there on that ice-cold street raising my right arm to the sky, I was looking for help in the moment of my desperation, and at the same time I was praying, too. I was reaching up to God. It was like a hurt child looking up to his mommy or daddy saying *"Hold me. Please, pick me up, Daddy!"* I was like a little boy reaching up to Mommy and Daddy to be picked up and held in their arms. I was reaching up to Him to be comforted and carried through this tragic storm!

I knew I did not have much longer to live, and I knew I was dying. I prayed for my son Jeremy and my only grandson at the time, Cameron. I asked God to be sure my son Jeremy someday surrendered his heart to Him, and that he would protect my grandson and lead him to a life of accepting Christ. I asked God to take care of my mom, Rose, and my dad, Dan. We were all so very close. My parents were a blessing to me all of my life. I loved them dearly and I knew just how devastating it would be to them to lose a child. I knew it would be hard for them to handle.

Those were my only quick prayers that I prayed as I was slipping out of consciousness. I did not pray that I might live. *I knew to get to Heaven I had to die,* but I did not want to go at this moment! There were so many things left undone, so many things that needed to be said. I did not want to go right now, but I was ready.

I was in real trouble and I needed that Trouble Grace now more than ever before in my life!

I remember the P E A C E! When it came it was so surreal it was just an amazing peace.

Just a quietness in my mind and a calming and a settling of my thoughts as a soothing warm feeling in the cold of the night came over me. PEACE. Just peace! My mind quieting down, my eyes were closing and my strength was all gone. God came on down at that moment and gave me rest. He gave me peace. He gave me *"Trouble Grace."* He sent me an angel at that moment when I was lying there in pain to be by my side and to comfort me. That is why I like to call him my *"Trouble Grace Angel."*

I truly thank God so much for that "Trouble Grace"! And thank you, Dr. Fred, for teaching me about it those years I was at First Bossier.

"God's Wonderful, Amazing, Trouble Grace."

When I was in Trouble He gave me a Special Grace!

<(((><

16

Biker Down! Biker Down!

Totally amazing.

I lay there on the ice-cold concrete road, going out of consciousness

I saw a man come running and drop to his knees there at my side. He reached down, scooped my body up off the pavement as he lifted me up and drew me close to him. I looked deep into his beautiful, deep ocean blue eyes as he had his arms wrapped all around me, and he placed his hand on the back of my head as he held me like a little baby. We were now cheek to cheek and I was bleeding all over him. He pulled me close to him and held me in his arms and chest in a warm hug and laid me back a little bit several times to look into my eyes. He gently held me in his arms and rocked me back and forth. I felt warmth, and a calming spirit. I saw the glow all around him. After a few seconds I heard a very comforting, sweet and gentle voice say, "Phillip! Phillip! Phillip...it's me, buddy...I am here for you. You are going to be okay! Hang in there. I am here!"

I opened my eyes and saw a familiar face and a radiant glow and shining bald head. I did not recognize him, but he looked very familiar! I looked at him and thought, Am I in Heaven? Are you an angel?

Then I asked him, "Are you an angel?" He did not answer for a few seconds, then he smiled at me. I saw tears forming in his eyes as he said, *"Phillip, this is Chad. I am here, buddy!"* After awhile I recognized the face but he had a shaved head and the Chad I knew had a full head of hair.

I did not know if he was a real person or an angel. I remember grabbing him and pulling his head down and kissing him on the top of his shinny bald head! I knew he was really an angel that God had sent to take care of me and he was to bring me to Heaven or to escort me to the opening of Heaven's gate to let me in. I was getting ready to see Jesus! No, I did not want to go yet! But I was ready to go.

Yes, he was an angel! But he was also my good friend, Chad Armstrong. God sent me a very special recognizable human angel that night to comfort and take care of me at that very moment. You may say no, he was a man directed by the Holy Spirit. Humans cannot be angels. You are correct, from what I have learned. God can send angels in human form, but everyday humans are not angels sent by God. However, God supplies all of our needs and God sends people rushing in to fill a need that we have. So, yes, that is a GREAT assumption that Chad was not an angel from Heaven, but he is still a human angel or messenger sent from God who was my friend. No matter what you think, there is no doubt it was a divine and holy appointment for both of us! This was truly a God appointment. I have to tell you the rest of his story for you to see why I knew God had sent me Chad in my desperate time of need. There was no doubt he was Heaven-sent!

As you already know, I was in so much pain and my body was so mangled, my whole left side was destroyed. I was in massive pain. My left leg hurt so badly I wondered was it even attached to my body. Do I even have my leg? My vision was distorted and all I could see was my blood everywhere.

I could hear the terror in everyone's voices as they began to come around me, now that Chad was there. I could see the horror in their eyes as some would come down close to my face peering, looking at me while Chad was holding me. I could hear voices. As they were drawing close to me and talking to each other, they were asking *"Is he alive?"*

There was an answer, *"Yes! He is alive. But I really don't think he is going to make it. He is in really bad shape, and he has lost so much blood, it is everywhere—just look!"* I heard someone say, "The woman over there, she is hurt really bad, too, but I think she will make it!"

I kept hearing people in the background say, *"Call the ambulances! Get the paramedics! This guy is dying over here! Hurry, this guy is **dying!**"*

I heard someone say, *"I called them already, but they will take her first because he is too far gone."* Then I heard another young man's voice come up by me and say, *"I saw it all...she ran that red light."*

Chad, in a very calming and sweet voice, looked into my eyes and said, *"You are going to be alright. Do not listen to them. You will be ok! I promise."*

I knew he was right. I knew it was true that I was going to be alright. At that moment I felt I was in the arms of God! I heard the quivering in his voice as he spoke and my eyes connected with his as he was looking deeply, directly into my eyes. He was trying not to look at all of the damage that was done to my body, but...I knew that I was dying! At that same time I looked back into his eyes and they were like looking into the deep blue ocean that was so clam and clear. I could see with clarity Jesus was in his eyes and I felt Jesus in his touch. It was just like I described earlier in Chapter one. It was so wonderful.

While Chad was holding me in his arms and my head was in the palm of his hand, I saw a glimpse of a young woman in her early 20's, a blonde girl, come up on my right side. She was looking down at me crying and trembling. She was crying her eyes out, saying, *"I am SO sorry! I am sooo sorry! I did not see you!"* I could not see very well at all, but I knew who it was.

Yes, it was the young lady who was driving the red car that hit me! Megan.

As I felt that I was lying in God's arms and looking in Chad's eyes, I remember telling Megan, "It is alright; it is ok!" At that point, I looked back at Chad in the eyes. I kissed him on that bald head again, and then I asked Chad,

"Please don't leave me! PLEASE! I need to tell you something!"

Chad said, *"I am not going anywhere, I am staying right here with you."*

I felt that amazing peace from God's "Trouble Grace" I described in the first chapter, and my pain was finally subsiding as I was now resting in his strong yet gentle and peaceful arms.

<((><

17

My Angel, My Buddy, Chad

The "Unbelievable" story about Chad Armstrong!

Friday, January 18, 2008, only 10 months before my accident! We met for the first time at Randy White's Restaurant in Frisco. Randy White is a retired Dallas Cowboys Football player and he had a nice restaurant with a live band that played at night. Chad and I were introduced to each other by a mutual acquaintance a couple of days after I moved back to Dallas from Kansas City.

Chad was not a believer in Christ. No! Not at all! So you ask me, "How he could be an angel?"

Well let me tell you the "Amazing Story!"

We met that night and we hit it off from the very beginning. We were like long-lost friends. We both loved to ride motorcycles, even though he rode one of those wimpy, rinky-dink sissy Honda motorcycles! (Hahaha...inside joke for us bikers! Harley guys LOVE to pick on the metric biker guys.) We laughed, we joked, we carried on all night long. We were the life of the room that night. We told stories all night. We had dinner and left like we had been friends since childhood. It was one fun evening.

The next morning I met Chad and all of his buddies at 10:00 a.m. and he introduced me to his group of friends who he rode with. We all connected, talked, and had a good time. Then we all loaded up and went for a ride in the cold air that January morning. It was an all-day ride all over Dallas and the outlying parts. We rode all day and into the night from one place to another, stopping in one small community after another having coffee and tea, lunch, dinner and the in-between snacks. Oh, I had tea and coffee; they had what most other bikers have when they stop for a drink. Anyway, let me tell you it was COLD! Even with all our leathers on. It was freezing cold by 9–10 p.m. that night.

We began to ride together a lot after that day, out on the country roads and all over the Dallas/Fort Worth Metroplex. Chad and I and his entire group of buddies got to be really good friends. I became known as the guy who drank iced-tea and coffee while they drank their "juice," if you know what I mean. I was the guy not using the four-letter words and telling the foul jokes, but I was still in the group. We had all connected and enjoyed riding together. God was doing something in all of those relationships from the very first day.

Now, God had placed me there in Chad's life at this point for a specific reason, and He placed Chad in my life for a specific reason, too. God was at work all along, we just did not know the entire plan!

At the end of the day after we would spend all day riding with our friends, we would all say our good-byes and everyone would get on their bike and head their separate ways home. I cannot count the times I would be riding home and I would be almost there, riding in the cold and dark, or freezing winter rain, almost home. After a 30-45 minute ride all alone at 9-12 p.m., all of a sudden my cell phone would vibrate. It was Chad calling. I would pull to the side of the road and answer it.

"Hey, buddy, it's Chad. Want to meet for some coffee? I really need to talk to you."

Needless to say, I would spin "Loudmouth Betty" around and back I would go, headed to whatever destination we had agreed on. God was working on Chad's heart and Chad was listening. Chad had been living a lifestyle so long and now he was ready to find answers that he knew I had. The Holy Spirit was convicting Chad in areas of his life and the funny thing is, Chad was so receptive from the very start. God was also busy working on the other biker guys in our group, too.

Chad and I would meet, have some small talk and laughter, then we would get to the reason for the call. We would begin to discuss his personal matters. He would always bring up God; I did not have to, and yes, the big, 6'2" strong man everyone looked up to as a leader of the group would sometimes tear up and cry like a baby, just like I did years ago. Ya' see, I remember those days in my life still to this very day. God was convicting Chad, and he was smart enough to know to get help—he knew he needed to talk to someone!

At this point Chad needed some help and he was open and willing to listen. God had been preparing his heart for a long time, and God had needed a messenger to deliver the good news to Chad. So God opened up His toolbox and chose an instrument, a tool to use. It was me this time. I was that tool that God decided to use. God allowed that Chad had to feel like he was the one in control. God had to allow Chad to feel he had found the answers on his own terms the same way I did, remember? Chad had to think he did it his way and God used me as the instrument. Wow!

But God was just getting started orchestrating a masterpiece of two lives to come together to make a beautiful melody. A new song was being written in Heaven, a song of redemption of another lost soul. The angel bells in Heaven were getting ready to ring. The angel choir was striking up a song to sing.

Chad was searching everywhere for the answers to his life and his career. He was looking for peace and true happiness, but knew what the answer was all along. All he needed was a friend to live it out in front of him. He needed someone just to be there and listen to him, and to have someone not to go blab his personal business. He needed an accountability partner. Chad needed a friend and a brother; Chad needed **Jesus, Biker Style**.

Chad was on a mission, searching for answers and his purpose in life after many late-night phone conversations, and getting away from all of our friends. While we were out riding, we would find a quiet place where we could talk and he could ask his questions and listen to the answers.

Chad would begin to say, *"Hey, say a prayer for me."*

I said, *"Sorry I don't say prayers, but I will pray a prayer for you."*

He knew I would pray for him, and he knew I would do it right then so he would hop on his bike and ride away as fast as he could, but he knew I was praying for him.

There were so many times when it was just him and me and we would stop right there and I would pray with him at that moment at the Starbucks or wherever it was. Just like my friend Ray Raney in Shreveport had done for me several times before. No, Chad would never say a word while we prayed, but I know his heart was talking and crying out to God. He would just bow his head and shed a few tears and say "thank you." Then he would say a fast goodnight because he was all choked up and could not talk. Then he would mount up as quickly as he could and ride off in the cold dark of night, headed back to a town named "The Colony" where he lived.

Here is the Really NEAT part!

Several months after we had first met, Chad accepted Jesus as his Savior. He accepted Christ as the promised Messiah. Woo Hoo. It was approximately June, about six months after Chad and I had met, and four months before my accident. Chad was a man like me; his was "a life that was changed."

Wow, what a privilege to get to lead Chad to Christ. The very man God would send to my rescue months later. God sent him this time not as my friend but as "my special Trouble Grace Angel."

So the man I got to lead to Christ, **God used, and sent him back to me as a first responder!** But as a first responder from God's care department.

Yes, Chad was a really great guy, but, he was a man who still had struggles to deal with, just as we all do as believers. But he was finding his way. Yes, this is the Chad God later used in my desperate time of need, in my time of TROUBLE. That is why I call him my **"Trouble Grace Angel."**

Arriving on the Scene

Normally, Chad would ride his motorcycle with us almost every time we rode. However, on this particular Sunday, Chad did not ride with us. He lived in The Colony, a small suburb of Dallas, a town approximately ten miles away from where I lay on the concrete that cold winter evening. Chad "just happened" to be driving by the intersection where I was and he "just happened" to be one of the first ones on the scene! I "just happened" to be the biker down.

Now you tell me if that is not a God thing or God's timing or what!

Yes, God showed up! He sent me a human messenger, a human angel at the EXACT moment when I needed help the most. When I was in the most troubling time of my life and there was no one there to help me at all, "God was there."

Besides God Himself showing up, He sent me something tangible that I could relate to and something I could hold onto. God sent me a messenger, someone to hold me physically while He held me, too. God sent someone to physically look me in the eyes and show me that Jesus my Savior was there, too. God came down and left me another comforter besides the Holy Spirit. God sent me Chad. That is why I call him my "Trouble Grace Angel." In my deepest trouble, God met my needs.

No, there is nothing that comes before God. He is all we need! But this time God opened His toolbox and chose an instrument to use, and God chose a new Christian who was willing to be used. That's my friend Chad.

Chad had been out just driving around in his Jeep, running an errand for his girlfriend, when he looked ahead and saw all the cars stopping really fast and coming to a screeching halt in the middle of the road, right smack in front of him. He continued driving on up through the traffic, weaving his way in and out. He finally got all the way to the intersection of the accident. He was almost completely stopped when he looked over to the left where all the commotion was and he saw a "Biker Down."

Immediately, Chad fired up the Jeep and cut right through the traffic, driving over the medians and over grassy areas. He was cutting in and out getting around all of the cars and trucks that were stopped in the middle of the street. He was dodging the people as they were getting out of their vehicles. Chad was focused on doing anything he had to do to get to the biker. Chad wondered why the biker was way out there all by himself. Why was no one helping him? As he got closer, he looked again quickly at the motorcycle, then at the biker lying in the street. All Chad was thinking was, "Biker Down, Biker Down! There is no one helping the biker! Why? Is he dead?" All of a sudden, he saw my biker jacket with all of my biker patches on it. He saw the John 3:16 patch as well, and he thought, is it him?

Is that Phillip?

Is Phillip the biker Down?

Oh, my God, NO, not Phillip! NO-no. Not Phillip!

Experiencing God Together

As soon as Chad got closer to the scene and could see everything clearly he looked hard at the crashed motorcycle down the way on the highway entrance ramp. He tried to see for sure if I was the biker. He looked again at the biker jacket now that he was closer. Then he knew for sure, it was me! He slammed on the brakes and stopped the Jeep right where it was; he jumped out and ran as fast as he could and dropped to his knees there at my side. Chad was the very first person I saw after the crash. I had been lying there on the pavement for what seemed to me like several minutes with all that went on in my head and the pain that I was in.

Now, you tell me God does not have a plan and sense of humor!

God had placed Chad in the exact place where He wanted Chad to serve. I needed someone at that exact moment. I was all alone and with all the people there, Chad was the very first one to come to me. This was a divine appointment made in Heaven above. Funny thing, isn't it? I was the one who got to lead Chad to Christ! Now God is using Chad to take care of me! Wow!

You see, God knew that Megan was going to make a life-changing decision for all of us that day! She made a choice that will affect her life and mine for the rest of our lives. But that is not all. She made a decision that will have a ripple effect for all of eternity. All of the people that I meet in this new condition, living disabled and as an amputee, affects you even today! If not, you would not be sitting here reading this story! There is a reason you are here right now reading this book! What is it?

God knew I would be living the rest of my life by her choice. Her decision. The choice she made to text and then to answer a cell phone call as she drove, then to run a red light! *Her choices affect thousands of lives forever! Think about it! The same is true for you. Every decision you make impacts someone or some situation.* You matter and you make a difference in everything that you do.

God always lets us choose! Megan made her choice. And I have to live with her choice! You see, we all live by other people's choices as well as our own choices. It is called free will. The way God designed the Heavens and the earth, we all make our own choices. We can choose to believe in God or not. However, that choice makes no difference as to whether God is real or not. The only factor here is do you believe in Him? Just because you may choose not to believe does not make it so. That is just your choice; free will to believe what you want.

That is what Jesus did! He made a choice to lay down His life and we live by His choice. Talk about a real ripple effect! Christianity has been rocking this world ever since Jesus was born.

Chad made a choice to accept Christ, but God directed Chad to be at that intersection in Dallas ten miles from his home on that Sunday evening at 7:26 p.m., and I "just happened" to be the biker down? No! There is absolutely no way that it was by chance or karma. It was a God thing! This is God at work! God was at work and Chad was joining Him, just like Henry Blackaby says in his *"Experiencing God"* series! Chad made a choice that affected my life and yours, too, at this moment. The crisis for you is to believe or not to believe if he was sent from God. Whether he was sent as an angel or as a man directed by God, or The Holy Spirit.

The funny thing is, Chad and I both were "Experiencing God"! Both of us in two totally different and completely new capacities! It was like a complete role reversal from the caregiver and the recipient. The genuine love of a new Christian man being used by God in a way he or I would have never expected.

Chad knew I was dying. His touch at that moment and time was like something I had never felt before in my life! It was a human touch with a divine, Heavenly power. Even though I could see the human emotions in him, I saw a divine composure and comforting as well.

Through his tears I could see Jesus communicating with me. Gazing into his eyes I could see Jesus looking right at me. In his arms I felt I was being held in the arms of God. At that moment, even though there was a quiver in his lips, there was the most wonderful and beautiful comforting smile only an angel could give. Chad was holding me close as I slipped out of consciousness. He never left me. He was right there all the way through that evening, right on up until the ambulance door closed.

Chad's mission at that point was done for the night!

Yes, I believe God was using a human that I knew as a messenger of His love and in staying with me to the end.

That's my angel, Chad Armstrong.

His mission had been accomplished!

<((><

18

Our Father in Heaven!

The ambulance came while I was lying in Chad's arms, unconscious!

I never even heard the sirens or engine or anything at all. I was completely at rest and unconscious and did not come to until they began to load me onto the stretcher.

I woke up with an oxygen mask on, IVs running into my veins; one paramedic was on a phone to the hospital and the other paramedics and firemen were trying to get me into the ambulance. They were all slipping and sliding all over the street because there was so much blood on the pavement and everywhere. I was then placed in the ambulance. I looked over at the black paramedic who was inside working on me; blood was all over him, too. My blood was all over the white shirt he was wearing. He was frantically working on me and smiling the whole time. I kept going out of consciousness and he was trying to talk to me and kept asking me questions. He was so loud it was like he was screaming and hollering at me.

"Wake up! Wake up! Do not go to sleep! Stay awake! What is your name? Where do you live? Talk to me!"

All the while he was scrambling to take care of me there was a huge smile on his face.

The paramedic woke me up; time after time he said, "Who do we contact for you?" I asked him for my cell phone. Chad handed it to the paramedic in the ambulance. That was the last I saw of Chad that night. The paramedic was trying to keep me awake and occupied while trying to find out who my family was and who to contact. He was trying to see if I could help out and keep me alert, awake, and occupied all at the same time.

I hit speed dial on the phone and called my mom, but there was no answer. I left her a message. I called my sister Sharon; no answer. I left her a message. I called my friend and my boss, Larry Speck. I got no answer so I left a message. I remember telling Larry I had been in an accident and wouldn't be at work the next day, that I was going to Baylor Hospital.

The paramedic interrupted, *"No, you are going to Parkland Hospital."*

I said, *"No. I have insurance. Take me to Baylor."*

He said, *"No, you are going to Parkland Hospital."*

I hung up the phone and the paramedic said,

"So, you are a believer? You believe in Jesus Christ? You asked each person you called to pray for you."

I said *"Yes, I am."*

The paramedic in the ambulance then asked me, *"Can I pray for you?"*

I said, *"Oh, yessss...please!"*

I do not know what he prayed, but he didn't just say a prayer. He was praying a sincere, heart-felt, genuine prayer from the very bottom of his heart.

He started his prayer saying, ***"Father in Heaven, I come to you..."***

That was all I heard! But it was more than enough!

Father in Heaven! Then I slipped out of consciousness again. That was all I heard of him praying for me, but it was such a beautiful and wonderful prayer! You just had to be there to feel the power in his words!

"Our Father in Heaven!"

<((><

19

Parkland Hospital Emergency Room

I was jarred awake as we hit some big bumps. I was jerked and jolted, sliding and sloshing all around on the stretcher as the paramedics and doctors and nurses were running down the hallways beside my gurney.

They were running as fast as they could down the halls of the hospital. Everyone was running, saying "Faster, faster to the emergency room!" They all ran as fast as they possibly could go. I felt like my body was flipping and flopping around as we were going down the hall. Then I lost consciousness again. I have no recollection of what happened from then on, just momentary, short glimpses of a few seconds at a time when I would regain consciousness over the next two weeks.

The Fight for My Life

The next several days I was literally in the fight of my life. There were days of many, many, surgeries. Emergency surgeries from the internal bleeding they could not stop, blood clots, and over 36 broken bones in my body. I was in intensive care for two weeks. Now **"The Fight of My Life was on."**

I was unconscious most of the next two weeks. I underwent ten different emergency surgeries as well as the amputation of my left leg three weeks later when gangrene and blood poisoning set in. The doctors said they almost lost me, or I almost died, seven times in those first ten days.

My left foot and ankle were completely crushed and shattered. The bottom of my leg from the knee down was all broken and shattered. I had 27 breaks in the bones of my leg, knee, ankle and foot. My femur bone, in the upper part of my left leg above my knee, was broken and literally snapped in two. The bottom half and the femur bone, the jagged broken bone that was still attached to my knee joint, was jolted and pushed all the way up and into my groin. My knee was completely demolished. All of my ribs on my left side were crushed and broken in several places. My spleen had burst. My colon was impacted and later it burst open. The bottom of my back was broken. I had internal bleeding as well as all the bleeding from my leg.

My abdominal area was opened up from my chest down to below my navel. I had three blood clots; one in my leg, one in my lung, and there was a blood clot in my heart, too.

The doctors could not stop my internal bleeding. I was told by my trauma doctor later that blood was coming out of my body as fast as they were putting it in. They could not get the bleeding to stop in the emergency room. Blood covered the emergency room floor as well as the doctors and nurses who were attending me. Everyone was slipping and sliding on the bloody floor as they all worked fervently to stop the bleeding. They just put whatever type blood they had in me because it was coming out as fast as it went in, from what I was told. My blood pressure was almost non-existent.

Amazing. Now, when I stop and think about it all once again, I see how God was there! Orchestrating every detail the whole time. He was The Master of the Symphony. God was still playing a perfect masterpiece that started with me lying on the street. I was in the Master's hands, as were all of the other players in the orchestra, too. They were all making beautiful music at a traumatic time. Every person in place, every skill was honed, every talent was on display, each one hitting their note perfectly and on cue with the perfect amount of crescendo. Not a note was missed, as The Master was playing His Masterpiece with all of the willing players of His orchestra that night.

Every person was there at the right time, in the right spot, and with the right expertise, all the way from Chad and the paramedics/fire department to the doctors and nurses. It was all in God's timing. Not to mention all of the other players I do not even know who were involved that night.

So do I believe in angels?

You Betcha.

I believe God has a beautiful orchestra playing with all His pieces and instruments playing in His symphony. He uses people, angels, situations and circumstances. He will use everything he has, even nature.

It was an awful and terrible night for me! But it also was a night when God was doing what He does. God was working through so many people. Yes, God was at work! He had an audience that was watching His power on display, too. They were all watching that day, as well as seeing the results today now almost three years later.

For me, November 9, 2008, is a new birthday celebration for me! It's the day I got life for the third time.

1. First time was May 13, 1959, my mother gave birth to a mischievous, chubby little boy.

2. Second time was on September 11, 1998, when I gave my heart to Christ in my 4-Runner on the side of that road.

3. Third time is this one! November 9, 2008. Through the fire of tragedy I got to LIVE!

All of these dates are so memorable to me, all except the day of my birth. I was a little bit too young to remember that one. Haha.

Since we are talking about dates, can I ask you a personal question?

Do you know the Date and Time?

I had become good friends with Zig Ziglar through all of the years, and he and I had talked many times. I remember having this talk with him several times and then he taught a lesson on it one Sunday morning at church. Zig was the teacher of the Encouragers Sunday school class I attended from time to time. The class he taught that day made such an impact on me that I still use it to this day. It goes like this...

Do you know the date or time you became a Christian? If you do not know when you got saved or became a believer, do you remember ever even asking Christ to forgive you and become your Savior? Do you remember a time, maybe summer or spring? Maybe it was July or August when you were 10 or 35 that you asked Christ to be your Savior?"

As Zig would say, *"You do not have to know the exact day but you would definitely know, 'It was when I was eight years old', or 'In the spring of 1982'. You may not know the exact moment, but you will have a very close approximation of when Jesus came into your heart."*

Now Zig knew this from his own personal "Firsthand Experience!" He was raised in church but did not become a true Christian, true believer, real follower of Christ until Sister Jessie, an elderly black woman, witnessed to him in his home on July 4, 1972, when he was 45 years old. See, there was a time when a marker was placed in his life. There was a time when he knew that he was a born-again Christian!

Growing up in church or attending church for 45 years does not make you a Christian. Attending or growing up in church with Mom and Dad does *not* make you a Christian. Living in America, a Christian country, does not make you a Christian. There is only one way to Heaven. Willingly, knowingly and consciously accepting Jesus as your Savior, asking for His forgiveness for your sins, acknowledging Him as Lord of your life, then believing by faith in your heart and accepting the free gift of grace. These are the markers of a genuine Christian.

If you do not know the answer to the question, "Are you going to Heaven?" or if you do not know your place or time marker, then please CALL ME! Send me an e-mail or text anytime, day or night. My contact information is at the back of this book. PLEASE allow me to introduce you! The Scriptures tell us that every knee will bow and every tongue will confess that He is Lord.

If you do not know Him, please allow me the privilege of an introduction!

TODAY is the DAY!

<((><

20

My Caretaker Angel

Out of ICU

It was very dark. I was finally coming into consciousness. I was waking up during the wee hours of the night and was in so much pain.

My lips were so parched and cracking from no moisture. I had not had any water or food for over a couple of weeks, and I was so thirsty. I had been on IVs and a feeding tube, and I was beginning to wake up and come out from being unconscious. I cried out "God, help me, please! God, please help me!"

I was totally lost, disoriented and incapacitated. I was completely and totally helpless. I could not move my body at all. It was dark, in the wee hours of night-time, and I was coming to. As my eyes opened and I tried to focus, I saw the shiny triangle-shaped pull-up bar above me, but my vision was blurry. I remember at that time crying out to God because I was in so much pain (I know it was a soft cry, as I had no voice, either, but I cried out again), "Oh, God! Help me, please!"

Even as I was asking for His help, immediately I saw a light, it had just appeared! The light was ahead of me and off to my left. It was very bright and low to the ground, almost on the floor. I was disoriented; things were spinning and blurry. I was woozy and tried again to focus my eyes. I did not know what was going on. I looked straight ahead and over to the left again, and the light just got brighter and brighter. It started at the floor and was rising and coming up. Higher and higher it was rising, straight upward, very slowly. The light got to the height of about what a man would be if he were standing up, then it stopped!

The light was much brighter as it started moving around the room and coming towards me in my hospital bed. It slowly moved to the foot of the bed then over to my right side. It looked like it was floating in the air. Then the light stopped! It was right beside my bed and it was close to me now, up by my chest and head. Then I heard a voice; it was very soft, but it sounded like a man.

It said, *"Phillip, hi, I am here...what do you need?"*

I said, *"Help me, please! God, please help me. I hurt so badly! Please help me!"*

He said, *"I am here! What can I do for you?"* as he reached over and clicked a button for more medication.

"Thirsty! Water! I hurt! Help me, please." I asked.

He leaned in to me and took a piece of ice with his hands and gently touched it to my dry, parched and cracked lips. He held it there for awhile and then he started going back and forth, side-to-side across my lips as it slowly melted away. I asked for more ice and a drink of water. He said, "Ice is all you can have; I cannot give you any water."

"More ice, please." I continued begging for water, too, but all I could get was ice. It had been over two weeks since I'd had any water and I was dying of thirst. I pleaded with him, "Water, please!" Then he took a paper towel and dipped it in a glass of water and touched it to my parched lips. He kept patting the wet paper towel on my dry lips, and moving it side to side allowing the moisture to soak in. Over and over again he would dip a paper towel in the water and hold it on my lips as he smiled at me. It was so good, but I wanted more and more and more. He never talked! He just looked at me and smiled while he was leaning over me, taking care of me.

All I knew was he was there! Who was he? He was so patiently serving me. Each and every time I would wake up all through the night until I would go out again, that gentle voice and tender male touch was caring for me. He took care of every need I asked for. He was doing simple little things for me that I could not do for myself. Both of my hands were strapped down to the rails of the bed. "Why?" I wondered, "What is going on? Why would I be tied down?"

Then I asked him again for help with the pain. He gently reached over my body and clicked the button on a hand control that lay at my side. It was a morphine dispenser. Then he gave me another piece of ice and placed it on my lips. He then tried to help me get comfortable in my bed again. "Why am I strapped down to the bed?" I thought. My hands were tied down to each of the handrails and I did not understand what was going on. I was on so much medicine that the doctors said I became violent a few times and that I was hitting people and pinching doctors and nurses. I would pull all the tubes and IVs out of my body. So they had to tie me down.

All night long I would go in and out of consciousness. I would be awake one minute then I would quickly go out stone cold again, just like the flipping of a light switch. I would be awake one second, then out again the next. I guess at that point it was all of the morphine and other medications that were putting me out. I remember having some pretty vivid and wild dreams, too, during this time. I still remember several of those dreams to this very day. I will tell you about them one day.

Sometime later during the night I woke up again and I cried out to God again. The pain was so acute again and I cried out,

"God, help me, please! God, please help me!"

Then it appeared again. I saw that light again! It was in the same place as the first time, low to the ground to my left, and then I saw the light rise up again! Then he came to my side and clicked the medication dispenser. He then quickly got the cup of ice and began wetting my lips. He never talked to me. He just did as I asked, taking care of my needs as quickly as he could. He was always helping me as I was moving and shifting in the bed again to get comfortable. The pain was so bad I could hardly move with all the broken ribs and broken lower back. My left leg was suspended in a sling with bars and pins sticking out of it. He jumped to fill all of my needs. While he was patting my lips again with ice and water, I would go out in a flash, just like a light again.

Yes, he was an angel to me. Whether a real angel or a man, being used by God and the Holy Spirit, I am not sure, but what I do know is God was taking care of me through regular people. This one was taking care of me in the wee dark hours of night while everyone else was at home fast asleep with their families. The angel God had sent my way that night was another new friend, Fred Pascarelli. Another man, a human just like you and I and I believe God sent Fred to me. Yes, you can say he was just a man used by God and that is ok, too, but the fact remains, this guy was giving and serving way above and beyond the call with strength and power that was beyond belief. This is why I call this book *Carried by Angels*. Listen to his story.

Fred was sitting there on the floor by the door. He was sitting by the door of my hospital room all night long where he could keep an eye on me. I was in his direct line of sight the whole night. Each time I cried out to God for help, Fred would rise up and come over to my bed again and again all night long. Yes, Fred is a regular guy, but God used him. In a different way he was my caretaker. He was ready, willing and available. So God used him.

That is exactly what God does, *He surrounds us with people in our everyday lives who will allow God to do a work through them, and to serve Christ by serving others.* Angels like this come out when least expected and they do not go away. People just like you, God uses as angels to bless others in their time of need. But remember, God is the only one who directs angels. So can an angel be a person?

God Calling Angels

Think about this for a second. Chad, Fred and I met at the same time in completely different social circles of my life. I met each one of them one day apart, almost the exact same time of day. I met Fred on Thursday night and Chad on Friday night. I met them in two different areas of Dallas. I met Fred in east Plano and Chad in North Frisco.

God placed two new men in my path one day apart and exactly ten months later each one would be serving in a way that people I have known for 20 years did not serve. Neither one knew the other. God brought both of these men into my life to use for this appointed time!

The first encounter after my accident was Chad, the second man I had met earlier. The second encounter God used Fred, the first man I had met. I know it means nothing but I think of the Scripture "The last shall be first and the first shall be last."

Fred stayed up all night long. He stayed in the most uncomfortable and inconvenient time to watch over and take care of me. God sent a different man with different gifts than the first one, Chad. Chad, my "Trouble Grace Angel," was there as soon as tragedy struck. God showed up as *"Jehovah-Jireh" (my provider),* as the Scripture Genesis 22:14 reflects, by sending Chad to bless and comfort me as well as provide for my immediate needs.

Fred is "My Caretaker Angel." He was there for the many days after my accident. Two totally different needs being met. Each one staying all the way through, never leaving until their mission was accomplished! *Yes, we are surrounded by angels on all sides.* There are people that are led by the Holy Spirit to do a work as well. This time God shows Himself as *"Jehovah-Rophe" (my Healer)* by sending Fred my way to care for me and help me to heal. Yes, God is "Jehovah-Rophe," which in translation means "The Lord who heals," as in Exodus 15:26.

God sent Fred that night to take care of me so my mom could go home and get some much-needed rest and sleep. My mother had been there by my side the whole time I was in ICU and all through ten surgeries and the seven times when I almost died while in ICU. She had been there at the hospital continually for well over two weeks straight, 24/7, and she was literally worn out both physically and emotionally. So God sent a helper, a special messenger, to serve when there was no one else available! I believe God empowered a normal human and gave him a special and specific mission. Fred!

My mom and dad were so exhausted. For over two weeks they'd had very little sleep at all. The life-or-death times came 24 hours a day for those first ten days. My mom was 76 at the time, my dad close to 79. They were in great shape; however, time and the stress were taking their toll. Mom needed rest. Fred piped up and told my mom, "Go home and rest, I will watch him; I will take care of Phillip." That he did. Fred was there all night long for several nights in a row and still would go to his job the next day. No, you cannot tell me he is not an angel.

I had not known Fred very long at all, about ten months total up to this time. But Fred allowed God to use him. He would never say he was an angel, but I know! *God sends people into our lives when we need them the most. God sends just the right person with just the right gift and expertise that is needed at that specific time, or He takes common, usable people and empowers them and does a work through them. But I think God sent a familiar human in my time of need and empowered Fred to do what he needed to do. So is he an angel, or used by the Holy Spirit?* You can answer that one for yourself!

Fred the Man

Let me tell you a little about Fred. He was the organizer of the meet-up group called Dallas Christian Singles—(DCS) remember, we talked about them already? I had joined them back in January that same year after I had moved back from Kansas City in January 2008.

Fred stayed right there by my bed, taking care of me that whole night with no sleep at all. All night long he was there in my room! He was sitting on that floor, working on his laptop and watching and caring for me at the same time. I remember at least three or four times a night I would call out in the night, and each and every time Fred would rise to the occasion. He would bring his laptop over and set it down, then would so gently tend to me.

Yes, there are angels! No doubt! I believe God uses ordinary people as well as His Heavenly celestial angels, too. I know without a shadow of a doubt God uses people like you to do a special work here on this earth! God sent Fred that night to care for me, watch over me, and to not get too relaxed but to be attentive and alert, because Fred knew his mission! He was the angel on duty. I know he is just a man and really was just used by God and possibly the Holy Spirit. But do not miss the point that God sent people into my life and surrounded me completely with His mercy and His Grace. To me he was my caretaker angel!

I know Fred is a regular person and is not a Heavenly being, transformed to come to this world. He is a man, a real flesh-and-blood man. But Fred had a mission to accomplish. He was on duty and was up for the challenge. No, I am sure it was not easy. I cried out many times in the night out of desperation and pain, and each time Fred responded with such love and compassion. Whatever I needed or asked for, Fred was there. Fred was so strong, yet he was ever so gentle. His spirit was calming, sweet, comforting, and helping. He had a transcending spirit, meekness and gentleness and yes, tremendous love, too. Fred was my angel of encouragement. He was engaged, attentive, and focused on doing his duty with a big smile every time and with those piercing eyes that looked dead into my eyes with a comforting look as if to say, "It is all ok, I am here and I am not going to leave you."

Yes, that was all in the look communicated in his eyes. The same look I saw in Chad's deep blue eyes, I could see Jesus communicating to me, "He would never leave me!" That is one of His promises in the Bible that He will never leave us or forsake us.

Yes, Fred was "My Caretaker Angel."

<((><

Instruments in "God's Toolbox"

Yes, your angels are in here, too

Have you ever in your life wondered about us Christians? We are imperfect, yet God can use us in supernatural ways.

He will work through us imperfect Christian men and women. Even at times when we least expect it or do not realize God is using us, He goes way beyond our human strengths or gifts.

Remember earlier we said, *"If we will do the possible God will do the Impossible"?* We are just common, everyday people like everyone else in this world. Just imperfect, everyday people calling ourselves 'Christians' and trying to live out a Christian life as best we can. Trying to live in a fallen world, all of us having made the same mistakes in our own lives as everyone else. We sometimes get trapped up in life situations like everyone else in this world. We are just common, ordinary people that God uses to do extraordinary things, because we have made those mistakes and we know the value of our salvation. God uses us because we are available and usable—and His!

We are just instruments in His "Holy Toolbox."

What a privilege to get pulled out of that box and be used to IMPACT lives forever! What if God did like we do, taking our tools, packing them away, using them every now and again and forgetting about a tool that could do the job so much better and faster? We have "paid the price" for the tool and then we forget about it! God does not do that. He knows the price He paid for us and how valuable we really are. He knows our true worth and He knows exactly what to do with us! Only if we will be available and usable then we can be blessed and be a blessing to so many!

God is always looking to see whom He can use and where He can use us. We just have to be "usable!" Are you usable? Why not?

Do you want to know the secret? It is no secret at all. We are just people. We are just walking by faith, that is the secret! Living in grace, and being available and living in communication and in fellowship with God.

Let me ask you, "How often do you talk to the people who are important to you?" I am sure you talk daily to those you love the most, and the people that love you. I would think you talk to them almost every day and that you tell them that you love them almost every single day, right? Sure you do. That is the secret to living this Christian life, daily communication with God, getting into the Scriptures every day.

If you will live in the power you are given through the Holy Spirit, you will have the power to overcome, and to not fall into so many of the traps set by Satan. We also have "The Fruit of The Spirit" as a gift, an extra portion as you can see in Galatians 5:22-23. We receive a supernatural portion of these human characteristics. Think about it: You have more! Look at this: "The fruit of the Spirit is more love, joy, peace, long-suffering, kindness, goodness, faithfulness, gentleness, and self-control." "Exercise your power" and listen to good, uplifting worship music. Get into fellowship and fall in love with God and Jesus. Search for God and His wisdom for your life. God wants to use you. You can be used to be someone's angel. If you do not think that you can be an angel, you are wrong!

Let me tell you, after what I have seen and experienced, I know God will use any of us who will allow God to be God. Angels are simply messengers sent by and from God. They follow His directives. How neat to know that God used you! Yes, rusty and crusty ol' you!

Fred was way more than an angel, he was the "Hands and Feet of Christ." Fred was being like Christ in the flesh, like Christ in action. Jesus with skin on! He stayed up with me all night long, still having to go to work the next day, taking care of a guy who was a new friend to him, and not even a close friend at that. He did this for several nights, not just one night.

Fred was usable. He was there in a gentle, compassionate way, helping. He was being a comforter, an angel by my side, sitting at the door keeping watch over me. Yes, there are angels watching over us!

Fred was not there to see or be seen. There was nobody there for him to impress! There was no one but him and me. Fred was serving. He was praying. He was hands in motion and feet in action! He was a compassionate and comforting friend. This is what the Body of Christ is all about. Not perfect men and women, but people willing to accept Christ and accept their responsibilities for the gifts that were given to them here on this earth.

Built in God's image

God designed and built you and me to be givers!

So give, just as God gave and just as Christ gave. You just need to have the compassion and the desire to be all that you can be. Be a giver and not a taker. After all, you are made in God's own image, and God is a giver! Look at Christ, the ultimate giver. He gave continually as He walked this earth. He gave of himself every day.

He gave us all that He had to give, "His very own life" at the cross.

Yes, you are made in God's image and you are not fulfilled in your purpose if you are not giving. The old saying, "It is better to give than to receive," is true! That is the way you and I are wired. To be just like God and Jesus! Do you ever wonder why your life is not fulfilling? Then be a giver! We only receive when we are giving. So, let me ask you a stupid question.

Have you ever wondered, like I have, "If I died today, who would come to my funeral? What would they say? How many of my friends would be there? Have I been a giver or a selfish person?"

Wow...what a sobering thought!

I have thought about this and I would say 30, maybe 60 people, possibly 100 would show up at my funeral, and most of them would be my family. Everyone would probably still be at work. And I may know a lot of people but I am not really that important in their lives. What about you? How many can you think of who would come to your funeral? Not that it matters, because we are not in that box. But what about the legacy that we leave and what about those who want to honor our memory and comfort our families?

"Angels?" you ask. "I am not one! And I do not know anyone who is, either!" Bah!-Humbug! God will use you where you are in whatever capacity He chooses. You can be a human messenger sent from God above with a specific mission and empowered by the Holy Spirit to make a huge difference in someone's life.

God will use you if you are usable! Truth is, He will use you no matter what, but what a privilege to be used in a powerful way to make a difference in other people's lives. Whether being used as an angel or a messenger or being used by the Holy Spirit, it is an awesome privilege, and the feeling is out of this world to know God used me!

Let God be able to reach down in His toolbox and pull you out and clean you up and put you on the top shelf of His toolbox. So He knows that you are the exact tool to use on a specific mission. Keep yourself ready and all polished up. Be in communication with him daily. Let Him know you are ready and willing and able to be used! Then follow Henry Blackaby's formula. Look around and see what God is up to and join in with Him. You will be being used in a mighty way. Then God will know when the time is for you to receive extra special blessing to be used on a specific mission. Who knows, when you are looking daily and joining God it could be that very time God impacts the world through you! Remember, we are made in God's image. We are givers. We have to be giving in order to live fulfilled lives and lives of "Purpose and Passion."

We are built in God's image and He is a giver, so to be all we can be, we have no choice but to become givers and be usable. Then we will find we are living lives of purpose and meaningful existence. We will then be able to live passionate lives.

Be Usable!

<((><

22

Carried By Angels

They were coming out of the woodwork

But wait...Fred was not the only messenger God sent into my life. They were coming out of the woodwork! There were people coming from everywhere! Most of them started appearing while I was unconscious, from the first night of the accident. I had no idea. Wow!

God was at work! Lives were being impacted from the very first call about my accident and lives were being changed. God sent people from everywhere. People surrounded my family, my mom, my dad, and my sister Sharon. My family was so overwhelmed taking care of my immediate medical needs, and the emotional stress of a tragedy in the family takes a toll on our human bodies. God sent each one of my family members a personal caretaker. Can you believe it? Plus all of the many other people that came running and rushing in to give, to serve and to encourage and pray.

God sent so many people running in! It was like a flood! Really, I hear it was more like a Tsunami of people came rushing in to give!

Everywhere you looked you could see people coming, one right after another. Then another wave would come rushing in to seamlessly fill the gap where others had left to take care of their own lives. God not only worked miracles in my life, but He provided through common ordinary people just like *you*!

When my family did not know what to do, God provided the right person with the right expertise. God was doing a work in each and everyone else's life, as well as my life! When I was unconscious, God had angels watching over me and people were working on me and for my behalf!

Hey, remember! This is about God! It is not about me! *I am so amazed God would use a sinner like me after how terrible I had been for over twenty years of being a God and Christian hate machine.*

It's an honor and privilege for God to use me as an instrument, just a tool. I was really doing nothing at all. I was just lying there. I was unconscious and in ICU, fighting for my life. God was at work, and brought hundreds of people together. Then God supplied an immediate need for my family and for me, too. He took care of us all! God sent regular ordinary people to perform extraordinary jobs. God also displayed His majesty of who He is to all of my family, too. God showed all of the people exactly who they are, too! Their true character was exposed. They were fulfilling the role of the Church. Perfectly! The Body of Christ was in action. God's design for the Church here on this earth was in motion all around us, displayed in each and every one of their lives.

God had just used me as the tool. An awakening for so many others is how fast life can change for any one of them, too. Yes, my plans for the day had now changed! I had no control anymore over anything. God was in complete control. God had taken a sinner like me, who also is a sinner just like you, unworthy of anything good, but He blessed me with everything and He used a wretched man like me to impact lives for Him.

Yes, God used me! Wow, what a privilege.

I am not disabled! I am enabled to impact a world for Christ. *"In my Tragedy comes Tremendous Responsibility"* for me to show God as the gracious and merciful God that He is! Yes, I was surrounded and then I was personally "Carried by Angels." How blessed we are to know Christ and to be under His protection. How awesome to be brought into His fellowship of believers, the church.

You are Cheating Yourself

How do Christians make it that say, "I don't need to go to church to be a Christian!" No, you do not. However, you are cheating yourself! You are missing all the wonderful benefits, all the blessings, all the friends, and all the support! You are missing your angels.

God has given you so much. If you are not plugged in then *you* also are cheating others of the blessing of *"you!"* No one can take your place. If you are not there to be a blessing to someone else, then you have cheated him or her. You have cheated yourself, and you have cheated God, too! If you are not involved, then you are squandering God's resources; you are not being a good steward! Ok, now *smile* real big, and let's "get in the game." Like I used to say when I was a kid playing sports, "Put me in coach, put me in, I can do it, put me in!"

Get FIRED Up! Get up! Get moving! Get involved!

All you have to do is get up! Get moving! Get involved! Get involved in people's everyday lives. Come on, smile. Today is the day to "Live, Love and Laugh, again!" Today is the day to live in the "Faith, Family and Friends network," as I learned at First Bossier. Let God bless you by using you like you never thought possible. You will have so much fun. You will love it. Allow God to use you as an angel to bring comfort to anyone and everyone all around you. You are the one. So bring good cheer to everyone everywhere in your normal, day-to-day, everyday life as well as in those tough times of tragedy. It is people like you who simply allow God to use them by the power of the Holy Spirit. He may have a mission for you to bless so many other people. Yes, it may cost you something, maybe some inconvenience or discomfort. But the reward is awesome.

Oh, yes! There are angels all around!

As for me, the angels kept coming and coming and coming! These regular people in our lives we sometimes call angels, they were doing work right here in Dallas. It brought them all personal joy and happiness to be used and to serve.

What about you? Take a moment and just think, meditate on all the times you have been carried. Times when you were experiencing a tragedy or at a loss of what to do, then "They appeared!" God either sent angels from Heaven, or He sent human messengers like your friends and family and empowered them, or He sent you angels to intervene.

Can you see now and remember a time when you were *Carried by Angels"* too?

<((><

The Face of Jesus

The Bible says no man has ever seen the face of God. However...if you ask me, I have seen the face of Jesus.

Let me explain.

I have seen the face of Jesus on so many people during this experience. *I have seen and felt the presence of God in a way that is totally indescribable.* I want to tell you where I have seen the face of Jesus! I have seen Jesus on faces that are round, some narrow. Some faces are black; some are brown; some white and some faces are yellow. I have seen the face of Jesus on so many nationalities, people from right here in Dallas, Texas, and from all over the world, serving my family and serving me.

Yes, I do believe in angels as well as I believe I have seen Jesus here on this earth! Absolutely! I know I have seen His face! It is so distinct yet it is indescribable! It could be *your* face.

Stay with me here. No, I did not go to Heaven; no, I did not die. I came very close to dying seven times in the first ten days following the accident. I did not have some vision or enlightenment. *I did get to see things exactly as they were.* I did get a small glimpse from time to time when I would be awakened for a few short minutes, then when I had really come to and Fred was right there, surrounding me with his service, comfort and protection. "Protection" you say?

Yes. Fred was praying for me and I believe those prayers, as well as all of the prayers of the many other people, kept my spirit and me safe from attack of the enemy when I was defenseless. My mom and my dad's prayers and all the prayers I had prayed all of the ten years before to keep me safe from the enemy and to be brought under His wings and for Him to be my Strong Tower, those prayers were all being answered now, too.

As all of the people were arriving at the Parkland Emergency Room that first night in November, everyone was praying, sharing, and comforting one another. They were there even before my family could arrive at the hospital! They were ready, armed with all grace and compassion and loving-kindness to comfort and help my family and me.

Yes, Jesus was there and God was at work.

Yes, I did sing those songs with all my heart and soul for God to *"Take my life and use it!"*

Yes, I sang the praise and worship songs, *"All I am is yours!"*

Yes, I remember singing the song that said, *"You are my Shepard, Strong Tower, my very present Help in time of Need."*

Yes, I have! I have sung the songs that say *"I want to see Jesus and see His face."*

Yes, I have seen the face of JESUS! But it was right here in Dallas, Texas, not in Heaven, where I expected to see him first. I got to see Him right here.

I saw so many people that were giving of themselves as never before. People were doing things that they never thought they would do, either! These people were donating blood, praying, bringing food, and caring for each other all at the same time. These people were sharing joy, happiness and peace in a time of major tragedy. They all made a terrible situation a time of ministry to each other as well as my family and all the workers at the hospital, too. I know, because all of the doctors on my trauma team at Parkland Hospital told me so.

All my orthopedic surgeons and intern doctors, all the nursing staff and nurse's aides, the physical therapist and speech therapist and the occupational therapist, all of them told me "they had never seen such an outpouring of love and support." They had never seen so many people acting the way they were.

These Christian friends of mine were impacting so many other lives. They were genuine. Real! This was all here in one of the busiest trauma hospitals in the country, where they see everything. And here it is now, three years later, and still to this very day. Yes, I can see the face of Jesus on so many of those same faces today.

I still see people serving each other from their very experiences of this accident. God started something that day in me as well as in so many other people. Lives would now be impacted and changed as never before. Now people have seen God working like many of us had never seen Him before! Yes. God showed up!

Yes, I am now a disabled amputee with a different life, and yes, there are some major struggles. But I am more alive today than ever before!

You cannot see what I have seen and experience what I have experienced and not be changed.

Once you have seen strangers, your friends and the angels come and go, then when you have seen the face of Jesus on so many faces, there is not a doubt in your mind that God saves us and then He leaves us here for a specific reason, and a specific purpose. We now have an even more distinctive purpose fused to our heart, to share Christ and His blessings with everyone and to live a life where everyone that you meet can see "Jesus on your face." So be an encourager to those that have lost their encouragement and be a booster of encouragement to those running hard in their personal race in this life! Let people see Jesus in your face. He is there.

Yes, there were so many faces where I have seen Jesus shine through! Yes, a glow, a countenance that is completely indescribable! But let me try.

24

Angels Rushing in Like a Flood

Yes, I have seen angels in action. Yes, there were real angels sent from God above, and there were those people that God used in a mighty way, too.

Here are just a few of those who came rushing in. You can say whatever you like, but these were human messengers that God sent with a specific mission. Some of these are people God used in their field of expertise, and some way out of their comfort zone, and some even out of their physical capacity like Stu.

And, there was Stu!

Oh, yes, I saw the face of Jesus on Stuart Berwick; he was there from the very first night. He was on the scene so lightning fast, yet he was the "disabled guy" with major severe health problems galore all his own. He has a realistic excuse why he can't do something or be available, yet he found that was the very reason why he could! Not only that he could, but that he SHOULD get involved!

The guy who needs help the most is the one giving and serving!"I saw the face of Jesus on Stu when I came to. Stu was staying right there with my mom, every minute, and every step. He would not leave her side. Oh, yes, Stuart was an angel sent from Heaven who shone so bright.

Stu was more familiar with sickness than anyone from a firsthand experience. You see, Stu needs a lung transplant, NOW! Stuart is terminal and at this point he is not able in his own strength to do hardly anything at all. He carries his own medicine pack everywhere he goes, a big black bag that is dispensing his medication all day long through a port going into his heart; a pic line. He also has an automatic medicine dispenser pack that has tubes running in his body to supply ongoing medicines that are essential to him taking his next breath and living. He even has to keep the refills under ice with him at all times, too. Yet Stuart, in the strength of Christ, and by his own faith, was working. He did not let my mom get too far out of his sight. He was my mom's cheerleader. He was advising her, counseling her on medical needs as well as emotional support. Stu patiently listened to her when she just wanted to talk.

Stu has come so close to death himself so many times before; he was and is still an expert in living with hardships and medical issues. Yet Stuart was there giving all that he had! Serving, and loving on my mom, Rosa, and on my dad, Dan, supporting them. God had sent my mom her very own personal human angel. Stuart!

Oh, yes, can you see?

Yes, I saw the face of Jesus in Stuart. Can you see it now?

Stuart was there all of that first night, and all day the next day as well. He almost lived at the hospital for the first two whole weeks solid! This is a man who can only be out of his house but just a little while at a time because of his own sickness and fatigue, who now had a supernatural strength and extra special sense of compassion and giving, all the while expecting nothing in return! He was on a mission from God.

He still took care of me for many months after my release from Parkland. He would call; he emailed me continually to check on me. Stu came many times to help me and give me advice and support. There he was, so sick and needing a lung transplant, yet still serving me and serving my family weeks later when I was back at work!

Oh, yes, my friend, Stuart! I have seen the face of Jesus like you might never have imagined.

I have seen "the face of Jesus" on Larry Speck

My dear friend and boss, Larry Speck, the vice president of the company I was working for at the time of my accident, he was there in the emergency room that same night—he got there so lightning fast! Remember, I called him from the ambulance that night and left him a message.

What can I say about Larry except—Wow!

Larry came into the emergency room where there was so much blood all over the floor from the bleeding that they could not get stopped, and he stayed as close as they would let him. I only remember coming to for a second and seeing and hearing Larry's voice. Larry told me I came to when they cut my boot off in the emergency room and they were working on my foot. He says it was so funny. The doctor was working on the worst part of my foot and he said I rose up and said, *"Hey dude! That hurts!"*

Larry Speck, a boss, and a "leader of leaders" and my friend.

Larry was sent from Heaven above. Larry was on a "Divine Appointment" and he knew it! Larry knew what his task was and he was on it like white on rice. Larry, a man who dropped everything in his personal life and in his business life and came RUNNING in to serve me and my family and it all started that same Sunday night, November 9, 2008. He came to the hospital as soon as he got the message.

Larry jumped in immediately and started taking care of all my personal business matters that needed urgent attention. He is my "Business Angel." No one else had his business acumen to know what to do, and Larry jumped right in. He took care of the wrecked motorcycle; he went down to the police department and the city's impound lot, he took care of my wrecked motorcycle and the business with the City of Dallas. Larry got all of my personal belongings, which had been left in my saddlebags on my motorcycle.

Then Larry called and got the corporate attorney for our company (John Browning) working on my legal issues that had to be dealt with immediately. Larry was taking care of my personal business, hospital business, and insurance for the hospital, insurance for me as well as for my wrecked motorcycle. Larry was getting all my affairs in order in case I did not survive the accident. My life was on the line! Larry was gathering all the life insurance papers and everything that we just do not think about at times like that. Larry not only took care of my personal matters, he also took care of my whole family. Larry was there serving! Being the hands and feet of Christ. Not talking about it, but doing it! He was serving and there was no one to look at him and say, *"Hey, look at what Larry is doing."* Larry was doing all the hard, behind-the-scenes stuff, and never thinking of himself in return.

Larry is a true man of character and integrity, a man of faith! He took over my business, my dealership in Mesquite, which I was responsible for. Larry moved into my office just a couple of days later and took over my business as well! Larry, my friend, continued to come by the hospital; he called often for progress reports and updates, and he came by to see me over and over, not knowing if I would live or make it through. Yet Larry was there! He still was taking care of his own personal family responsibilities, taking care of his own job and doing my job, too. After I was released from the hospital and having my leg amputated, Larry not knowing if I even had the right mind or the drive in business to make it, still held my job open for me to return! Larry held down the fort at my dealership and housing display center where we had 18 model homes and a sales staff, finance office and construction crews. He ran my business for me. Larry was also the vice president over another nine dealerships just like mine, all scattered in Texas and Oklahoma. Yes, Larry Speck had his hands completely full!

Larry coordinated with my company, communicating with everyone at the company of well over 1,100 people to pray, and he updated them all continually. He got with Laura Wilson of Western Insurance, a division of our company. Laura immediately set up prayer warriors from her Houston office. She even had her sister here in Dallas sending people over to Parkland Hospital to help and pray for me. They were sending cards and letters of encouragement from people I never even knew.

Larry set up Steve Comstock of our parent company to see what the company could do to help with my mounting hospital bills right from the very first day. Steve was on it. Steve Comstock and American Homestar helped with a hospital bill that was astronomical. Steve Comstock and the CEO Buck Teeter, with Larry and Laura Wilson and all of the company Oak Creek Homes/American Homestar, Inc., immediately supplied over $47,000.00 to assist with all the hospital bills. Megan, the driver of the car that hit me, did not have nearly enough insurance to cover but just the first day of my hospital bill.

Larry set up even more prayer warriors still, at work and at his church, Lake Pointe in Rockwall, Texas, as well as people from all over the world. Larry was active in missions in Cuba. He even had the Cuban church and mission teams there praying for me! CUBAN Christians, praying for me? And I did not know any of them! Get that, people of Cuba praying for me here in Dallas, Texas.

I cannot even begin to tell you everything Larry did. I will tell you he did have faith in God and in me. He allowed me to come back to my position as the general manager of the dealership, a one-legged amputee in a wheelchair who still did not have all his senses about him yet. I was still struggling with short-term memory loss, cognitive and communication skills. I could not even remember anything about my computer except how to turn it on. I could not remember my passwords or e-mail address or anything. It all came back little by little, very slowly with the help of my business manager. Kim Stafford, at Oak Creek Homes who was so wonderful to me.

Larry made adjustments in my office for me to get in and out of the office, and to get to construction sites when I needed to. Larry was there to lead, guide and direct me. He did not see a disabled man; he saw a man with a heart, a passion to come back and recapture my life; a man who was driven not to take disability income and live off the system. Larry gave me the opportunity to be a complete man again, even though I was missing a part of my body. He believed in me, trusted me, and yes, he prayed a lot, too, I am sure. To me, Larry was not only an angel. He was the hands and feet of Christ. I could see God at work and Jesus on Larry's face.

Larry "The Boss" was serving me!

Oh, yes, and what a messenger God sent to me in Larry, a man on a divine mission from God above! A man who stayed on point all the way through until his task was completed over two years later after the first starting point!

Oh, yes! Larry, I have seen Jesus in your face!

Larry's Motorcycle Accident

Let me tell you more about Larry Speck. Larry was still surviving a serious motorcycle accident in March of the same year, 2008!

Larry was still walking with a cane and not long off walking with a walker while he was doing all that he did for my family and me. This man never stopped, never let up. He was working so hard just at getting back to his own life! This is the stuff I am talking about! Angels have a mission and they will achieve maximum results. They will achieve their goal! They will see the mission they are on all the way to completion! No exception and no excuses!

Larry was on his Harley and was riding with the Lake Pointe Riders, a motorcycle ministry and riding group from his church, when he had a terrible accident, just seven months before mine. Larry was flown in on a Life-flight helicopter to the same hospital I was in, Parkland Hospital in Dallas, approximately 60 miles from point of impact. Parkland is where they take all the serious trauma patients in North Texas.

Larry was in the exact same hospital room I was in, too, Room #222! Now, if you think that is amazing, wait until you read about Kyle Webb in a later chapter!

Larry had severe and life-threatening injuries, too. He broke his pelvis, among many other things that I am not aware of. I just know it was by the grace of God that he survived the same as me. Larry had been walking with a walker until I was admitted to the hospital with my injuries. Larry was still recovering from his trauma, and was maybe 80% mentally healed and 60% physically healed, as well. So the amount of strength Larry had to serve my family and me throughout my recovery was truly a miracle from God!

Can you see how God brings people into our lives at times when we have no idea who they really are and what they really do? Then God uses them to perform duties in a supernatural way.

Oh, yes, Larry Speck, a mere man was on a mission from God.

Larry had just gotten back from his mission trip to Cuba on a Friday night in March when he had his horrible accident the following Sunday. When the believers in Cuba learned about Larry's accident, they began to pray. The funny thing is, the next March, when I returned in my office working and healing in my wheelchair, Larry went to—guess where? On another mission trip to Cuba!

God used Larry in a mighty way. This time there were even more hugs and camaraderie with his people from Cuba, but on this trip Larry got to preach! Larry shared the miracle of his accident and the miracle of my accident with the Cuban church. God was using Larry and me both to strengthen the faith of the new church planted there in Cuba. The victories gave the Cubans great hope; they could see their prayers being answered and coming back now to minister to them, there in Cuba. They were affecting lives here in the USA. These prayers gave the Cubans a new purpose for their mission. The Cubans were now being missionaries to America, serving Larry and me both! And we were thousands of miles away in another country!

Oh, yes, Larry, I see Jesus in your face, my friend.

I love you so very much and I respect you and the character you display and live out!

Thank you, my friend, Larry Speck!

I could see God was all over; God was literally everywhere, in hundreds of people. I could see God in people from my church at Prestonwood and my Sunday school class; the people from Dallas Christian Singles, the people from my work and people from my past; my current and former employees, all coming and rushing in to serve. Wow.

That is why I had to write this book! I have to tell the stories or no one would ever know exactly what God does when tragedy strikes and you are a believer. He sends His angels all around you on every side and on every front with expertise that you would never even begin to imagine.

There was Rob Lowe

I saw the face of Jesus in Rob.

He was the leader of the band we went to see that fateful Sunday at Strokers, the day of the accident. Rob was also a member of the Dallas Christian Singles and Rob was there at the hospital day after day. He was one of the first people I remember seeing when I was regaining consciousness. I guess it was a drug-induced coma. Rob would come every day, even though I was unconscious. He was there, just sitting sometimes and praying, encouraging and talking to everyone.

Rob came to see me every day while I was in the hospital. I had been on a feeding tube for so long my body didn't know how to digest food. I would ask Rob to bring me something when they took the feeding tube out, and every time from then on he would bring me Chicken McNuggets from McDonald's down on the first floor of the hospital. They were always hot and fresh, and I wanted them so much! But I would get sick every time because my body had to adjust to eating food again. Still, Rob brought me chicken nuggets every time he came to see me. Rob would sit in my room and pray for me, often bringing other people with him and crack his corny jokes. But this guy Rob is the real deal. He was there serving relentlessly.

God used Rob because he was the venue for the day at Strokers. Rob was one of those tools, one of those instruments in "God's Holy Tool Box." God was using Rob and his music to reach lost bikers that day as well as to entertain them. Rob was not a biker but he played the biker scene.

We may be bikers for Christ but Rob is a "guitar player for the Kingdom."

Yes, I saw the face of Jesus on Rob. Not only then but still to this day.

He is sold out for the cause of Christ.

Mark Worrell

There was my friend Mark Worrell. Yes, I saw the face of Jesus on Mark, too. Mark was constantly at the hospital, spending numerous hours there, as did many other people. After I was released from the hospital, I was afraid to go to church by myself at first.

I didn't know how to get in the car and how I would get my wheelchair disassembled and loaded to the back of the car with one leg, then hop to the driver's seat to get in and drive to church. After all, I had only one leg. Then how would I hop from the back of my car to get my wheelchair out? Then I had to get it out of the car and reassemble it. Then get in it and wheel around! Can you see the difficulties of the disabled? I had NO idea myself, but *now* I know! Hey, I even have a whole new ministry now!

I thought there was no way I could get around a huge church with over 30,000 members and one million square feet under roof, then get three stories up to my Sunday school class. How would I have the strength to do all that and then wheel myself in from the huge parking lot all the way into the building, then get all over the church? There was just no way possible for me to do all of this! After all, I had just gotten out of the hospital after a few months' stay, and I was still very weak even though I thought I was Superman now.

Mark called early that first Sunday morning and said, "I am picking you up in two hours to take you to church." He came to the door of my home knocked and opened the door right on up. He helped me get in my wheelchair and pushed me out of the house and to his truck. He helped me get into the passengers side, then loaded my wheelchair into the back of his truck. Once we arrived at the church, he drove to the door. It was pouring down rain by this time, so he drove right up as close as he could get and he helped me out of the truck and into the wheelchair. He pushed me into the building as fast as he could in the rain. Then Mark ran out and parked the truck about 800 feet away from the door where I was and he ran in the pouring rain all the way back. With a church of almost 30,000 members, the church and parking lot were huge.

Then Mark was soaking wet, I mean soaked, all the way down to his underwear and his socks. He pushed me everywhere. He did this over and over and over again, week after week for a couple of months! There was never any thought that he was not going to be there! For Mark, this was his mission. This is what God led him to do. Mark had a mission to accomplish and he did it in high fashion, style, and commitment to do his part.

There were many times Mark would just show up at my door, standing six foot two, all dressed up in his crisp look with a big smile and cowboy hat, and say, "Time to get out of the house for awhile." Then off we would go to wherever Mark had in mind. It was sometimes to dinner and sometimes to friends' homes or sometimes just out for a drive. Mark was always being sure to keep me active and involved in life.

As I was recuperating and gaining my strength, I was learning how to take care of myself. However, God used my accident to grow Mark in his faith. Mark had such joy in taking care of me and knowing if it were not for him I would be doing it on my own. That made him so happy to know he was making a difference.

Mark gave of himself, his time, his gas, and his resources. He had such great satisfaction, knowing God was using him to bless someone else. Big, tough, strong Mark Worrell was just like Jesus; giving all he had to someone he had barely known before. We now were connected as lifelong friends. Before my accident, Mark was a good acquaintance and as he befriended and helped me through those first rough months, I got to see him grow in his faith.

Sounds like Fred my "Care Taker Angel" and Chad my "Trouble Grace Angel," doesn't it? God had placed new people in my life right before all this tragedy! God put His people in place. Not perfect men, just men.

Yes, I saw the face of Jesus all over Mark Worrell.

Mark had his mission and he was not going to let anything keep him from achieving his objective.

Mr. Rob Dorman

I saw the face of Jesus in Rob Dorman.

A friend, yes, another new friend in my life! Just like the others! Rob worked at Brinker International, the company that owns Chili's, Macaroni Grill and Maggiano's restaurants. Rob was a construction coordinator and supervisor of construction. He and Brenda Ross would bring food to the hospital when I was relearning how to eat. Yes, I had to learn how to eat. Rob and Brenda would bring a feast fit for a king! Then after I was released and was at home, he would just show up at my house, ring the doorbell, then come in and say, "Come on, we are going to lunch" (or dinner). He would help me into my wheelchair and push me out to his truck, load me, put me and my wheelchair in the back, then off we'd go. He would unload me, then wheel me into a restaurant, take care of me, order for me, pay for me, load me back up and take me home and get me settled in. He did this 20 or 30 times!

I got to see him grow in his faith. We would talk about his life and what he saw God doing through my accident and how so many people were being impacted, how all he wanted to do was to serve and to help. All the time, God was doing a work on Rob and inspiring his faith walk. Rob was so filled with the servant's heart.

Yes, now a big, six-foot, four-inch man with a soft, gentle heart, a real man's man, loved serving me! The love of Christ shone all over and through him, he was so happy to be giving and serving and to know that God was using him to make a difference in my life. He was proud of our relationship as we grew closer as men of God, and just as with my friend, Mark Worrell, we were relatively new acquaintances of just a few months before my accident. But God grew Rob and his faith, and Rob was happy to serve. His face was always glowing and always he had a big ol' Texas smile!

You could just see Jesus in Rob's face.

My Buddy Tom

I saw the face of Jesus on my friend, Tom Merricks. He knew that I could not get in his BMW; it was too low to the ground and I could not get in with a newly-amputated leg. He was my best friend, and we were always buddying around together. He knew I was going to be in a wheelchair for a long time, so Tom sold the BMW and bought a four-door truck so I could get in. He did this for me. He could get me in the truck and put my wheelchair in the back of the cab if it was raining or in the back of the truck on sunny days.

So many more!

I saw the face of Jesus on Michael Perron, my Singles Pastor, and Janelle Spearman. I saw the face of Jesus on GiGi, Rose, Ken Woods and Ken Hackman, and so many more people who touched my life through my time of recovery.

I can still see a special countenance on thousands of people's faces. I can still feel the presence of God when I am with them. I can sense the peace in everyone's demeanor. I see people serving with a purpose now like never before in their life.

Yes, I saw the face of Jesus on so many people!

I can now answer the question I asked you a couple of times earlier, how many people would be at your funeral?

The real question I should have asked is what will your eulogy be? What will your legacy be? What will be said about how you lived?

Well, if this accident is any indication at all, my answer now has changed from the time before. From what I have seen with my own eyes and experienced, God sent me so many people, that "It Just Blows My Mind!" I am still amazed by how many people showed up to the emergency room. Well over 100 people in just a few short hours on a Sunday night after 8 p.m. Past midnight they were still coming to the waiting room all night long and they stayed. I was unconscious in the emergency room and the operating room all night, and then in ICU, with no idea of what was going on at all!

They just kept coming and coming and coming and *coming*! The people did not ever stop. The biggest thing is, it was the people who I did not expect to be there! They were the ones coming out of the woodwork, running in late, late on a Sunday night still coming and staying for several months. Serving. Yes, I believe in angels. You can bet your bottom dollar on that one. Whether they were angels or people that were available to be used by God makes no difference. They were all there being the "Hands and Feet of Christ." But I know without a doubt I have seen real angels from Heaven as you have read in this book.

We never know just who or how many people our lives impact. We can only think of a few, but in reality there is a huge ripple effect. There are thousands! We just think we are going through life all by ourselves, living day to day, trying to be genuine, and trying to be a real Christian, listening to people then trying to help when we can. We then work at trying to encourage as many people as possible. We go to our jobs and try to be good employees, good bosses, and good workers. We go to church and try to learn and to contribute to the body of Christ.

We get involved in our community and civic events. We are just living a busy, normal life. Then **BAM**, when tragedy strikes, we are amazed at the lives we have impacted and how people want to give anything they can and they want to help us in any way possible; to serve us in whatever capacity is needed. It is all a GOD thing! The Holy Spirit is working through people when we have been investing in people for years and now, all of a sudden they are investing back in us. But it is not about us. They are serving God.

It is the most humbling experience ever! To know God is using you to impact lives.

I can't help but think about and be thankful for all the people who came to support my family while I was in the emergency room, and then the whole time I was in ICU and all through my recovery.

There were literally hundreds of people. I believe there were a couple of thousand people or more there, from the beginning to the end.

Yes, the hands and feet of Christ were in action!

Yes, I believe God's Angels surrounded us all.

My Legal Eagle Angel, John

My "Legal Angel" came running in. John Browning was right there, protecting my family, my assets and me. That attorney, who went to work for free, was John Browning—John was serving another brother in Christ and expecting nothing in return. He was there. God supplied a "Legal Angel" for me. He had lots and lots to do while I was there in the hospital, and then for two years afterward he worked and worked and negotiated and negotiated with all the hospitals and insurance companies. You see, we did not have enough insurance from Megan or on my motorcycle. The cost was so high we may have had enough money for a total of three or four days in the Intensive Care Unit or the emergency room and emergency surgeries that all started as soon as I rolled in the hospital door. Not to mention all of the doctors, etc.

So you want to tell me God will not supply our needs? What's wrong? Cat got your tongue on that one?

Yes, John had a very intense mission that was over two years long. You may say, "Nope, the Holy Spirit worked through John." I do not care what you call it. Really, it does not matter at all. It was God at work, The Holy Spirit at work and everyone falling in line and doing whatever there was to do.

God sent "experts" in their own career fields, so their natural born gifts and talents were definitely God-inspired in them from the very beginning many years ago. All of the people God sent to do their specific task seemed to have that gift as well as that profession!

Yes, God supplied experts in every field. From the first few minutes, John was on the scene late Sunday night and early the next Monday morning, working for

FREE! For ME! He took care of me while handling all of his other paying clients.

Each person God sent in assumed their roles and expertise and got to their tasks. *No one* was duplicating another! Each one had a specific mission and each one carried it out to completion!

My Sister Sharon

Oh, and there was my sister Sharon. I am at a complete loss for words here! This one makes me cry. I never knew just how much my sister loved me and I cannot in three books tell you all that she did.

There is so, so much! My older sister was taking care of my every need! She was coordinating everything from every angle, answering all the questions and making the real life and death decisions that had to be made in a split instant sometimes. There were surgeries that had to be performed immediately, consent forms to be signed over and over and over again. She was constantly tracking my mom down; it seems that when my mom would think all was ok and she could rest or just go get a cup of coffee then *bam*, another emergency surgery was needed. Mom had to sign the consent form. There were two or three times that the doctor himself went running through the halls of the hospital to track my mom down and get the consent forms signed. The doctor was not getting results fast enough from his staff and he knew it was a life or death situation, so he took off himself, running all through the halls of this huge hospital!

I have a question for you: how many doctors in a hospital as large as Parkland, who really do not even know you personally, will run out of the operating room where he is waiting for the approval and chase down a family member? This was amazing all in itself! You would have had to have been there to see the magnitude of just what happened at the time and in the urgency.

Sharon and my mom and making those life and death decisions in those first ten days and carrying them out!

Yes, I have seen the face of Jesus in Sharon, too!

There are hundreds more stories about Sharon I can tell you. She is a professional, master social worker and again, not only did God use her sister attributes, but He used her professional skills, too. She was navigating my case from a social worker standpoint as well as that of my loving sister.

Thank you so much, Sharon.

I see God in a whole new light today.

I now can see God at work everywhere, literally.

I have "Experienced God" in a whole new, awesome and powerful way. Yes, He is real. Yes! I have now seen and experienced the church in action as it was designed to operate, too.

Yes, I have seen angels in action. Yes, there were real angels sent from God above, and there were those people that God used in a mighty way, too.

Yes, I have seen the face of Jesus on faces just like yours!

I have almost touched the face of God…

…through His people.

25

John F. Kennedy and Parkland Hospital

Three years after the accident, I went back to Parkland Hospital. You know...that famous hospital here in Dallas where President John F. Kennedy was taken after he was shot back in 1963.

Yep, that's it, the same one. *I went in through the same emergency room doors, down the same halls to the same emergency room, and then into the same operating room.* It is like reading the Bible from Genesis to Revelation. In Revelation we know how the story ends, or as Paul Harvey said, "Now you know the rest of the story." Yes, I lived. I survived that dreadful night. I won in the battle of life and death. I survived by the grace of God and by His mercies. That night I received the greatest blessing ever. LIFE AGAIN!

The Adventurous Mischievous Boy

My mother gave birth to a chubby little fireball baby boy who would bring into her life lots of fun, love, laughter, and oh yes, hmm... I think I caused her quite a few tears, too. After all, I was a mischievous little boy! I really was a good boy, but I did have an adventurous side, too. I loved to laugh, play and have fun, but I also liked to see how things worked.

Hmm...what makes that wind-up clock work? How does that radio work? Hmm...I would take everything apart and see! I would always find a treasure. Now, what is that thing? How does it work? What makes the clock sound like tick and tock? How do those hands go round and round? How does that thing do that?

I had questions, questions and more questions and lots of answers to find. Yes, life was an adventure for me, even back then.

As I would be exploring the clock, I would hear my mother coming down the hall, looking for that clock! I would know I'd better put it back together and FAST, too! Okay, so what do I do with all of these leftover parts? Where can I put them? I know…under the bed! My mom would be looking for her clock or whatever it was at the time. I would pop up right out of nowhere and say, "I found your clock! Here it is." Yep, I was a mama's mischievous little helper, too (wink, wink). I told you I was a good boy.

Another adventure for me was my mom telling me that something was hot. Like a hot frying pan. My mom would say, "Don't you touch that! That pan is HOT!" "Hmmm…hot?" I would think to myself, "Oh, it can't be that bad. I think I will touch it real, real fast. Naaa…nope…that ain't that hot." So I would think to myself, "Let me touch it again! This time I will touch it just a little bit longer with my pointing finger." You know, the pointing finger. As we get older we learn the pointing finger is actually our index finger. Well, at my house we called it the pointing finger. I wonder why that is? Now, just who would ever point at anyone, anyway? Who, besides an angelic, mischievous, inquisitive, fun-loving, adventurous, chubby little boy, me?

You guessed it; I touched it again and OUCH! Yes, it was **H-O-T**!

Now, if you think the pan taught me a lesson about hot, or about listening to my mother…well, nope, not at all. It just made me stop and think a few seconds longer the next time I was told something was hot. As a matter of fact, let me tell you about that hot fire! Now, THAT was H O T! Okay, so now back to the story.

Introduction to Christ

My family and I went to church as I was growing up and I went to Sunday school, too. Did I tell you that I loved Sunday school? They had lots of neat stories, skits, plays, and games and, of course, snacks and red Kool- Aid!

Okay, okay…I know if you are younger than 30 years old you have no idea what Kool-Aid is. I always did like that glass Kool-Aid pitcher where you could see the ice inside the pretty, clear, curved glass pitcher; you could see all the way through it, and you could see how much Kool-Aid was left in it…for me! I liked that cool, curved handle, too! You may remember the TV commercial of the cartoon guy in the costume; he always had a pitcher of red Kool-Aid in his hands in the TV commercials. I really thought he delivered that red Kool-Aid to my mom. I even have one of those Kool-Aid pitchers to this day.

Okay, back to Sunday school. We went to church as I grew older into my teen years, and I never really heard about grace. We went to a strict, legalistic church back then. There were rules upon rules, and rules for the rules that the rules had to be followed. There began to be rules and things that I did not see in all of the Bible stories that I was taught in Sunday school. They only told us of The Ten Commandments and all the "thou shalt not's" and not about all the fun, exciting things you could do as a young child growing up.

In junior high and high school we had some do's and lots and lots of don'ts. As for me, being that little mischievous boy and becoming a teenager, I heard the word *"No"* an awful lot! I began to wonder if "No" was part of my name. "No-no!" "No!" *"No, you can't do that!"* *"No, you cannot go to the movie theater."* *"No, you cannot dance."*

"No, you cannot go swimming with girls….they wear bikinis!" Duh…yes, yes, I know!"

That is why I want to go swimming! **Hello.**

I liked to go swimming, yes, even with my guy friends, too. We would swing from the rope and dunk all the guys and we dunked a few girls, too. We would have chicken fights, where you fight with your buddy sitting on your shoulders. I just wanted to go swimming in general with all our friends, and the girls, they just made it fun.

Now let me explain an important fact. I really was not a swimmer; I was a water splasher and a game player. I was a great swimmer…only if rocks could swim! I would sink, just like a big ol' boulder or a rock. No, truthfully, more like a big boulder thrown into the water, landing with a huge splaaasssshhh, then plunging straight to the bottom, fast. Yep, that was me. I would try to dive in and instead I would do that good ol' belly flop!

Ouuucccchhhhh!

Anyway, no…No!!! No dancing allowed. *"If you go dancing you are going to Hell!"* Like in the game Monopoly. No stopping at Go, and no collecting $200.00. Just going straight to Hell.

Now I knew Hell would definitely hurt worse than the belly flop. I knew Hell was super-hot, high-intense fire and it would hurt worse than that hot frying pan. And no, I will never forget that fire, I just had to test out. To see how hot it was. Oh, that fire! Ohhhhh…and let me tell you how hot! That fire was HOT, HOT, HOT!

Burning Down The House!

By the way, I did burn the house down when I was three or four years old, too.

So I can tell you all about hot fire and playing in the gas space heaters. I loved to light up and run with my flaming Olympic torch waving with its long, beautiful, smoking flame trailing behind me as I ran all through the house with my Superman cape on. I saw it all on the cartoons.

Well, I ran until the fire got too close to my hand and I felt how hot it was. Then I ran into the bedroom that I shared with my three other brothers and *I threw my hot flaming Olympic torch behind my bed*, so no one would find it! YEP, that flaming torch was now burning behind my bed. So you guessed it, the whole house went up in flames. I burned down the house!

Growing up and going through my high school and college years, I came to the obvious conclusion I was a sinner and I was going to Hell.

I could not keep all the rules. I loved church and I liked the girls and having fun with my friends. I was good most of the time but I was a teenager, so I made some not-too-good choices sometimes. I had heard so many times before, "You are going to Hell if you do not abide by the rules of church membership and the advice to members completely. After all the Church is the bride of Christ." I got the message I was going to Hell, my brother was in prison and our church friends all abandoned us so, oh well, *I might as well have as much fun as I can now before I get to Hell!*

So come on, where are the girls? Let's rock 'n roll! Where's the party? The party was now on! And it went on…and on…and on. Yes, it was a lot of fun for a few years. At first I had a BLAST! But then the realism set in; it was all catching up with me after just a few months. All of that fun and partying, the friends and doing things my way was no longer fun. After a few years the consequences of my actions were all around me. Through my own selfish ambitions I had begun to hurt my friends and my family.

No, I never did any drugs; I just lived my life my way in the "Fast Lane."

As I got older, I did pretty well for myself in the business world. I actually became a good businessman, too. However, I was still on my own journey, living my life my way. I was living the good life, fast and furious. Now, I did have lots of fun. But I was accumulating so much baggage all along the way! However, some of the business deals I did really were selfish for me. I was not always looking out for the welfare of others. Business was about making money. So the party did continue to go on from the time I was approximately 19 years old until I was 39. I had a party for approximately 20 years! I had way overstayed my welcome. I did not just have baggage, now I had several sets of luggage bags all filled up and stuffed in the closet.

Today

Today I live in a suburb of Dallas in a community called Rockwall/Heath, Texas. I attend Lake Pointe Church (it's a Baptist church). Yes, there has been lots and lots of restitution; I had to get busy. I had phone calls to make, people I had to go see eyeball to eyeball. With some people I had to just sit awhile, explain what I did and why and ask their forgiveness, and explain what was going on in my life. Some of them were Christians, but most of them were not. Yet, I had wronged many people through those 39 years.

Over time, as people from my past surveyed my life, they knew something had happened to me. I was no longer the same. It was an awesome relief for me to go see people I knew and had wronged and say, *"Hey, I have to make restitution here!"* I lied to you, I hurt you, or I cheated you. I had to face as many people as I possibly could. I could not possibly see everyone; I could only see those I could find, and the ones God laid on my heart. There were just way too many people in all those 39 years to remember each and every one of them, so I had to accept my grace.

I now know that I live under the grace dispensation, the sacrifice of Jesus, and not under the umbrella of legalism. The do's and don'ts of legalism do not exist for me anymore. But I do try to live a righteous and pure life. I do try to love like Christ. I no longer want to do anything hurtful, because I know that if I do, it will hurt my relationship with Christ, and my peace with Him. I choose not to do things so I do not hurt my wife, or my kids, or my grandkids.

I choose everything. There are no rules only choices. For the first time in my adult life, I know Jesus loves me. Jesus died for Phillip…ME! Can you say that? If not, you know what I am going to say next; pick up the phone now and call me, no matter what time it may be, or email me, or contact a Bible-teaching church right there close to you.

The Gift of Life Again

Wow. What a night. November 9, 2008! At Parkland Hospital I received the blessing to live again. I really received the gift of life!

I hear it said that three times is a charm! This new life will be a whole new journey with new excitement, new challenges as well, too. However, at least I made it all the way through. I made it past all of the surgeries and out of Intensive Care to *room #222.*

John F. Kennedy

President John F. Kennedy's life journey ended just a few feet from where I was given another chance at life here at Parkland Hospital in Dallas, Texas.

We went in the same emergency room door and the same hallway and into the same emergency room. JFK and I both stared directly into the face of death. I was given a whole new life again at 49 years old. Ten years after accepting Christ, I was given a gift from God, *life* again.

President Kennedy and I had both come to an impasse! What a thought! A life lost and a life given! Both of us were in the exact same place. You would think God would save a man as important as the President of the United States, and a regular ol' Joe's life like mine could be taken instead.

That is just the way God is. You never know just what His plan may be for our lives. We may think, *I am just a regular person, and I am not of any real significance,* I have no real importance. But God has a plan we know not of.

Room #222

My first hospital room when I was released from Intensive Care after those first two weeks was room #222. WOW. That is the same room my friend Larry Speck was in back in March 2008 when he had his motorcycle accident. Later, I found myself going back to that same room #222, to see my new friend, Kyle Webb.

All three of us, three men, three motorcycle accidents, all rushed in by either Life Flight or by ambulance, all of us seriously injured, Phillip, Larry Speck and now Kyle. Wow. I wonder about that. What is the significance? Maybe it's the number three? Maybe it's all three going to Parkland Hospital? Maybe it's three motorcycle accidents? Maybe it's all three injured with life and death injuries, but all three of us staying in room #222? Maybe all three of us having a whole new outlook on our lives. What do you think? I would like to know. There may be no significance at all but it surely is something to think about if you are one of us three men. Okay, let me tell you "the rest of the story," as Paul Harvey would say. Then you will have more pieces to this puzzle.

Room #222, Again

My wonderful bride Erika was looking at the list of prayer requests at church for the week. Donna Webb had requested prayers for her nephew, Kyle Webb. Kyle was in the hospital and had just had his leg amputated, OUCH! I know that one all too well. We went on to our Bible class and then sat through the sermon by our assistant pastor, Todd Phillips, at Lake Pointe. We went to lunch and then I called the hospital and asked for Kyle Webb's room. When the operator said, "Room #222, Sir," I could hardly believe it! That was my room!

With a big lump in my throat and my heart skipping a beat, I had to stop and take a minute to catch my breath. I made the call to his room and talked to Kyle's wife. I told her who I was and that I was an amputee, and, as a matter of fact, that I had been in that same room some two and a half years prior. We talked for a few minutes and I told her we would try to come see Kyle the next day, which was Memorial Day, Monday, 2011.

Tomorrow came…wait did I say that? "Tomorrow came." I guess I have to tell you that's what I always say…tomorrow…because I am always starting a diet "tomorrow"…and when the next day comes, my daughter Emma says, "I thought you were starting a diet today?" I would tell her "No, Emma, no, that's TOMORROW, not today."

Tomorrow came and we entered the hospital foyer through the big revolving door, and walked past the reception desk, down the main hallway and stopped to use the restroom. My son Christian and I had come out and we were waiting for Erika. While we were waiting in the hall, a family was looking at me and staring at my prosthetic leg. They were about to pass by us when the man stopped all of a sudden. He looked down directly at my prosthetic leg and said, "Can I ask you a personal question?" "Sure," I said. He asked, "Um, how do you do with that prosthetic leg? I am only asking because my son just had his leg amputated and I want to know what to expect." I asked him what his son's name was and he said, "Kyle Webb." I said, "Hello, Mr. Webb, that is who we came to see." I explained that Erika saw it in our church bulletin in Rockwall and he said, "Yes, my sister goes to church there." "Well, that is why we are here, to introduce ourselves to him, and to try to give him encouragement." With huge smiles way bigger than Dallas on his and his wife's faces, he said, "Well, you can just follow me on up."

Isn't it amazing how God works? All of these pieces of the puzzle, finding out about Kyle and the time we chose to go, then the timing of his family coming in at the same entrance to this massive, humongous hospital all at the same time.

We followed them on up, and had a nice conversation as we went down the hall and up the elevator. Then we arrived at room #222.

My heart skipped a beat. I had millions of thoughts running through my mind. My heart, mind, and emotions all were racing! We went on in and looking at Kyle as he lay there with no leg, at first glance he looked just like me in the face 25 years ago! But mostly he really looked just like my oldest son, Jeremy, who lives in Bossier City, Louisiana, who is 29 and yes, he is a biker, too.

As I talked to Kyle, he asked me some questions and I answered as best I could. But my mind and heart kept pounding. I wanted to put him at ease and give him encouragement. But my mind was racing from being back in the same room for the first time since my accident. It was all coming back to me. I really was thinking and reminiscing more about my own stay in that room.

I wanted to let Kyle know that God had spared his life for a reason and a purpose and now was the time to search for that purpose and not to have a pity party and feel sorry for himself, like 99% of amputees do. I just wanted to give him the source for my hope. We go through all kinds of things in life to be able to bless others, so please look at where you are and what gifts God has blessed you with. For me it is an amputated leg and the gift of life extended, as well as a salvation experience 13 years ago! The visit was only about ten minutes long but it was great. To come back and to remember so many great things about that room and how God blessed me and left me here a little longer! I could remember seeing so many things for the first time again. I remember seeing God do mighty and awesome things in that room. I was reenergized to the fact that I have responsibility to bless and encourage others with my blessing of life again, in room #222.

You have the responsibility to bless others with the blessings that you have been given!

<((><

My Wonderful Angel Bride

"The Chase!" It Never Ends!

This angel I had *to chase!*

I was sitting in the restaurant area at church called the commons/atrium at Prestonwood Baptist Church. We have a restaurant and a Starbucks in the church, too. It is way cool. So this is where we go to lunch after our Sunday morning service.

The Zig Ziglar Factor

I looked over at the table where Zig usually sat. He always sat at the same table every Sunday with his Encouragers Bible study class and I did the same. I sat with my class at the next table over. We had the same tables, side by side, for several years. I looked over and Zig was still there. It was about 1:30 p.m., and everyone was wrapping up and going home. I went over to say hello to Zig. I had not had a really good personal conversation with him for quite awhile. I thought this was a good time for me to set up an appointment in the next week or two so we could meet and have a good heart to heart talk. I needed some of his advice!

I was reasonably confident I would get an appointment with him because Zig always took the time, no matter how busy he was. I did not want to hold him there at that moment. I wanted a good 30-45 minutes with him later in the next week or two.

I really had missed talking to Zig while I had been in Kansas City for the past year with my job transfer, and I was happy to be back home for good. As soon as I asked him for an appointment he invited me to sit down and said, "I have all afternoon, it is just me and the Redhead today."(Everyone who has ever heard Zig knows that is what he calls the love of his life. His wife, Jean, is The Redhead!)

We discussed my return from Kansas City where I had met John Caton. John had been a good personal friend to Zig for a long time, and it was a "God thing" that he and I just happened to meet while in the business world in Kansas City. John and I were both taking care of our own businesses and in time John and I had hatched a plan to possibly work together on a major business project. We worked hard, negotiated a plan and worked out all of the details; however, we nixed the deal at the very last minute. It just was not in God's timing for us. John is another man like Zig. John is a man of character, integrity, drive and ambition; a professional with a great personality and a wordsmith/communicator, too.

Zig and I were talking about my new career goals when he asked me, *"When are you going to write that book?"* As usual, I told him I am not a writer. He then asked, "When are you going to start speaking on the platform?" I told him I did not have that talent or gift. Again, Zig the encourager gave me a really good pep talk to start writing and speaking and we then finished our talk on business. He began to ask me point-blank some personal questions in his loving, gentle, kind yet professional, authoritative and personable way. That's what I really wanted to discuss with him all along, my personal life! We were discussing life. Life in Kansas City and life back in the North Dallas area of Plano/Frisco. In this conversation we had some pretty frank discussions! We discussed why I was happy, yet not really achieving the personal goals that I wanted to achieve in my own life, and yes, we discussed some of my bad decisions and misjudgments, too!

Well, I really had a great conversation from that moment on! Honestly, it was a listening session for me. He had lots to say and that is what I really needed at the time, honesty from Zig.

Zig is a gentleman; however, he also can be very matter-of-fact and get right to the point, too! He can get directly to the point in a very nice and encouraging way and he does not mince words, either. He has always been the same to me. He just always shoots it straight to you. No sugar, just the hard, cold facts sometimes. The thing with Zig is, what you see is what you get! There are *not* two Zig Ziglars, from what I have experienced in my relationship with him. There is only one, the same man you see and have grown to love and admire. He treats everyone the same way.

He will take time with anyone and try to guide them through and help them to make better decisions. He seems to live to impact lives, to encourage people and see them thrive in their personal life, as well as in business. He believes in a fully balanced system of faith, family and business, keeping Christ first in business as well as at home. He is always exactly the same man in person as you see him on the platform.

As we were talking, Zig got right to the point and asked, "Phillip, how old are you now?" I replied I had "just turned 49."

"Now, just why have you not married yet?" Ouch, Zig! Touchy subject!

I answered his question with all of my good Christian, Godly, and church knowledge and book/seminar relationship wisdom. After all, being a Christian for 10 years now, I had been reading all of the books and studies on relationships, the single life, and finding a Godly mate. Oh, yes, and I went to all the seminars, Song of Solomon, Love Languages, etc. I seemed to have all the right answers and I had it all down with every "i" dotted and "t" crossed! It all sounded so perfect in all of my responses, as far as me giving him the textbook answers and textbook ways of remarriage in a Christian environment. Now, if only there were a remarriage test, I could take it and make 100% every time, too!

Zig just sat there and smiled as he listened to me talk (as he always does) or I should say my meaningless rambling. He finally had heard enough of my reasoning! Then quietly and calmly, with his methodical body movements I could tell he was getting ready to get right straight to the point. He said, *"Phillip, we were not designed to live alone, unless we are called to live as single people. The reason I see for all of your personal problems is you are missing the other half of you."* As he went on into the creation story of Adam and Eve and the helpmate scenario, he pointed out that he is the man he is only because of Jean or, as he calls her, "The Redhead." His advice was simple. Pray about God leading me to my helpmate and then listen and keep my eyes wide open and watch to see what God is doing.

Zig has this concept that he believes we all should have "The Home Court Advantage." Keep Christ in our homes and family relationships. He liked to talk about courting his Redhead. How blessed to have the love of your life and at his age (at the time, he was approximately 81) still in love! Talk about "The Home Court Advantage," ZIG LIVED IT!

Zig Ziglar passed away approximately 6:00 am on November 28, 2012, here in Plano, Texas. The "Home Court Advantage" was a lifelong commitment and Zig celebrated it right up to his last breath here on this earth and his first breath in Heaven. He and "The Redhead," as he calls her, celebrated their 66th wedding anniversary two days before he went to Heaven. He had Jean and all his kids there, Julie, Cindy and Tom, while he made that journey. Yes, as Julie says, "*How sad for us, but how happy I am for dad,*" to finally reach his goal. As Zig taught us for over 40 years in his "Born To Win" seminars, you have to plan to win, prepare to win, then and only then can you expect to WIN. Well, Zig WON. He got to see Jesus face to face on that day. My family and I were so privileged to get to spend a few hours with Zig and the family a day or two before he left, and today I have my most precious picture of him and me taken that last day. There are no faces in those pictures; just me holding Zig's hand.

So you ask me if I believe in "The Home Court Advantage"? Well, I have seen it modeled and lived out right before my eyes. So YES, I believe. The only court better than that is the courtyard of Heaven.

My List

After that meeting we had in the early spring of 2008, I began to start evaluating my list that same day. Ok, I know I better start striking things off my list of requirements. The problem was that I was still in control of my own list. I really needed to give up my list and let God do His thing. Ok, but this is the beginning stages.

Here was my list:

Number one, she had to be sold out to Christ and God had to be her #1 priority.

Then came all of my requirements. She had to be short and pretty, 5' to 5'2," she had to have dark hair and nice, dark, smooth skin; she had to be really sweet, nice and polite with good manners; she had to be smart, intelligent and articulate. We had to be able to discuss God, church, family, kids, business and sports.

She had to like riding motorcycles and ride with me sometimes. She had to be active and athletic. She had to like flying in airplanes, boating and water sports. She had to like Christian music, not drink at all or smoke at all. She had to have a nice, calming voice. She could not be a hollerer or a screamer. She had to be able to discuss our personal issues as they came up and not let them build and fester up.

*I did not want a woman who was a "**history major,**" someone always bringing up* *my past history of all my flaws and mistakes, things like "you said….you did…," etc. I am sure you get the idea of what my list was like!*

I did not want a woman with kids!

My son Jeremy was all grown up and I had a grandson now, Cameron. So I did not need to get back in that kids game again.

So, as you read this, let me ask you, what was your list like? Or what IS your list like?

I know what you are thinking, *this guy is a jerk!* Naa, I am baring all my heart and soul here remember. So honesty has to be transparent.

Back to Rebuilding a New Life

My accident happened in November of 2008, the same year I had that conversation with Zig, and all I can say is my perspective changed. Now, since my accident I was happy just to be alive! It seems that now all my wants, needs and cares had changed. For the rest of 2008, I was in Parkland Hospital.

After being released from Parkland and getting back to my life in the winter of 2009, I was adjusting to being a new amputee. Having only one leg was a major adjustment. I was trying to get back to having a normal life, trying to be productive in my job. After all, I felt I'd better do well because who wants to hire a one-legged man in a wheelchair or a walker, hopping around the office or on construction sites? I was trying to get used to my new way of life.

There were some major fundamental changes for me. I was now disabled as an amputee. I was still on the walker/hopper. Yep, as you can see, I am a short, fat, one-legged man on a hopper. So now I have a new requirement on my wife list!

I now knew what her name was to be, too. I needed her name to be "I'lean," so I would have someone to lean on, my I'lean and me! Oh, yes, and if you and I are going to breakfast, please let's not go to…I-Hop! After all, I-hop all the time now! Hahaha! Truth is truth, no reason to sugarcoat it. Just have fun and go with it.

Now for me the walker was really my hopper. Hey, Hop-along Cassidy! Yes, a one-legged man has to hop, then slide that walker forward right on up a little bit and hold on tight, because you've got to hop again!

What a mode of transportation, one hop at a time. I needed to change my name to I-Hop!

Naaa…no, no, hopscotch is not a game for me! Now I got to play hopscotch all day long but I never seemed to win! I was always playing all by myself, too, and that is no fun. Or, I could sing that Easter bunny song…"Here comes Peter Cottontail, hopping down the bunny trail, hip-pity, hop-ity, Easter's on its way."

Hey. Life is good. We have to laugh! Yes, I do laugh at myself an awful lot, too. You just have to roll with the flow. I was really happy to be a hopper. I was alive, and yes, I can take myself lightly and not have a chip on my shoulder! It is what it is, so let's have fun and go with it! I did have a wheelchair to use, too. I would have to use it sometimes…well, most of the time. However, a walker/hopper helped me to gain strength and balance as well as agility, so I would hop as much and as far as I could. Then, when I'd get tired, I would get in my wheelchair and wheel it around awhile.

Now, if you really want some funny stories, I can tell you quite a few about people and being disabled! Like, the view is surely better hopping behind someone standing up, rather than the view sitting down in a wheelchair. I always seemed to get the rear end of the deal. Yes, the view is completely different down here.

The Chase is on!

Around March or April of 2009 I began to see a picture of this beautiful lovely blonde-haired lady, who had the most beautiful eyes and a perfect smile. She was on the meet-up group website for "Dallas Christian Singles." DCS is not a dating site but a Christian connection calendar of events. I looked at her picture and thought, Hmmm…*I like her. She is cute! No dark hair but I just love those pretty eyes and that nice beautiful smile is all too captivating. But I am just a short, fat, one-legged guy on a hopper trying to survive and get back to life. Who would ever want that?*

Oh, well, hey, I am just as happy as I can be. But wow! She sure is cute! Nice to have a dream anyway! Especially since I now have a new lease on life and I have a new journey. I am going to have a lot more fun and I am going to enjoy it to the max, too.

I am going to laugh more, smile more, dream bigger and reach for the stars. Hey, I might even grab me one of those stars up there and pull them down here, too.

A short time later, in May, at La Madeline's restaurant at the Park and Preston intersection in Plano, we were at the same assistant organizers meeting for the group and I wanted to go and meet this girl. I arrived a little late with my new prosthetic leg. "Hey, hey, hey!" as Fat Albert would say. "Got me a new leg!" I was just beginning to learn how to walk again. And when I say, "learn how to walk," that is exactly what I mean! It was a job, so yes; I was now on my walker, one slow step after another slow step. I went in the front door, all the way through the lobby and the restaurant, all the way to the very back into the meeting room. I opened the big, old, heavy wooden door and…there she was!

The girl in the picture!

She was there! Sitting in the back of the room at the end of the long table, and I was on the other side of the room at the opposite end of the table. I was just in front of her so I could look at her all through the whole meeting. As the meeting progressed I could look over at her any time I wanted to. I watched her mannerisms, listened to her when she spoke, and when she started making suggestions and asking questions, I thought, "Hmmm, I like this girl. She is a smart chick and very pretty. She is articulate, nice, polite, and I love that beautiful smile. Hmmm…

After the meeting was over I sat there thinking, *I'm going to make my way over* and…

NOT!

That really was not a good idea for me, in a small meeting room that was full of people and furniture, and me a guy on a walker trying to navigate through the people and the obstacles, not to mention all of the other guys in the room had the same idea. They were on their way to her before I could even stand up! Whoosh! You could feel the swirling of the air as the guys flew right on by me. They were gone! After all, she was the newbie of the day and the herd of single men was lining up. They were on their way over to check her out! Me too, they just beat me to the punch!

I did mix and mingle for awhile, and then I went on home. I'd had a good day. Then I thought, "I think I will send her an e-mail" and…she replied! Erika was putting together an event at Rockwall. Now I had an opening line! I was looking at doing exactly the same thing! Free concerts at Lake Ray Hubbard at "The Harbor." Now, in the world of single parents, a free event always draws a crowd. That is the magic word—FREE.

I texted her a couple of times, starting a line of communication, and she replied. She was getting ready to leave on a trip to New Mexico; it was a singles family trip. So I texted her a couple of times while she was on her trip, just to get her attention and keep open that line of communication. After she got back to town the next week, she was hosting her event with her church, Lake Pointe in Rockwall. It was a free Chris Tomlin concert. (There's that word free again.) So there was a huge turn-out from the church and the community as well as the meet-up group of the DCS.

I arrived for the concert about three hours early at Harry Meyers Park. I had to park my car as close as I could and I knew I would have a long, slow walk. I waited in my car for awhile, reading a book and waiting for time to pass. The people started arriving and it was getting close to time for the concert to start, so I texted Erika to see if she had made it there yet. "No, I am on my way." She gave me instructions where to find the spot on the grass where we all would be sitting; close to the sound engineers' booth.

I put the fold-up chair in my bag and slung it over my shoulder and it was off to the races. I went as fast as a turtle could go! I was slowly racing just as fast as I could go on my new prosthetic leg and my walker. I was so proud of my new $27,000.00 leg with my motorcycle graphics! Let me tell you it was a cool-looking leg, too. You know me—one of a kind!

I was taking one short step at a time in the grass. I was not used to walking on grass or any terrain at all. It was all a new experience and it was totally different from walking on a solid surface. About 15 minutes later I finally arrived at the spot where a normal person could have been in about two minutes.

By the way, just so you know, a prosthetic foot has no feeling in it. It is a German foot made of steel and titanium with a rubber coating on it and shoved into a shoe. So you really don't know how solid a footing or surface you are on as you take a new step. There is even more uncertainty on the grass. Talk about a faith walk, this was definitely a "prayer walk" for me.

When you are placing your foot down and not feeling the ground beneath you, you are feeling the spike of pain in the nub of your leg from all of your weight on the amputated stump pushing down in the cup of the bezel of the boot of the leg that has a foot attached to the bottom. The newly-cut amputated stump at the bottom of what leg you have left is where the weight goes to support you in the prosthetic leg. Now, that takes some major concentration at first.

With each step you feel the pain on your leg and you don't feel that nice, soft, grassy terrain beneath you. Then you take a step on your good leg and your brain has to adjust to the right foot landing perfectly normally, sending the all-ok signal to the brain and all the right signals saying, *all is well; you can take another step now,* and then the pain of another step on the prosthetic leg again, and so on.

Yes, it is a major learning experience! But I am alive, and now I get to walk! I get to stand up! I get to look people in the eye! I can feel like a man again! Not that I didn't feel like a man; it's just a new learning and adjustment phase. And it felt so good to be able to stand up and walk! And yes, I was so proud of myself! My chest stuck out a little, my shoulders were pulled back; I walked as tall as I could—well, as tall as a short guy can stand up! However, no one could see the pain of walking. I looked as normal as I possibly could on a walker!

I got there, opened up my fold-up chair and started looking for Erika to arrive. I was watching the guys set up the stage for Chris Tomlin. As I sat there, I kept looking at the way for Erika to arrive. Then I saw her! She was way across the park, walking in my direction. She was wearing a light-colored, almost-white sundress with a brown stripe at the very bottom. The dress would sway to and fro as she walked. It would flow with each step she took. I saw her as she approached the wooden walkover bridge, and I just watched her. I looked and I thought, "Now that is what I want...PERFECT!"

For me the thought brought hope that someday God would bring a special lady like that into my life. Knowing all along that she would have no interest in a short, fat, one-legged guy, I still said "Lord there she is! Send me one just like that. PERFECT!"

The concert was awesome, lots of fun and fellowship. The next event Erika scheduled was at The Harbor on the Lake the next Thursday night. Hey, I am going to that, no matter what! And I am going to walk, too, with no walker! I arrived and was walking on my own for the very first time. Really....truthfully...I was wobbling, bobbling, and walking like a duck, but I thought, "I am walking and I look good!" It was a very nice evening and before the concert we all went sailing on a huge sailboat called The Sea Wolf, docked at The Harbor. I was determined, so I went on the boat without my walker! I was walking on my own for the first time. I was so excited! I know I had a smile on my face as big as all of Texas!

We boarded The Sea Wolf sailboat and off we went, sailing with Captain Scott. We went aboard the huge handmade catamaran that Scott built himself. It was nice! Here, take a look for yourself, *www.sailwithscott.com.*

"The Closer" is Moving In!

Erika was busy being a social butterfly and making her rounds on the boat, and I loved just sitting there and watching her.

It was a thrill to see her get around, talking to everyone, taking pictures, laughing, smiling, and, oh yes, by this time a guy had started to move in. Okay, no name here, but an acquaintance in the DCS group was making his play. He was putting the close on this girl. I thought, *Hmmm…I'd better move quickly before he closes the sale!* (Oh, I'm sorry—before he steals her heart!)

Now the closer, as we will call him, was a great guy and I knew it. He was a very nice guy, professional with good manners and skills, too. And buddy, he was working it hard! But then she came over to where I was. A-haaa. Then she sat down with me! Mmm. Erika and I talked a few minutes, and then here comes the closer! He was coming over, working his game, turning on the charm, smiling that big-ol toothy smile and closing the deal. Erika said to him as she sat there with me, "Hey, take a picture of us together!" *Wow…*I was now in hog Heaven (and I do not mean HARLEY hog Heaven, either!). Yes, there it is, another one of those Texas colloquialisms. Hog Heaven. To this day, that is my favorite picture! She and I, sitting on Scott's sailboat on Lake Ray Hubbard at The Harbor in Rockwall, with the water and sun in the background, her beautiful smile and that blonde hair blowing in the wind. Erika sitting right beside me!

After The Sea Wolf docked at The Harbor, we went up and had dinner at an outdoor restaurant, called Dodie's, there at The Harbor. Here, take a look at The Harbor, too. *www.theharboratrockwall.com.* Nice, isn't it? That is home, this is where we live.

We sat at a table of four. I was across from Erika and got to look directly across the table at her, right into her beautiful eyes, while the closer sat beside her! Now, Zig! I have to say I did learn from you. "Sit across from your prospect; look them straight in the eye! Eye contact—that is what closes the sale! Listen. Pay attention. Read their body language. Be calm, cool, still; slow motions when you move; be patient; be positive, use your manners and smile." After all, I had the eye contact! I was in the power seat now!

We were all having a good time and a great conversation. Then the closer piped up and said, "Phillip, you are a grandpa, aren't you?" Now, if looks could kill, well, he would definitely be…injured, for sure! Maybe even an amputated leg or something like mine. I said, "Yes, I am," knowing that he was the same age I was but he had teenage daughters, and they were the same age as Erika's kids. And that makes me the old grandpa. At this point I did not know Erika was ten years younger than we were; however, I knew he was eliminating the competition—me. Even though I was really no competition. After all, I was the one-legged guy! Hey. Gimme a break here!

The Toga Party

The next time I saw Erika was about a week later I think, and you will not believe it…all right, we were at a Toga Party! The ladies were having a ladies night out at one of their homes. It was a toga-themed party and the guys were having a guys night out. We really were just wasting time so we could catch up with the girls later on! We were talking, laughing, playing pool and watching a ballgame. There we were, everyone was just waiting, watching his watch and looking for a clock, checking the cell phones for a text or a sign that we could come on over! We were all getting together later that night at the ladies' toga party. We guys did our thing, just killing time, waiting. Then, finally, someone got the all clear! We all loaded up and headed to the parking lot. We were lined up like a train, headed out. This was a private invitation only, so most of us did not know where we were going. We had to follow the leader and the leader was a little lost, too. This was another DCS event, and it was neat! After all, I had never been to a Toga Party.

All the ladies were dressed in their Greek toga attire. Yes, you got it, bed sheets ripped up and sewn together!

They were all decorated and wrapped around with their leafy crowns. They were all adorned like Greek goddesses! Really, it was pretty neat! They all were stunning. They looked beautiful. And the guys, well, we just showed up, like we were the Toga Party crashers! It was a neat and fun event. I walked in—oh, I am sorry, I hobbled in on my prosthetic leg and walker/hopper, and there she was on the other side of the room. She never even noticed I was there. Well, at first, anyway. I found a nice, comfortable, strategic place to sit and talked to everyone. But she was in the house, and I kept my eagle eye out for her, too!

The night went on and it was a lot of fun. Later I found out that night that one of the ladies there, Olivia, said, "Erika, what do you think about Phillip?" I never did get Erika's response! Then, on her way home, one of her friends, Tiffany, who rode with her from Rockwall, said, "Erika, what about Phillip?" All right! Wow! Two unpaid, unsolicited endorsements in one night! YEE HA!

I am sure she must have thought, "But he is short! And he has only one leg!" I really don't know exactly what ran through her mind, but God was working for me! YEE HA!

I knew no one really wanted what I had to offer. However, when I quit the doing and dropped the list then **Bam**! God comes on the scene! Did I say **Bam**? Let me say it so you can hear it—**BAM**! God shows up!

What List?

Do you remember my list? I did not want a woman with kids. Well, Erika had two kids and she was not anywhere close to the physical description I listed. But when the list went out the window, God took control!

I turned loose of the reigns and let God be God. I was happy to be alive, but I sure would like to find the love of my life! And…that I did! Here is what I did.

First, I threw that list out the window!

The Chase is On!

Erika was going on vacation the next week to Atlantic City where Doc Block and her mom (whom we all call Oma) Brunie Block, own a nice house on Chicken Bone Beach. Yes, that is a real beach in Atlantic City, "Chicken Bone Beach." You know I could not make that one up. Erika was going to be gone for a whole week! And I LOVED it!

Okay, I thought, I've got to keep her busy, get her attention while she is captive away from Dallas and Rockwall, away from all da' playas, so none of the other guys can get their foot in the door. Oh, yes, I forgot all the other guys have two legs and two feet, and I only have one foot! Okay….I'd better get my foot in the door, and now!

I saw the opportunity to get my groove on. (Oh, no! Here I go, showing my age!) I started making a play. The chase was on. I started closing the sale! I was doing the assumptive close. I assumed while she was gone that the other guy pursuing her would be busy, so I assumed I could take advantage of the situation. I knew I had one week to capture her heart. That was it, I had only one week, so I'd better get a plan and get that plan in motion, fast!

I started by sending her a text message; then she texted me back. WOO HOO!! I texted her again, she texted back again! I sent another text, and she texted back! I like this; it's like tennis. Boop—ball in your court; boop, ball in my court, boop,

boop, boop. It was a texting volley. Okay, that was one test text, then a confirmation text. Then the game is on text. (I still have copies of all those texts for one whole week, too!) I worked it, baby! I poured it on. I was giving it everything I could think of and, oh yeah, I prayed, too!

I knew from conversations we were having she was everything I wanted, a lady who had a good sense of humor, intelligent, beautiful, nice, sweet, and polite, she loved to laugh, and she was a great mom, too. She was the whole package I had always wanted and I was just now figuring it out. Ahh yes, the "Ben Franklin Close" I learned from Zig years ago, also known as The Balance Sheet Close, and it was now in play! I compared all my pros and cons, did my two columns, and saw all the options and I was now set on GO! She is not the dark-haired or deeply dark tanned girl; she is a 5'4." blonde with pretty light, fair skin. She was not 4'11"to 5' 2." She has kids, too! My perception had completely changed overnight, and I knew she was the one for me! So I worked it!

I asked Erika for a date, on text. I know, I know…you are thinking, Oh, no, you didn't! Yes. Yes, I did! I asked her for a date by text and she said yes! That was the first time I had ever done that, gotten a date by text. I had never tried to get a date by email, either, and I cannot believe I asked on text, and mostly I cannot believe I got a yes!

Guess what? The chase was on big time now! We set a date and a time and I was to pick her up at home the night she arrived back in town at 6:30 p.m. I knew she would be tired from traveling, but she and I both wanted to go out that Saturday night, so I went to work as soon as I had a yes, for a date. Well, that is not true! I started planning a date from the first text. I knew I had to make this the best date she had ever had! I had four days to get it planned out now! This has to be the best date ever, especially since I am now a short, fat, one-legged guy!

The Plan

First things first, I have to take care of the kids, so I called the local pizzeria. The kids loved Palio's. I ordered the kids a pizza and sub sandwiches. I ordered two kinds of cheesecake for Christian (who I later nick-named Cheesecake—do you wonder why?).

I ordered a chocolate dessert for Emma. Now, what girl does not like chocolate?

I gave Palio's the exact time for delivery; I paid them up front and gave them a very nice incentive to be sure it was all perfect. I wanted it to arrive on time and be fresh and hot, too!

So…I had the kids all taken care of.

I called the limo service and talked to Scott. I told him what I was doing. I asked him to wear a black tuxedo and white shirt with a nice black tie. He agreed and he was excited to be a part of this first date. After I gave him all the details he said, "This is going to be FUN!"

Erika's flight arrived at 4:30 p.m.; we needed to be at her house at 6:30 p.m. She thought I would be coming to get her and she was not expecting a limo at all. I made all the arrangements and got the details to Scott. He was going to pick her up. However, I would not be there with him!

I gave Scott an invitation to dinner for him to deliver to Erika! He was to take it to the door, ask for Erika, hand her the envelope with an invitation sealed inside, stand there and wait for her to accept the invitation! Do NOT assume anything! WAIT.

When she said yes, Scott was to escort her to the car and open her door where another envelope and a red rose would be waiting for her lying on the back seat of the limo. I had placed some of that rose-smelling oil on the envelope and on each page of the contents. Then I gave Scott a CD I had made for her and asked him to have it playing before he exited the car to give her the invitation, and to be sure it kept playing the whole time she was riding in the car.

I instructed Scott that once they arrived at Three Forks Restaurant in Addison, he was to pull right up to the front door. The valets would be expecting them. I wanted him, with all the exquisite fanfare, to escort Erika into the restaurant as if she were someone super-famous and he was her date! Then tell the maître d' to escort her to my table where I would be waiting for her.

Scott did not miss one beat! He was perfect.

Three Forks was ready, too, on that very busy Saturday night. I asked them to have me seated in the dining room so I could see her walk all the way from the time she came in the front door and started walking through the aisles to be seated at my table. Perfect plan! It went off perfectly, too.

As I was watching, I knew the exact second when she had arrived. I could see the waiting crowd moving to the side, getting out of the way. They were opening an aisle up to let her through. Then they were all looking back as if someone super famous had just come in the door. Then I saw her! She was walking towards my table, dressed in a black, elegant evening dress with thin straps over the shoulders. She looked absolutely beautiful.

There she is!

It was a beautiful and a magical night! That was the most fun date ever to plan, and to see her enjoy it so much as she walked down the aisle of the restaurant with all eyes on her. The lady who arrived in the limo was escorted in, and the maître-d' escorted her through the dining room. It was just an absolute joy to my heart. She looked so beautiful and she knew it, too. All eyes were on her, every step she took. I knew then that Scott and the maitre d' both had done an awesome job. I could see her big smile and her beautiful bright eyes. She was extravagantly, yet, simply stunning!

What a first date!

Perfect. Ahh, yes. The adventure of "The Chase." The chase was on, full throttle! No holds barred, pedal to the metal! Don't let up! Full steam ahead! Go get this girl! Do not let this one get away!

We went out several more times, and it did not seem to bother her at all that I hobbled, wobbled and bobbled like a duck!

We dated for awhile and I knew that I wanted to marry this girl.

Erika had a really good friend who was a pastor, Brad Strand. I met Brad the next Sunday morning right after our very first Saturday night date. We went to his church in Cash, Texas, that Sunday morning. It was a nice country church in a little country town, and I felt like I went back in time 40 years! This was a mega-church of the '70s. Erika had been talking to Brad all week, "Help, this one-legged guy is coming in like a whirlwind! He is chasing after me. He says he is going to get me! Brad," she said, "I need help! I need advice! I told him I was not going to have a relationship for seven years and he said ok, but he is still coming! Help, Brad. This guy only has one leg and he is chasing me down."

Brad was a very special and dear friend to Erika. After Erika had moved back to the States in 2004 from Germany, where she had been living for the prior 15 years, she had started searching for clear direction in her life. A friend of Erika's, Anna Keith, had invited Erika to a Bible study at her home. Erika met Anna while they were at work. Their meeting was another "God thing," Erika and Anna both working at the same place, sitting right next to each other, a one-hour drive away from home. They worked in the up-town area of Dallas, yet they lived in the same community, Rockwall, Texas. They lived about two to three miles from each other. What a coincidence. Naaa.

Brad Strand was leading the Bible study at Anna's home and he became a good friend and mentor and advisor to Erika. What Erika did not know at the time is that Brad was a Bible scholar. He was completing the first edition of "The Strand Study Bible," his own version of a study Bible that is now entering its second edition of printing. It's a pretty neat study Bible and I have quoted from it here some as well. Brad had become like a spiritual father to Erika over the years. He advised her and counseled and took care of her.

Wes Hartley was another mentor to Erika. Wes was a lot younger, in his 30's. Wes is the media pastor at her home church, Lake Pointe in Rockwall. Now this guy is funny and a real cool pastor, too.

As Erika began to grow, she felt the desire to serve. She got involved in the media ministry team working with Wes. Hmmm…interesting…before I surrendered my heart to Christ, I hated TV and radio preachers. Now I am a fully devoted follower of Christ, and I am a product of both TV and radio ministry…and…no…I am in love with a media person? What? Someone who helps put these preachers on the airwaves.

No way!

Aaaaah, but yes, He did! Amazing! The very things I hated as an un-believer are what God used to bring me to Him. Now I am dating someone in that very field of ministry. He is such a funny God sometimes.

Besides serving as media pastor, Wes taught a Bible study class for the media team after the Saturday night services. He is a dynamic teacher, too. Erika grew from the relationships in the class as well as from relationships within the media team and the Bible study with Brad Strand. So Wes Hartley was her local church associate pastor, Bible fellowship teacher, friend and counselor. Wait, he is another of those media guys, too, who puts people on TV and radio? *No way!*

When the time had come and I decided to ask Erika to marry me, I knew I had to ask these two men for her hand in marriage, too, Brad Strand and Wes Hartley.

Oh, my! I had to pass the Erika tests, too. The family test, the kid test, the friend tests, the Brad Strand test and the Wes Hartley test. What's a guy to do? Hey…this is one confident one-legged guy! Somehow it will all work out! Remember, I am the optimist! I knew I was blessed and I knew this would be like a walk in the park for me! Oh…but I forgot…I have only one leg, so a walk in the park for a one-legged guy is like climbing Mount Everest for a perfectly normal able-bodied person. After all, I was still a hopper on a walker. Oh, well, the chase was still on! Come on, hop-a-long, let's go.

I was in my car in downtown Rockwall; I was close by and waiting for the time to pass. I still had an hour to wait for Erika to arrive in the limo at the restaurant, Zanata's. Yes, I did it again! I called the limo company again.

This time I had them pick her up and bring her to—you guessed it—another nice but local restaurant, this time so I could propose. I had talked to Al Lefere, the owner. I set it all up in advance. I gave him a very nice ring to bring out at the perfect time. He had it placed inside the cork-covered menu, dangling inside from a pretty yellow ribbon that lay perfectly in the crease of the fold so when she opened the menu to look, she would have no idea what it was or what was coming next. Out popped a ring dangling there.

Ohhh! Let me tell you about this little bitty ring I got her!

I looked for a little while and did not see anything I liked, so I called a jeweler friend of mine, Rios, in Fort Worth. I talked to his wife, Roberta, and made an appointment to drive to Fort Worth and design a ring that he would make for me to give her. I love to design stuff and I used my creative mind to conceive of something special. Roberta and Rios worked with me on it.

Roberta said, "Oh, no! That diamond is going to be too big!" I said, "What? I didn't know a diamond engagement ring could be too big." She said, "Oh, yes, you have to remember she will wear this every day for the rest of her life, and this is too big. It will get caught on everything and snag, and eventually become loose and fall out and you will have caused her to lose the first diamond you ever gave her! Plus, it's so big it will obscure the beautiful setting we're making for her. It all has to be balanced so she can see every angle of the ring and it has to sit perfectly on her small hand!"

Now, I have never heard any girl showing off her engagement ring and saying, "Look see…and look at the ring way down here!" Nope. They all say, "Ohhh, let me see the diamond ring! It is beautiful!" The next question women always ask seems to be, "How big is it?" referring to the weight of the diamond.

Roberta and I went back and forth. Rios made a couple of mock-ups for me and some computer drawings with the square princess-cut stone in the center. We kept tweaking it until the ring was perfect and he was ready to make his wax mold. Now I had to decide on the size of the stone so we could design the wedding band.

Oh, I forgot. There was a wedding band to go with it, too. So I made a decision on the size of the stone. Roberta was completely right, the ring looked a lot more balanced, the smaller stone looked more natural, it was exquisite and radiant, and, after all, Roberta had been doing this for 40 years! I hated to admit it, but the smaller stone actually looked so much better. So I made my decision based on all the professional information and advice, and Roberta was right! The smaller diamond was perfect. Now it is definitely a good jeweler, when they tell you to buy smaller instead of bigger. Plus, I liked the idea financially, too.

I wanted to make a statement but Roberta was right; guess what? She lost! I wanted the bigger diamond! I wanted to make a huge, big, bold statement! However I must have forgotten to take my meds. I had forgotten that the bigger the diamond, the smaller the balance in my checking account when it was all said and done. But I didn't care. I wanted a showpiece. I wanted to announce to all the future guys, "You can't touch this. Don't even try! She is taken! She is loved and cared for. She is mine!"

Now that bigger stone decision was causing a really big problem with the wedding band. We had to design it so there is a cut-out or an indentation to go around one side of the engagement ring. Well, we did it. It was a beautiful design. Then Rios said, "This is too difficult for me to make. I need to send it off and have it made by a friend in New York." So off it went. It was back in plenty of time and we had made it to fit perfectly! The first fit was so funny because Erika has tiny little fingers, but we got it right the very first time!

This ring is my pride because it was a labor of love and it was designed especially for her with the thought in mind of the two of us marrying our two families together. It is also a representation of her two kids, Emma and Christian, and my son Jeremy and his kids, Cameron and Matthew and us. We were all one family marrying another family to become one happy blended family.

The Proposal

The limo came and picked up Erika and she thought it was just another date to go see the Christmas lights. Now, if you want the truth, I really had to plan three dates to get the one special night to work out!

I made three restaurant reservations and three limo reservations all for this one night at different times and three different places! I was ready for whatever popped up. I had a plan and we could work around whatever situation arrived and still have a nice, calm, fun evening. I was prepared.

Okay, here is the story: I wanted to surprise her and every time I would make a plan for us, something would come up with the kids. Every time, something else popped up and I would have to cancel the plans I had made for this special time! So I had to reschedule.

I wanted Erika to be completely and totally surprised. I wanted her to have no idea what I was doing. Tonight, she thought we were just going out to dinner. So, this was my third time to plan this special night! Then with three different time slots and restaurants, I figured I had better at least make one local reservation in Rockwall, just in case I had to cancel our reservations in Dallas again. At least I would have done everything I possibly could do to make it work out for tonight. However, I still had two more reservations made just in case! I really wanted to get this done as soon as I possibly could. As they say, the third time is the charm. Yep! Sure is!

So back to where I was, sitting in my car downtown Rockwall, and I had already talked to Wes and passed the test. I had Wes's approval! All clear! I waited until the last minute to get the last approval that I was so sure of. Well, I thought I was so sure. Maybe I really was a little worried about Brad, after all! I pulled into a small parking lot behind one of the buildings in downtown Rockwall and called Brad on the phone. I asked for his permission. I said, "Brad, I need to ask you a question. I am downtown in Rockwall and I have Erika coming to meet me; I want to ask her to marry me."

Brad just laughed and chuckled. He said, "Well what are you doing sitting here talking to me?" I said, "Brad, I need your permission." He said, "Well…what are you waiting for? You'd better hurry up and get there before she does if she is on her way. Yes! You both have my blessing and I know God has put both of you together, so yes!"

I *got* it! I got the final approval! Whew…I surely cut that one close!

Okay, so on to the restaurant to get her ring to Al so he could get it prepared. I called the limo driver and did the same thing once again. This time when the white limo came pulling up to the restaurant, I could see right through the plate glass window of the restaurant. Well, everyone at the restaurant in the little town of

Rockwall, Texas, could see the limo pull up ever so slowly! Like he was making an announcement: Clear the way, special delivery here! VIP coming to Zanata's. Please let us through.

Scott got out, went around slowly, opened her door and escorted her in the door of Zanata's. Then the lady maître d' took over. I could see Scott grinning as big as Texas as I was nodding my head of approval for a job well done through the plate glass window. He picked me out of the crowd somevhow and my eyes were fixed on him. Scott knew he had done a perfect job.

I looked and watched Erika. I took in every moment and every step, every glistening and sparkle in her eye. The flowing of her blonde hair as she walked to the door. I surveyed each and every move, every step she took. Oh, yes. It was perfect, and the chase was still on. I had to propose and get her to say yes.

Once again, as Erika arrived at the restaurant in the limo all eyes inside and outside were fixed on her from the first second; however, this time, it was in Rockwall, this small but quaint, revitalized downtown happening restaurant called Zanata's. It had become a place to see and be seen, but it was Erika's favorite restaurant because it had a nice and quaint, small hometown feel, yet a special atmosphere. Zanata's has a personality all its own. Erika had lived in Germany for 15 years and she loved the small old-town, quaint, homey atmosphere. So this was her place.

As Erika was escorted to the table she had a big smile. As she sat down, I had her favorite drink waiting for her. After approximately three minutes, Al sent the waitress to our table with the menu. I watched as she opened it up, not knowing Al and the wait staff had told everyone in the restaurant that evening what was happening.

So, as the menu came and Erika opened it, there was no menu at all!

Only her big, beautiful diamond ring dangling inside!

Then I had written a very personal handwritten note just for her, letting Erika know I was about to ask her to marry me.

As Erika sat there in the dimly lit restaurant, with the glistening and twinkling of Christmas lights on the Christmas tree behind her, she had a glow all about her. As she looked up, she lit up like a Christmas tree. Then I asked her if she and her kids would marry me. And she said…Y E S!!!

I finally had found and captured the heart of the love of my life!

It took me until I was 50 years old to grow up, but I had finally found my bride.

My one and only! Everything I did not want from my proverbial list had now become the whole world to me!

My beautiful bride came at the very time when I least expected God to bring her to me! After all, picture this: a one-legged guy chasing after the love of his life, hopping around on a walker saying, "Hey, YOU, Pretty Lady! Stop. STOP!! S T O P ! I've got to talk to you! Hey, slow down. Wait for me! I am coming! Slow down."

Hey, Zig! I now have "The Home Court." I can now flirt with my bride! And yes, I will take care of the *"The Home Court Advantage."*

No! The chase will never end!

I still chase her to this day and I am going to chase her around until I am a 90-year-old one-legged man, flirting with the love of my life!

The chase will never end!

Three-Dog Night Wedding

Erika and I were now trying to figure out all the logistics for a wedding. Where to have it, who could come, when would be the best time for everyone, you know the drill.

There were lots of things to consider and lots to do, and all the time needed to make arrangements. We were in the beginning stages, and discussing all the issues, so we were in the evaluation process and it was a daunting task.

Christmas came and went and it was New Year's Eve. I had to work. I was working at Oak Creek Homes where we have a retail display housing center to show all our homes. It was the same place where I was after the accident. We worked out all the financing, closing of the loan process (we did land procurement, appraisal orders, title work). This was also where we managed the construction process. From the dirt to a completely finished home ready to move into, we did it all. It was a one-stop shop in a large organization. We were the leader in our field of factory-built homes; and there were 26 company-owned locations.

Our company also owned two factories here in the Dallas-Fort Worth area, and another factory in Alabama, where we would build the modular homes and HUD homes. We would build them in the factory and send them to the construction site for final completion of construction. I had the responsibility as the general manager of the Mesquite/East Dallas and North Texas location where we sold the homes for all of North Texas. However, we delivered homes to Baton Rouge, Louisiana, up to McAlester, Oklahoma, and way south to McAllen, Texas. Because we were a leader in the industry, our operation in Mesquite was required to be open on New Year's Eve.

Being the businessman I am, I always try to help all of my employees get personal and family time, as well as holiday time. Of course, just about everyone wants to take vacation days during the Christmas/New Year's holidays. I decided to run a skeleton crew, and I was going to work there with them as well until about 2 p.m., then if things were slow I was going to close down for the rest of the day. So I put myself in the lineup and worked the 9 a.m.–2 p.m. shift that day.

Erika works as an analyst for a large, worldwide banking company. They had a communication breakdown and all the bosses took off for the holidays and left the department with no one to do analytics. Someone had to be there. Erika usually works from her laptop from home or at the corporate offices, but on this day she was required to drive in to work at the office and be there all day. I was wrapping up my day and was ready to leave, and let Erika know; she was ready to wrap up her day, too, so we met at my office and went to dinner at Chuy's on I-75 in Plano.

Chuy's is a really neat, locally-owned Mexican restaurant. We were discussing our wedding options and Erika said, "What about your ring?" I told her I just wanted a cheap gold band. After all, she was wearing a stone that was as tall as the new Dallas Cowboys football stadium and was just as bright, too, so I did not need a building on my hand, too! After all, I had to help her carry that big ol' boulder she had around, so I had to hold her hand!

We had an early dinner from 4 o'clock to about 5:15 p.m. We pulled out headed north for the turn-around to go back south on I-75. We saw a Costco and Erika said, "Do you want to look over there for a ring?" Sure; we had plenty of time and nothing else to do, so we spun around, turned to the right and into the parking lot. We went in and it was a little slow, not many people were there, we had Costco almost all to ourselves. We walked straight over to the jewelry counter and found a ring in just a few seconds. The guy asked for my size, then he said, "Go to checkout. I'll bring it to you there." Sure 'nuff, he did, too! We checked out and were back in the car in all of 10 minutes' time. Now, that was easy!

Erika and I had no more gotten on the entrance of I-75 going south when she said, "Let's just do it now!" I said, "Okay, let's do it!" She called Wes Hartley, her friend (whom I had asked to marry her!) and said, "Wes, would you marry us tonight?"

Wes said, "Well, I'm leaving at seven for a New Years Eve party. Do you want to come to the house?"

We said, "SURE, we are on our way! We will be there at 6:30!" WOW!

That was some quick decision-making! We decided it would be easier than everyone trying to adjust schedules later, getting all the busy family members there; it would save all that planning and time so we decided, let's do this!

Erika and I were laughing and having fun and it was pouring down rain outside! We were on I-635, going around the loop at the Jupiter Road exit and I said, "Okay! What are we going to say next week after the holidays when we get back to work?"

"Hmm...so Erika, what did you do on New Year's Eve?"

"Ohhh...I worked until two, had dinner at Chuy's, went to Costco, bought a wedding band for Phillip, drove to my friends house and got married!"

Oh, boy, did I mess up! I was just making a funny! Then, all of a sudden with no warning, there was no thunder or lightning, but now came a downpour in the car. There was more water pouring in the car than in all the pouring down rain outside! BOO HOO HOO! Erika had burst out in big ol' hippo tears; she was boo-hooing BIG TIME! Oh, no. What did I say? I was laughing out loud a big ol' belly laugh. Well, I was laughing! Yes, I stopped laughing, real fast! But inside I had cracked myself up!

Erika said, "We sound like a bunch of hillbillies!" There was dead silence in that car...for all of thirty seconds. "Oh, no! It's okay! Really, this is fun! I love it! After all, Erika, you are marrying a Hatfield...like the Hat¬field's and the McCoy's!" Okay, so now I had her back to at least a slight grin!

We continued the drive; Erika got the happy feeling back pretty quickly. We drove up Wes's long driveway. It was very dark. We jumped out in the rain and ran to the door, well, she ran, I hobbled and wobbled as fast as I possibly could. Christy opened up the door and we walked right in, like people on a mission, like we had a purpose! Wes said, "The kids are all gone; it's just us!"

We said. "Great!"

Wes cut right to the chase. "Okay, where do you want to do this?"

Erika and I looked around the house from where we were standing and the Christmas tree was right there in the foyer where we stood. So we said, "Right here! This is the spot!"

Wes was ready, he opened up his Bible. Christy Hartley, his wife, stood facing us. Oh, yeah, we had her three dogs sitting there, too, staring, and watching us as we exchanged our vows. We exchanged a covenant between God and us…"Until death do us part" This is what we call a "Covenant Marriage."

It was so funny, though. It was just like a movie. See, we even have our witnesses, too—three dogs!

So it was a Three-Dog Night!

After all, God spelled backwards is D O G, right?

And we had all three of the Godhead there for our wedding, Father, Son, and Holy Spirit. Right? Just a funny thought that ran through my mind and I love to tell the story. Now, that was the fastest $100.00 Wes had ever made in five minutes! It was done! In-N-Out! Then GONE!

Guys, I want you to see what we knew all along. It was about the marriage. Our marriage, our lives and not just about the wedding! It was about God, our families and us, Erika and Phillip joining our hearts and lives and families. Becoming a family.

This truly has been a marriage orchestrated in Heaven. I adore my bride! I love my kids—ALL of them: Jeremy, Emma and Christian! They are all OUR kids, ya' see. We do not have "step-moms" and "step-dads" or "step-kids." We have a family.

See, I am *not* going to step on them and they are not going to step on me! We are going to have a life together!

No steps in this family!

Oh, yes…The Chase!…it never ends!

<((><

A Chip off the Old Block!

This is what we are to do. Help wherever we see there is a need.

"Encouragement" The Next Generation

I was in my hospital room after surgery December 22, 2011, when the internal medicine doctor came in my room and looked at me lying in the bed with my newly-amputated leg sticking out of the covers. He walked right up to the foot of my hospital bed knowing I had my left leg amputated, looked at me head to toe and then he said:

"Mr. Hatfield, how tall are you, 5'10?"

I looked right back at him and said, *"Well that all depends; if I am standing on my right leg I am 5'6."*

"If I am standing on my left leg, I am 4"8.""

That poor doctor cracked up and was dying laughing. He could hardly catch his breath, he was laughing so hard! I am beginning to think Bryan Flanagan is rubbing off on me with his quick-witted one-liners and jokes out of the clear blue.

Yes, I was just released from the hospital in January 2012 this time. I had an infection in my leg and it kept getting worse. I had to have reconstruction amputation surgery. I was in the hospital from December 22, 2011, until January 12, 2012. Yes, I was there all through Christmas, New Year's and also my anniversary, too. Yuck!

I have a quick story I want to share with you.

I am a Bible study teacher at Lake Pointe Church here in Rockwall, Texas. Erika and I got a call that a lady in our class had a tragedy in her life. Her name was CeCe.

Thursday morning December 1, 2011, CeCe got a call that her dad had just passed away at 11:30 that morning. It was a long day for her as she got with the family and her sister and her son Josh, and they made plans. They were getting ready to leave town and travel to Mississippi the next morning to be with the family and bury her dad.

CeCe's sister came over from Fort Worth and was going to be spending the night. They were all going to get up early the next morning and drive to Mississippi. They had some quality family time that evening and were getting ready to go to bed when CeCe's son, Josh, decided he needed to go to work and drop off the key to the kiddie train and plug it in so the battery would be all charged up for the next day. He was leaving town and he knew someone else would be driving all the kids around the mall area all day and he wanted it to be problem-free. That was Josh's job, driving the kids around the mall. He loved it, especially now with Thanksgiving just past and Santa had already come to the mall. Christmas was now in the air.

Josh left in his new Mazda Miata and was on his way. While he was driving he lost control of his car and had an accident. Josh was killed about one mile from his home at 11:30 p.m. that very same day. CeCe was devastated, as you could only imagine.

Josh, a 19-year-old young man, was killed. He was not paying attention and was distracted. Josh was texting and driving at the same time from what we understand.

Our Bible study class jumped into action as soon as we got the news. Erika and Becky Seymour took off work that day and we all went to CeCe's house. We spent some time there all that day, talking and helping, delivering food, etc. We contacted the church for advice for a funeral home and tried to help CeCe with all that we could. Becky and Erika jumped right in and helped her out. CeCe was shaken and at a loss, but God sent her ladies that were on a mission. Caretaker ladies. You could even say they were like angels. Trying to help do any and everything they possibly could to help.

The following morning my friend, Tom Merricks, and I with my son Christian who is 14, and Brennen Basset who is 17 and Matt who is 12, all went over to help clean up the outside of the house and mow the lawn and trim the hedges. We knew she was going to have lots of company and we all wanted to help in any way that we possibly could. No one asked if we could come, we just knew what we needed to do and showed up, never knocking on the door, just doing our part and moving on out of the way as swiftly as possible. We were all just trying to serve. We wanted to be the hands and feet of Christ for her. We wanted her to see the church in action. We all just wanted to serve in any way that we could.

The funeral for Josh was the next Tuesday, December 6th, and we all pitched in again. We were trying to help and do a reception at a church banquet hall, since there were too many people to go to CeCe's house. Erika and Becky got all the ladies together and made a plan. The ladies cooked and put together a care calendar, sending food every day, and many other services they were doing to help CeCe as well. Becky was awesome at organizing and facilitating for a couple of weeks. They cooked and put together a very nice reception for the family so they would not have to do anything in their time of grieving.

Everyone was working, serving and talking to people. Emma and Christian, our kids, were right there with us giving and serving 100% all evening long with our Bible study class. I was sitting on the sideline. My prosthetic leg was bothering me and I sitting there while everyone else was working. I felt horrible doing nothing, so I got up and helped pick up and clean up. My leg was giving me problems from the very beginning, being on it so much the past few days, and my prosthetic leg was not fitting right, either. That was the last day I walked. I rubbed a blister that got infected and that is how we wound up back in the hospital in December.

I was amazed at how well the kids did in serving that rainy Saturday morning, mowing and working for two to three hours! The kids were used to serving and helping out, but this was a different service for them. Helping a lady who had just lost her dad and her son 12 hours apart. My son, Christian, serves in the media ministry. Brennen Basset serves all over the 10,000-plus member church where his dad is on staff. Matthew Belmonte, a neighbor and a friend of my son, Christian, came along to help as well. Our daughter Emma, who is 17, was there serving with us at the reception, too. Kids all pitching in. They saw a need and saw God was doing something and they joined Him and got busy being a blessing to other people who were hurting. Yes, Henry Blackaby, our kids are "looking for what God is doing and joining Him," as you have taught us all for so long now. They were now "Experiencing God" in a whole new light.

This is what we are to do. Help wherever we see there is a need. And these ladies and kids were doing that! Please pray for CeCe and for each of these servants I have mentioned, that they will be strengthened and KNOW what a difference they are all making at a time of tragedy! I am sure CeCe will tell you that she, too, has been "Carried by Angels."

29

The "Apple" Does Not Fall Far From the "Tree"

Thank you, Tom, for being like this tree that is planted by the water and bringing forth fruit in its season...

While I was in the hospital I was amazed at the visitors who came to see me and take care of me this time. It was a completely different group than before, three years ago.

There was my friend from Ziglar Corporation, Bryan Flanagan, the funny man. "Coach," as I call him! He is the king of one-liners. This guy can crack you up all day long. I call Bryan "coach" because he is my speaker and training coach at the Ziglar Corporation.

There was Tom Ziglar, the son of Zig Ziglar. There was Joey Sammons and Tim Hartwell, friends from the Ziglar group that I had become friends with, too.

Bryan came and brought me some crazy funny games and puzzles to keep me occupied through the Christmas holidays. He knew there were going to be some boring days in there through Christmas time. All the guys came by several times to visit and encourage me. But what really surprised me was Tom Ziglar!

Tom is very busy, as well as Bryan, flying all over the world, but Tom came several times and was just like his dad, Zig. "A chip off the old block," Tom and Bryan came one day and brought his blender from home and some fruit. Tom started making all of us fruit smoothies right there in my hospital room. We all sat there laughing, talking, and had a great visit. That was so nice and fun, having smoothies in a hospital room with your friends.

But on **Christmas Day 2011**, when everyone is at home with their families having Christmas dinner and opening gifts, having family over, Tom Ziglar was at the hospital with me!

Tom Ziglar came and spent two to three hours from 12:00 to about 2:30 talking and spending time with me and encouraging me on Christmas Day. I was so blessed.

Tom was never in a hurry, just like Zig. He was calm, cool and collected. He was funny, telling his stories and we were laughing and having a nice day!

Yes, Christmas was a slow day at the hospital overall. My wife Erika and my son Christian came to see me and had just left to go see a movie when Tom just showed up out of the clear blue! It was a tough Christmas and holiday time for Christian, too, with me being in the hospital his whole Christmas break from school. Christian was not at home much; he was there at the hospital with me almost every day. He did really well taking care of me, too. Now that is not to say that he did not take my wheelchair and go up and down all the halls on every floor, popping wheelies everywhere! Yep, he wore that wheelchair out; it was almost smoking when he would spin in the room on two wheels. He was in and out of my room on that wheelchair all day long.

I was still so amazed that Tom Ziglar would spend so much time with me on Christmas day in the hospital *when everyone else was at home with their families!* Here was a busy man who travels the world and took time for me. That was such a blessing that I will never forget. Yes, Tom is "Encouragement: The Next Generation" for the Ziglar corporation.

Not just lip service of telling people what to do but actually giving more of himself, just like Zig always has! Yes, I am writing this chapter several months after Tom wrote the Foreword to this book. That is all the more reason why I am writing this chapter, so everyone can see he really is a "Chip off the Old Block" in every way!

Tom has the natural ability and gifts of his dad. He is a natural born encourager, too!

Now that was not the entire Tom Ziglar story!

After I got home from the hospital and was on home health care for over three weeks and confined to my home, I had three weeks on a strong IV antibiotic called vancomycen.

Tom called on the first Monday after I got home and said, "What do you want for lunch? I am coming to Rockwall Thursday to have lunch with you."

Mr. Healthy "Pure and Simple" Tom Ziglar stopped and got a nice salad and came all the way to my home an hour away from Ziglar offices to have lunch with Erika and me. Wow, once again another time Tom is putting legs and feet to what he says and what he teaches at Ziglar, Inc. I have been so blessed to get to know Zig for the past 20 years, and now a new friendship has developed with his son, Tom Ziglar, for the next 20-plus years!

I would say Tom is directed by his character and integrity as well as being led by the Holy Spirit. Certainly he was an angel to me in my Christmas holiday hospital stay.

The family tree of Zig Ziglar is still growing and expanding in many more ways than one.

Psalms 1:1-3 *(ESV)* says

> *Blessed is the man who walks not in the counsel of the wicked, nor stands in the way of sinners, nor sits in the seat of scoffers; but his delight is in the law of the LORD, and on his law he meditates day and night. He is like a tree planted by streams of water that yields its fruit in its season, and its leaf does not wither. In all that he does, he prospers.*

Thank you, Tom, for being like this tree that is planted by the water and bringing forth fruit in its season, a new season for Ziglar Inc., and remember the promise that all you do will prosper.

Thank you, Tom, for continuing the Zig Ziglar Legacy!

Thank you for being my friend.

No, the "Apple" Does Not Fall Far From the "Tree"

"Encouragement: The Next Generation"

Tom Ziglar

"A Chip off the Old Block"

<(((><

WOW! What a Life!

I now live a new life as a disabled amputee, a one-legged, middle-aged man with some tough physical limitations.

A Perfect Life? NOPE!

But it has been a great journey. Everything has not been absolutely perfect through my life, but it surely has been one awesome, fantastic ride so far. But take time to STOP, and take a quick look at just how blessed we are. Look at how wonderful and merciful God has been to me. I hope you get a tiny glimpse of how blessed I am and how blessed you are in the scope of real life.

I now live a new life as a disabled amputee, a one-legged, middle-aged man with some tough physical limitations. Yet I still can see a God who has blessed me beyond anything you can possibly imagine. God has allowed me to stay here on this earth and spend more time with my new bride and my new family.

Stephanie (who was on the motorcycle) recovered very well. She had a broken pelvis and was in the hospital for about two weeks. We stay in touch continually and as I write this piece right now, telling you about Stephanie it is 7:26 p.m. November 9, 2011. Three years to the exact second from the time of our accident! WOW!

Yes, Stephanie has had some struggles getting back to living her life. Recovery is not easy and it takes some time and lots of help from our friends and family members and many hours of rehab learning to reuse muscles again and relearning how to walk after a broken pelvis. But we both know we are blessed to be alive. Stephanie had a beautiful grandson born not long after she was released from the hospital and she spends time with him every day.

God has a plan and I have no idea what it is, but I know it is going to be one fantastic ride. God left me here for a reason, or possibly for just a season of time. That is why I have the passion and the drive to share that "God works in our deepest, darkest despair."

That is when the blessing of the "Trouble Grace" flows! When we are in real trouble. When we are in our absolutely deepest and darkest moments and facing all of our worst fears. When staring death right square in the face, eyeball to eyeball. When it looks like it is time and we are ready to meet our Creator. That is the most blessed time of all!

Ya' see, ain't none of us getting out of this world alive!

Heaven!

The Master is Ready!

The trumpeters are queued up. The organist and the string orchestra are ready to play! The cymbals are ready to ring out loud! The banquet table is set and everyone is waiting for you to join with them in the banquet hall. It is getting close to time for "your" grand entry to the most wonderful place that we cannot even begin to imagine. A new journey is ready for us on the other side of the door! Magnificent! And then…we get to see JESUS!

It really is a blessed time.

We are all so used to looking at it from our own human and selfish perspective. **While you are in that dark tunnel**, *God is doing a miracle! Right out in the open, in front of the entire world and all the critics to see.* God is out there in front of everyone. He is there looking down, then He comes on down to wrap His arms all around us, to hold us tight. He comes to cradle us in his arms and gently rock us to and fro. He comes to grab our family members and friends and cause them to think and to reflect on their own lives, and to reflect on the joyous and the happy times, the memories. Looking back, they all can see the blessing of YOU!

You are being celebrated in Heaven as preparations are being made and you are also being celebrated on this earth, too. You are being celebrated by having those special people in your life all around you in one place or in one frame of mind remembering YOU and what God has done through you. Then God either takes you on into the celebration of Heaven, or He opens up the door for a new celebration of you here on this earth. Your work is not done yet!

You get the privilege to go back and see everyone and share the blessings and the lessons that you have learned in your own tragedy. You are there to share and invest in their lives once again so they can get prepared for their own banquet and their encounter with JESUS one day! See, not everyone is ready yet. God needs YOU to be the messenger. That is why He gave you the gift and blessing of extra time here on this earth, a new life; a new journey!

Yes, trouble brings "Trouble Grace." Ahhh, but without the trouble you would never be celebrated, neither here on this earth nor in Heaven! There is only one way to get to Heaven. We call them sad times; Trouble times; however, they really are "parties in Heaven!"

Tragedy is not all bad. Yes, it is hard. Yes, it is tough. Yes, it is painful. No, we do not want it. I honestly can say, given the choice to have the accident and go through it all again, I would say NO!

Seeing now what God has blessed me with and seeing what God has done and is doing in my life today, as well as in the lives of all of those around me, I can now see perfectly clearly. YES! I will do it again!

NO, I do NOT want to go through it again.

But, the answer is, YES, I am yours, Lord. I am yours, and as the songs say, "Take my life and use it," and "Just as I am." Then we can sing, "Shout to the Lord, all the earth let us sing; power and majesty, praise to the King!"

I love the blessings I have received from this life-changing event and the new experiences I have had. I would not trade them for the world.

YEP, I am now disabled and I have a prosthetic leg that always sticks out from under my pants leg. I hobble and wobble and bobble like a duck. I fumble around with my balance and cannot do the things I used to do. However, I can do things now that I never could do before!

This prosthetic leg of mine opens up new doors every single day! It keeps opening new doors all throughout the day. People want to know what happened; why; how; where; when, and on and on the questions go.

See, God has given me a tool. A visible tool to open doors! This is my tool. This is my blessing. This is my pride and joy to carry. As Paul had a thorn in his side, this is mine. This is my cross to bear; my thorn in my side. What a small price to pay for all the rewards I get in return.

God has given me a tool to spark conversation, to encourage others, to share how blessed every day is. To live my life now with a purpose and a passion daily!

It is such a small thing to have endured the accident and all the pain, to work hard with physical therapists, to learn how to get around and how to walk on a walker, with crutches and on a new leg. It has been a challenge and still is a challenge.

I had to work with the occupational therapist in relearning how to do the regular activities of daily living. I had to learn how to shave, how to coordinate my hands to accomplish my task. How to pick things up with my fingers again and place them where they needed to go at the time I needed them to be there. See, trauma affects your brain and nervous system. It was a tough job, but I had to do it! I had to work hard with the speech therapist to learn how to process information in my brain again. I had to relearn how to reason and how to process information in difficult situations, in regular life as well as in my professional/business life.

I had to relearn how to think like a professional businessman. I had to relearn how to understand my numbers adding, subtracting, dividing and working on my percentages. Most of it came back with some hard work and great patience from my boss, Larry Speck, and help from my business manager, Kim Stafford.

After all the hard work and dedication, God blessed me. I got almost everything back that I had lost. Everything is almost like it was before, except I now have a new way of life! Not a bad way, but a different way of life.

I see life from a whole new perspective now that I would never have seen before. Had I not gone through what I have had to endure, I would have never learned all that I have. I would not know now all that I have learned from all of the wonderful people in my life—my friends and my family and the Church.

Had this accident not happened I would not know how much I am really loved and appreciated if it were not for the tough times.

God has held me up the whole time. God carried me through this incident the same as He has done or will do for you someday.

I have been *Carried by Angels* and Held by God!

YES, and I have seen the face of Jesus, too!

I love all the many different doctors I had, the trauma team, orthopedic team, psychologists, etc. All of the different nurses and their nursing specialties in their specialized fields of nursing. And all of those nurse aides. All the people who took care of me while I was unconscious and in ICU. What about the janitors there at the hospital, the secretaries, the cooks down in the kitchen and the dishwashers? I appreciate so much what each of them does! They are all on the same team. It took all of them to do their part to allow me the opportunity to live.

YES, God heals through medicine and God heals through people, too. God heals with the touch of His hand. Sometimes the touch of His hand is the PEOPLE who allow God to use them!

Zig has a saying, "Most accidents are caused by people, and most people are caused by accidents!" Hahaha that is really funny, when you think about it!

NOPE! God don't make no junk! However, for everything I lost and did not regain from this accident, I got a double portion of something new. Things I never would have known or things I would have never experienced before, and how all the people responded.

Now I have so many more tools in my new toolbox of life and my business toolbox to share, too.

YES, this leg is a tool that opens the door for me to share with the entire world!

Yes, I have been "Carried by Angels!" Yep, I may walk with a limp and hobble and wobble like a duck; however, I am proud of each of these waddles that I have.

"My Greatest Tragedy is my Greatest Blessing!" And I can say I have been *Carried by Angels.*

Do you want to know what I am going to share when people ask the questions like:

What happened?

Why do bad things happen?

What is that? (When they look at my prosthetic leg)

Why did God let this happen to you?

Hey: Just Ask Me! I will tell you!

Yes, I have been…

Carried by Angels!

&

My Greatest Tragedy is My Greatest Blessing.

<(((><

Book Phillip to Speak
at Your Next Event!

Bring Phillip and his EXCITING message of inspiration "from Tragedy to Triumph" to your next church meeting or business event.

Phillip Hatfield "The Real McCoy"
A Zig Ziglar Certified Presenter
Keynote/Conference & Church Speaker*

High Energy • Humorous • Fun • Engaging
Dynamic Presentation & Communication skills

All conference and breakout session topics are specifically designed and tailored for each individual, conference, business, church or school setting.

Venues include: Association meetings, non-profit organizations, sales meetings, business meetings, leadership conferences, schools and special events!

A few customizable topics for your event:

#1 My Greatest Tragedy is My Greatest Blessing!

Hey Mom, Look! It's a "Transformer"

OUCH! "That Hurts, Dude."

Triumph over Tragedy!

What's in Your Wallet?

"HEY" Are You a Cripple or Something?

The Ripple Effect

Go Ahead, You Can Pull My Leggo!

Toes go in First!

Chiseled Character "Charasso"

Get FIRED–UP

Hey Mister, You Walk Like a Duck!

Business or Busyness?

Nuts, Fruits and Flakes YES, You can Get-UP!

Self-Worth Beats Net Worth

Stand Up and Lead!

Change Happens So GET UP and Start Over Again!

Living Life with a REAL Purpose and Passion

Are You a Transformer or Terminator?

WHAT?...You are Texting and Driving? No WAY!

For Speaking Engagements
Travels from Dallas, Texas
www.PhillipHatfield.com

SPEAKING TESTIMONIALS

Thanks so much for the blessing you gave our camp in your presentation on last Thursday. I cannot tell you how wonderful it was to hear your testimony. I talked to many of those present and each one was very pleased about your presentation and told me so. So thanks!!! Your presentation was excellent. You were articulate, your enunciation was excellent, transitions were good, and you were organized. I will let other Camp Presidents in the area know about you.

Blessings, Dick Porth
Allen Camp President
Gideon's International

Phillip Hatfield is one of the most dynamic people I have met. He is well worth listening to...and being motivated by. He and I both appeared at the Texas Courier and Logistics Association's Annual Conference, which had the theme "Moving in the Right Direction." I was the opening keynote speaker and Phillip was the concluding motivational speaker. Among the messages that I got from Phillip:
- *Grabbing your own gold means different things to different people.*
- *We must celebrate the journey, the hard work and the process of getting there, not just the moment of glory.*
- *Having people believing in you makes all the difference.*
- *True champions will support and nurture others.*
- *No champion made it without good coaching. Having a qualified, experienced business mentor is the sure path to your success.*

Phillip Hatfield is a true champion for others.

Hank Moore
Futurist, Corporate StrategistT
White House Advisor to 5 US
Presidents: Lyndon B. Johnson,
Jimmy Carter, Ronald Reagan,
George H. Bush, George W. Bush

Received 4 Presidential Citations from Johnson, Carter, Reagan, and Bush.

As usual, you Ziglar guys deliver. I thought we were in the delivery business. Phillip was SUPER. I loved knowing that he has a PHD.

Rod Steinbrook, Vice President
Supershot, Inc.
The Delivery Service

Phillip had us on the edge of our seat the whole time. That was GREAT!

Bob Gilliam
Gideons International
LakeRockwall Camp

I have known Phillip Hatfeld for several years and seen him in many different situations. He is an energetic, passionate communicator. He has a GREAT life's story and communicates it with passion and humor. His detailed discription of the things that have affected him is priceless. As a motivational speaker he is outstanding and has an expert use of presentation skills. He encourages participation and is actively engaged in the audience during his presentations. A consummate listener, a detailed proactive worker that provides a high level of quality in all that he does.

Gene Scott PMP, CPF
Sr. Partner / Lead Instructor
at Facilitative Project Leadership
Dallas/Fort Worth Area

Out of GREAT pain, comes great PASSION. When that passion is focused on a greater purpose for good, AMAZING things happen. Phillip's message and delivery is just that, "AMAZING."

Scott R Tucker
Radio Host/ Author & Life Coach

Phillip is God's man! And everybody can "feel" his love!

Julie Ziglar Norman

"Phillip is an awesome speaker and motivator. His story is inspiring. He moves you to action. He helps you to think about where you are and move forward with intention. He is a gifted presenter, born to share his story and encourage others. I'd recommend Phillip to speak at any event where you need to set the room 'on fire'. His light will spark a fuse in your audience and move the crowd to action."

Bethany Williams
VP Marketing ZirMed
Results oriented executive at ZirMed

This year I was not feeling the conference, I have had many personal "bumps in my road." I had made my appearance and was heading out of the door when I stopped to say hello and introduce myself to Phillip. At that very moment, I knew I had to stay. We sat for hours visiting and chatting. His story, his passion, his appreciation for the blessings he has and those that Zig and then Tom shared, they radiate from this man! Meeting Phillip Hatfield, I am convinced, has changed my life. I don't know exactly how just yet, but I can assure you, he has. To all those at Ziglar, rest well at night, because Zig has passed the torch and it's burning brightly in men like Phillip Hatfield.

Eric Donaldson
President Hot Shot delivery

Phillip Hatfield is truly amazing! His from the heart passion and total gratitude for life and his Lord come through in every word he says. Whatever your need may be, Phillip will inspire you to take the next step in your journey towards success.

Tom Ziglar
CEO-Proud Son of Zig Ziglar

Recently I was privileged to hear my colleague and friend Phillip Hatfield speak at the Zig Ziglar Born To Win Mega Conference in Dallas, Texas. As Phillip shared how he overcame what seemed like insurmountable odds I was inspired and challenged to not only do more but be more. Phillip is a powerful communicator and encourager who shares the lessons he has learned and applied while fighting for his life and returning to a successful business and personal life. You will be challenged and changed as you hear Phillip Hatfield share his message of hope for one and all.

David Wright
Partner at The Growth Coach

Phillip Hatfield's commitment and dedication to his Lord and Savior Jesus Christ are far from "surface"—they have been tried in the fires of adversity and only strengthened as a result. He effectively relates to challenges in the world of business as he does struggles in one's personal and spiritual life. The power and depth of his experiences come through clearly when he shares his messages with his audiences.

Laurie Magers
Executive Assistant
to Zig Ziglar

Philip Hatfield's story is a story of courage, faith and overcoming obstacles and Barriers! Your organization would benefit greatly from having him speak of his life lessons. He will motivate your team to become stronger and better within themselves! I have had the privilege of hearing him speak and recommend him highly!

Dave Kauffman
Founder of Empowering Small
Business
www.EmpoweringSmallBiz.com

Phillip is a humble but bold person. As Phillip related his incredible motorcycle story, those of us in the room were sitting forward in our seats listening to this incredible account! As Phillip spoke, he took us through the details of this accident and his awesome recovery. He has truly become a gifted speaker with the amazing ability to hold the attention of a small or large audience. I would highly recommend Phillip Hatfield if you or your company has need of an accomplished speaker.

Wallace L. Edge, PH.D.

I know Phillip Hatfield to be a man of great integrity and character. His actions speak for themselves, but you should also hear his story. His message will inspire you, challenge you, and motivate you to embrace the "attitude of gratitude." No matter where you are on life's continuum, Phillip's experiences will apply to you. Whether it is in your personal, your family, your professional, or your faith journey, you will greatly benefit from Phillip Hatfield's message.

Bryan Flanagan
Vice President of Sales
Ziglar, Inc.

CPSIA information can be obtained at www.ICGtesting.com
Printed in the USA
BVOW030443100413

317762BV00001B/1/P